The Dog Lover's Companion to Oregon

1ST
EDITION

Val Mallinson

GRRRRR

AVALON
TRAVEL

D0057323

THE DOG LOVER'S COMPANION TO OREGON
THE INSIDE SCOOP ON WHERE TO TAKE YOUR DOG

Published by
Avalon Travel
a member of the Perseus Books Group
1700 Fourth Street
Berkeley, CA 94710, USA

Printing History
1st edition—March 2010
5 4 3 2 1

ISBN-13: 978-1-59880-548-2
ISSN: 2151-7460

Editor and Series Manager: Shaharazade Husain
Copy Editor: Kay Elliott
Designer: Jacob Goolkasian
Graphics Coordinator: Elizabeth Jang
Production Coordinator: Elizabeth Jang
Map Editor: Brice Ticen
Cartographer: Kat Bennett

Cover Illustration: Sean Bellows based on the artwork of Phil Frank
Interior Illustrations: Phil Frank

Printed in Canada by Friesens

ABOUT THE AUTHOR

This is the story of how a washed-up copy-writer, a puppy-mill puppy with a broken back, and a dog who lived in a cage in a barn overcame all obstacles to bring more joy to people and their pets.

Leading the charge is Val Mallinson, who believes that beauty and hilarity are every-where you look. Bitten by the travel bug early, she has explored all 50 states, a dozen European countries, Mexico, and the Caribbean.

© J.Nichole Smith / www.dane-dane.com

Val's love of dogs began even earlier, thanks to her childhood companion Keegan, who waited, nose pressed to the window, for her to come home from kindergarten. Her favorite bedtime story was *The Pokey Little Puppy,* which also forecast a love of dessert. After being seduced by her mother's adopted dog Thumper, Val adopted two miniature dachshunds, Cooper and Isis, from purebred rescue.

Cooper spent the first year of his life locked in a cage in a barn. When he broke free, he vowed from that day forward to chase as many squirrels through the world's forests as the length of his extendable leash would allow. Isis spent her working years as a dog-bed demo model and nanny to eight fussy Italian greyhound show dogs. It was back-breaking work, literally. Post surgery for spinal cord injuries, she chose to retire to a life of leisure in the back seat of the Mallinson Prius.

Before devoting herself to the position of chauffeur and stenographer for the Wonder Wieners, Val survived a decade in the fast-paced and glamorous world of advertising and marketing copywriting. She penned snappy copy for extinct dot coms, as well as for a large software company in Redmond, Washington. She helped author the stylish travel guide *Moon Metro Seattle,* and her writing and photography appear in *Bark, Seattle Metropolitan, Northwest Travel, Northwest Palate,* and *CityDog* magazines. With her husband, Steve, she has lived in Seattle for fifteen years.

In the course of writing *The Dog Lover's Companion to Oregon,* the Dachsie Twins have slept in the car in a downpour and eaten kibble off the cold, hard ground. They've learned how to navigate using the (bleep)-ing GPS, endured the admiration of excitable toddlers, and scratched at rashes caused by field grass allergies. It's been worth every moment.

For those who rescue dogs and other innocents

CONTENTS

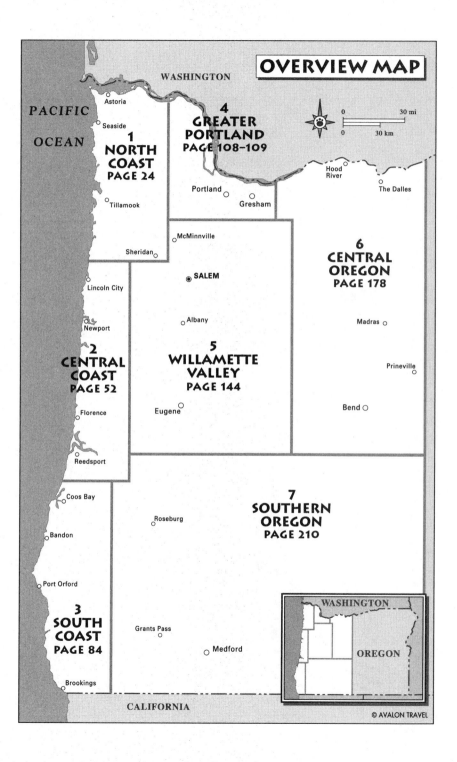

Introduction

In our demand-filled lives, the faithful creatures who sit at our feet expect so little of us. In exchange for lifelong devotion, all they ask is to be fed and to have someplace warm and dry to sleep. For bringing joy and laughter into our lives, all they hope for in return is an occasional tummy rub and some play-time. For unconditional love, they demand only to remain glued to our sides, always, always, always allowed to go wherever we are going. That is, unless we are going to the v-e-t.

At our house, going on a trip without the dogs is rarely an option. We can't handle the guilt. Copernicus Maximus the Red, a.k.a. Cooper, or Coop for short, mourns our departure from his perch at the picture window, his devastation clearly visible in his hangdog posture. The Goddess Isis is much more direct in expressing her displeasure. At the first key jangle, she runs to the door to the garage. As the door closes behind us without her, she protests, using a high-pitched, staccato bark reserved for these occasions. I-can't-be-lieve-you-are-leav-ing-with-out-ME!

Why shouldn't they protest? They know the big wide world out there holds more wonders than they can possibly fit into their short dog lifetimes. For the Dachsie Twins, even a trip to the dry cleaners is full of new sensory pleasures.

Truth be told, we don't want to go anywhere without the kids, for the dogs are our children, hairy, four-legged, and speech-challenged though they may be. Seeing Oregon through the eyes of the Wonder Wieners makes the region's natural beauty and endless recreation opportunities seem even more wondrous. Every city looks prettier from the perspective of its parks. They are right, there are marvels out here.

Native Americans treasured the secrets of the Pacific Northwest for thousands of years. Their oral legends and petroglyphs tell of its abundance. Of giant forests sheltering elk and wildlife to hunt, hillsides thick with brambles yielding sweet blackberries, and oceans and rivers teeming with steelhead and the sacred salmon. The Lewis and Clark Expedition of 1805–1806 brought the mysteries of what was called the Oregon Territory to the attention of European settlers back east. Meriwether Lewis explored Oregon with his faithful Newfoundland named Seaman at his side, and his journals are bursting with drawings and details of native flora, fauna, and natural phenomenon the likes of which the Corps of Discovery had never seen. From 1843 to 1869, hundreds of thousands of pioneers endured dangerous journeys and immense hardships to reach this promised land at the end of the Oregon Trail.

Thanks in part to this book, our hope is that you don't have to suffer any hardships traveling Oregon with your pets. Coop 'n' Isis worked their weenie hindquarters off for you, to sniff out romps with the highest fun factor, the choicest eats where dogs are allowed, and the nicest digs for slumber parties. They discovered, more often than not, that dogs are a natural fit into the relaxed, casual, outdoor lifestyle of the region.

"Oregon is dogs' country," said a park host at a tiny county oasis in the Coquille River Valley. Well, if dog utopia is measured in trees, he's right— nearly 60 percent of Oregon, about 30 million acres, is forested. If dog heaven includes room to roam, Oregon wins again, with a population that's little more than half of Washington State's. There are extensive wilderness areas and rural farmlands. Extremely tough standards protect all of the state's natural resources. Much of Oregon remains wild, untamed at heart.

Water dogs seeking paradise will be beside themselves to learn that every inch of Oregon's 360 miles of beaches are public lands. The beaches fall under the jurisdiction of the State Park system, which requires pets to be on leashes of six feet or less. This rule is *absolute* in the campgrounds, but you'll see much more freedom of movement on the beach.

Also in state parks, a 2007 survey of 10,000 people showed an overwhelmingly positive response to allowing pets in yurts and cabins. A test program that allows pets for stays started May 1, 2009, at South Beach on the Central Coast, Stub Stewart in the Willamette Valley, and LaPine in Southern Oregon. Reservations can be made by phone at 800/452-5687. Let's hope all goes well and they decide to allow pets statewide.

There are thousands of miles of riverfront waterways for swimming, boating, whitewater rafting, and the state's seemingly most popular pastime, salmon and steelhead trout fishing. Perhaps to avoid gender complications, the word fisherman has been universally replaced in Oregon with the word angler. If dogs had opposable thumbs, surely they would be anglers.

With the exception of the I-5 Highway Corridor, all roads are head-out-the-window, tongue-hanging-out scenic. Add in 14 national forests, almost 200 state parks, and dozens of dog events, and it sure starts to sound like somebody up above had canines in mind when designing Oregon.

Humans enjoy a few extra perks in the Beaver State, too. Most recreation areas have park hosts in the summer, valuable resources to answer your questions and help you with things like campfire wood and trail maps. In Oregon, all shopping is free of sales tax, and you don't even have to pump your own gas.

Cooper and Isis hope that this guide will help make traveling with your

dogs a way of life. Every park, place to eat, and place to stay has passed the inspection of these hounds' fine-tuned senses. Coop 'n' Isis dug up dog events, unearthed the fanciest pet boutiques, and scratched under the surface of dog day care centers to include a few they deemed most worthy. Each pupportunity has been carefully rated and described to make your travels easier. You can fit your dog into your favorite outdoor passion, whether it's hitting every farmers market and roadside fruit and vegetable stand in sight, climbing every mountain, or fording every stream. As we researched this book, we fell in love with the region's beauty over and over again, from the mountains to the prairies to the oceans white with foam. The Wonder Wieners hope your discoveries in Oregon will be no less wonderful.

The Paws Scale

At some point, we've got to face the facts: Humans and dogs have different tastes. We like eating chocolate and smelling lavender and covering our bodies with soft clothes. They like eating roadkill and smelling each other's unmentionables and covering their bodies with slug slime.

The parks, beaches, and recreation areas in this book are rated with a dog in mind. Maybe your favorite park has lush gardens, a duck pond, a few acres of perfectly manicured lawns, and sweeping views of a nearby skyline. But unless your dog can run leash-free, swim in the pond, and roll in the grass, that park may not deserve a very high rating from your pet's perspective.

The lowest rating you'll come across in this book is the fire hydrant 🔥. When you see this symbol, it means the park is merely worth a squat. Visit one of these parks only if your dog can't hold it any longer. These pit stops have virtually no other redeeming qualities for canines.

Beyond that, the paws scale starts at one paw 🐾 and goes up to four paws 🐾🐾🐾🐾. A one-paw park isn't a dog's idea of a great time. Maybe it's a tiny park with only a few trees and too many kids running around. Or perhaps it's a magnificent national park that bans dogs from every inch of land except paved roads and a few campsites. Four-paw parks, on the other hand, are places your dog will drag you to visit. Some of these areas come as close to dog heaven as you can imagine. Many have lakes for swimming or hundreds of acres for hiking. Some are small, fenced-in areas where leash-free dogs can tear around without danger of running into the road. Many four-paw parks give you the option of letting your dog off-leash (although most have restrictions, which are detailed in the park description).

In addition to finding paws and hydrants, you'll also notice an occasional foot symbol 👣 in this book. The foot means the park offers something special for humans. After all, you deserve a reward for being such a good chauffeur.

This book is not meant to be a comprehensive guide to all of the parks in the state. Oregon suffers from a happy problem of excessive recreational opportunities. We struggled not to become overwhelmed or jaded as we selected the best, largest, most convenient, and dog-friendliest parks to include in the guide. We had to make tough choices about which to include and which to leave out. A few places have such a limited supply of parks that, for the sake of dogs living and visiting there, we listed parks that wouldn't otherwise be worth mentioning.

Since signposts are spotty and street names are notoriously confusing, we've given detailed directions to all the parks from the nearest major roadway or city center, but it certainly can't hurt to pick up a detailed street map before you and your dog set out on your travels.

He, She, It

In this book, whether neutered, spayed, or au naturel, dogs are never referred to as *it*. They are either *he* or *she*. Cooper and Isis insisted we alternate pronouns so no dog reading this book will feel left out.

To Leash or Not to Leash...

This is not a question that plagues dogs' minds. Ask just about any normal, red-blooded American dog if she'd prefer to play off-leash, and she'll say, "Arf!" (Translation: "That's a rhetorical question, right?") No question about it, most dogs would give their canine teeth to frolic about without that cumbersome leash.

Whenever you see the running dog 🐕 in this book, you'll know that under certain circumstances, your dog can run around in leash-free bliss. Some parks have off-leash hours, marked by the time 🐕 symbol. We wish we could write about the parks where dogs get away with being scofflaws.

Unfortunately, those would be the first ones animal control patrols would hit. We can't advocate breaking the law, but if you're tempted, please follow your conscience and use common sense.

Also, just because dogs are permitted off-leash in certain areas doesn't necessarily mean you should let your dog run free. Unless you're sure your dog will come back when you call or will never stray more than a few yards from your side, you should probably keep her leashed. An otherwise docile homebody can turn into a savage hunter if the right prey is near. A curious wet-nose could perturb the rattlesnakes that are common in high desert areas or run into a bear or cougar in the woods. In pursuit of a strange scent, your dog could easily get lost in an unfamiliar area.

Crowded or popular areas, especially beaches, can be full of unpredictable children and other dogs who may not be as well behaved as yours. It's a tug of war out there. People who've had bad experiences with dogs are demanding stricter leash laws everywhere or the banning of "those mongrels" altogether from public places. When faced with increasing limits, dog lovers want more designated places where their pets can play without fear of negative consequences. The rope is stretched thin and tensions are tight.

In short, be careful out there. If your dog needs leash-free exercise but you don't have her under complete voice control, she'll be happy to know that several beaches permit well-behaved, leashless pooches, as do a growing number of beautiful, fenced-in dog exercise areas. As for general leash restrictions, Oregon State Parks require dogs to be on a six-foot or shorter leash.

There's No Business Like Dog Business

There's nothing appealing about bending down with a plastic bag or a piece of newspaper on a chilly morning and grabbing the steaming remnants of what your dog ate for dinner the night before. Worse yet, you have to hang onto it until you can find a trash can. Blech! It's enough to make you wish you could train your pooch to sit on the potty. But as gross as it can be to scoop the poop, it's worse to step in it. It's really bad if a child falls in it, or—gag!—starts eating it. The funniest name for poop we heard on our travels was WMDs—Wanton Mongrel Defecations—but there's nothing funny about a poop-filled park. Have you ever walked into a park where few people clean up after their dogs? You don't want to be there any more than anyone else does.

Unscooped poop is one of a dog's worst enemies. Public policies banning dogs from parks are enacted because of it. Good parks and beaches that permit dogs are in danger of closing their gates to all canines because of the negligent behavior of a few owners. A worst-case scenario is already in place

in several communities—dogs are banned from all parks. Their only exercise is a leashed sidewalk stroll. That's no way to live.

Be responsible and clean up after your dog everywhere you go. Stuff plastic bags in your jacket, purse, car, pants pockets—anywhere you might be able to pull one out when needed. Don't count on the parks to provide them. Even when we found places with bag dispensers, they were more often empty than not. If you're squeamish about the squishy sensation, try one of those cardboard or plastic bag pooper-scoopers sold at pet stores. If you don't like bending down, buy a long-handled scooper. You get the point—there's a pooper-scooper for every preference.

And here's one for you: If your dog does his business in the woods, and nobody is there to see it, do you still have to pick up? Yes! Pack out what you pack in, and that includes the poop. As forest lands get ever-increasing usage, the only way to keep them pristine is to do your part. Here's a radical thought: Pick up extra while you're out and about—garbage, dog droppings, whatever. Cooper and Isis have the convenience of having very petite poop, so there's usually room left over in the bag. If enough people do it, we might just be able to guilt everyone into picking up after themselves and their pets.

Etiquette Rex: The Well-Mannered Mutt

While cleaning up after your dog is your responsibility, a dog in a public place has his own responsibilities. Of course, it really boils down to your responsibility again, but the burden of action is on your dog. Etiquette for restaurants and hotels is covered in other sections of this chapter. What follows are some fundamental rules of dog etiquette. We'll go through it quickly, but if your dog's a slow reader, he can read it again: no vicious dogs; no jumping on people; no incessant barking; no leg lifts on kayaks, backpacks, human legs, or any other personal objects you'll find hanging around beaches and parks; dogs should come when they're called; and they should stay on command.

Nobody's perfect, but do your best to remedy any problems. It takes patience and consistency. For example, Isis considers it her personal duty to vocally defend the car from passersby. So, we keep a squirt bottle on hand to quench her tendency to bark. In Cooper's mind, he's obeying the "Come!" command as long as he's vaguely and eventually headed in the right direction, and you can forget about it altogether if there are squirrels in the general vicinity, which means he's on leash more often than not. Every time there's a problem between someone's dog and someone else, we all stand to lose more of our hard-earned privileges to enjoy parks with our pets. Know your dog's limits or leash him. If you must, avoid situations that bring out the worst in your best friend.

The basic rules for dog parks are fairly consistent as well, and we've compiled a master list from our experience: no puppies under four months or females in heat; keep dogs from fighting and biting; leash your pets on entry and exit and in parking lots; be aware and keep your dog under voice control; ensure that your dog is properly vaccinated and licensed; and, you guessed it, pick up poop.

Safety First

A few essentials will keep your traveling dog happy and healthy.

Beat the Heat: If you must leave your dog alone in the car for a few minutes, do so only if it's cool out and you can park in the shade. Never, ever, ever leave a dog in a car with the windows rolled up all the way. Even if it seems cool, the sun's heat passing through the window can kill a dog in a matter of minutes. Roll down the window enough so your dog gets air, but not so much that there's danger of your dog getting out or someone breaking in. Make sure your dog has plenty of water.

You also have to watch out for heat exposure when your car is in motion. Certain cars, particularly hatchbacks, can make a dog in the backseat extra hot, even while you feel okay in the driver's seat.

Try to time your vacation so you don't visit a place when it's extremely warm. Dogs and heat don't get along, especially if your dog is a true Oregonian who thinks anything over 80 degrees is blistering. The opposite is also true. If your dog lives in a hot climate and you take him to a cold and rainy place, it may not be a healthy shift. Check with your vet if you have any doubts. Spring and fall are the best times to travel, when parks are less crowded anyway.

Water: Water your dog frequently. Dogs on the road may drink even more than they do at home. Take regular water breaks, or bring a bowl and set it on the floor so your dog always has access to water. We use a thick clay bowl on a rubber car mat, which comes in really handy on Oregon's curvy roads. When hiking, be sure to carry enough for you and a thirsty dog. Those folding cloth bowls you can find at outdoor stores are worth their weightlessness in gold.

Rest Stops: Stop and unwater your dog. There's nothing more miserable than being stuck in a car when you can't find a rest stop. No matter how tightly you cross your legs and try to think of the desert, you're certain you'll burst within the next minute… so imagine how a dog feels when the urge strikes, and he can't tell you the problem. There are plenty of rest stops along the major freeways. We've also included many parks close to freeways for dogs who need a good stretch with their bathroom break.

How frequently you stop depends on your dog's bladder. Cooper can hold it all day, whereas Isis is whining for a potty stop at every park. If your dog is constantly running out the doggy door at home to relieve himself, you may want to stop every hour. Others can go significantly longer without being uncomfortable. Our vet says to stop every two hours as a matter of course. Watch for any signs of restlessness and gauge it for yourself.

Car Safety: Even the experts differ on how a dog should travel in a car. Some suggest dog safety belts, available at pet-supply stores. Others firmly believe in keeping a dog kenneled. They say it's safer for the dog if there's an accident, and it's safer for the driver because there's no dog underfoot. Still another school of thought says you should just let your dog hang out without restraint, and hey, the dogs enjoy this more anyway.

Because of their diminutive stature, Isis and Cooper have a car seat in the back that lifts them to the level of the car window and secures their harnesses to the seat belt. That way, they can stick their snouts out of the windows to smell to world go by with some level of security. There's still the danger that the car could kick up a pebble or a bee could buzz by, so we open the car window just enough to stick out a little snout.

Planes: Air travel is even more controversial. We're fortunate that our tiny bundles of joy can fly with us in the passenger cabin, but it still costs $75 a head each way. We'd rather find a way to drive the distance or leave them

back at home with a friend or at the pampered pets inn. Val lost a childhood dog due to a heat-induced stroke from being left on the tarmac too long in his crate. There are other dangers, such as runway delays, when the cargo section is not pressurized on the ground, or the risk of connecting flights when a dog ends up in Auckland, New Zealand, while his people go to Oakland. Change can be stressful enough on a pet without being separated from his loved ones and thrown in the cargo hold like a piece of luggage.

If you need to transport your dog by plane, it is critical to fly nonstop, and make sure you schedule takeoff and arrival times when the temperature is below 80°F and above 35°F. All airlines require fees, and most will ask for a health certificate and proof of rabies vaccination.

The question of tranquilizing a dog for a plane journey causes the most contention. Some vets think it's insane to give a dog a sedative before flying. They say a dog will be calmer and less fearful without a disorienting drug. Others think it's crazy not to afford your dog the little relaxation she might not otherwise get without a tranquilizer. Discuss the issue with your vet, who will take into account the trip length and your dog's personality. Cooper prefers the mild sedative effect of a children's antihistamine.

The Ultimate Doggy Bag

Your dog can't pack her own bags, and even if she could, she'd fill them with dog biscuits and squeaky toys. It's important to stash some of those in your dog's vacation kit, but other handy items to bring along are bowls, bedding, a brush, towels (for those inevitable muddy days), a first-aid kit, pooper-scoopers, water, food, prescription drugs, tags, treats, toys, and, of course, this book.

Make sure your dog is wearing her license, identification tag, and rabies tag. We advocate a microchip for your dog in addition to the ever-present collar. On a long trip, you may want to bring along your dog's rabies certificate. We pray it'll never happen, but it's a good idea to bring a couple of photos of your dog to show around, should you ever get separated.

You can snap a disposable ID on your dog's collar, too, showing a cell phone number and the name, address, and phone number of where you'll be staying, or of a friend who'll be home to field calls. That way, if your dog should get lost, at least the finder won't be calling your empty house.

Some people think dogs should drink only water brought from home, so their bodies don't have to get used to too many new things at once. Although Cooper and Isis turn up their noses at water from anywhere other than a bottle poured in their bowl, most vets think your dog will be fine drinking tap water in U.S. cities.

Bone Appetite

In many European countries, dogs enter restaurants and dine alongside their folks as if they were people, too. (Or at least they sit and watch and drool while their people dine.) Not so in the United States. Rightly or wrongly, dogs are considered a health threat here. Health inspectors who say they see no reason clean, well-behaved dogs shouldn't be permitted inside a restaurant or on a patio are the exception rather than the rule.

Fortunately, you don't have to take your dog to a foreign country in order to eat together. Despite a drippy sky, Oregon has restaurants with seasonal outdoor tables and many of them welcome dogs to join their people for an alfresco experience. The law on outdoor dining is somewhat vague, and you'll encounter many different interpretations of it. In general, as long as your dog doesn't have to go inside to get to outdoor tables and isn't near the food preparation areas, it's probably legal. The decision is then up to the local inspector and/or restaurant proprietor. The most common rule of thumb we find is that if the patio is fully enclosed, dogs are discouraged from dining. Coop 'n' Isis have included restaurants with good takeout for those times when outdoor tables are stacked and tucked away.

The restaurants listed in this book have given us permission to tout them as dog-friendly eateries. But keep in mind that rules change and restaurants close, so we highly recommend phoning before you set your stomach on a particular kind of cuisine. Since you can safely assume the outdoor tables will move indoors for a while each year, and some restaurants close during colder months or limit their hours, phoning ahead is a doubly wise thing to do. Even for eateries listed in this book, it never hurts to politely ask the manager if your dog may join you before you sit down with your sidekick. Remember, it's the restaurant proprietor, not you, who will be in trouble if someone complains to the health department.

Now, we all know that the "five-second rule" for dropped food does not apply in most dog households. You're lucky if you get two seconds after uttering "Oops!" before the downed morsels become the property of your dog's maw. However, we're aiming for some better behavior when eating out. Some fundamental rules of restaurant etiquette: Dogs shouldn't beg from other diners, no matter how delicious the steak looks. They should not attempt to get their snouts (or their entire bodies) up on the table. They should be clean, quiet, and as unobtrusive as possible. If your dog leaves a good impression with the management and other customers, it will help pave the way for all the other dogs who want to dine alongside their best friends in the future.

A Room at the Inn

Good dogs make great hotel guests. They don't steal towels, burn cigarette holes in the bedding, or get drunk and keep the neighbors up all night. We've seen a positive trend in the number of places that allow pets. This book lists dog-friendly accommodations of all types, from affordable motels to bed-and-breakfast inns to elegant hotels, and even a few favorite campgrounds—but the basic dog etiquette rules apply everywhere.

Our stance is that dogs should never, *ever* be left alone in your room, even if crated. Leaving a dog alone in a strange place invites serious trouble. Scared, nervous dogs may tear apart drapes, carpeting, and furniture. They may even injure themselves. They might bark nonstop or scare the daylights out of the housekeeper. Just don't do it.

Bring only a house-trained dog to a lodging. How would you like a houseguest to relieve himself in the middle of your bedroom?

One of the hosts we met recommended always entering a new place with your dog on a short leash or crated, unless you've inquired ahead otherwise. We think that's a splendid idea. There are too many factors beyond your control.

Make sure your pooch is flea-free. Otherwise, future guests will be itching to leave. And, while cleanliness is not naturally next to dogliness, matted hair is not going to win you any favors. Scrub your pup elsewhere, though; the new rule we've heard quoted frequently is not to bathe your dog in a lodging's bathroom.

It helps to bring your dog's bed or blanket along for the night. Your dog will feel more at home having a familiar smell in an unfamiliar place, and will be less tempted to jump on the hotel bed. If your dog sleeps on the bed with you at home, bring a sheet or towel and put it on top of the bed so the hotel's bedspread won't get furry or dirty.

After a few days in a hotel, some dogs come to think of it as home. They get territorial. When another hotel guest walks by, it's "Bark! Bark!" When the housekeeper knocks, it's "Bark! Snarl! Bark! Gnash!" Keep your dog quiet, or you'll find yourselves looking for a new home away from home.

For some strange reason, many lodgings prefer small dogs as guests. All we can say is, "Yip! Yap!" It's ridiculous. Isis, bless her excitable little heart, is living proof that large dogs are often much calmer and quieter than their tiny, high-energy cousins.

If you're in a location where you can't find a hotel that will accept your big brute, it's time to try a sell job. Let the manager know how good and quiet your dog is (if he is). Promise he won't eat the bathtub or run around and shake all over the hotel. Offer a deposit or sign a waiver, even if they're not required. It helps if your sweet, immaculate, soppy-eyed pooch sits patiently at your side to convince the decision-maker.

We simply cannot recommend sneaking dogs into hotels. Accommodations have reasons for their rules. It's no fun to feel as if you're going to be caught and thrown out on your hindquarters or charged an arm and a leg and a tail if discovered. You race in and out of your room with your dog as if ducking the dogcatcher. It's better to avoid feeling like a criminal and move on to a more dog-friendly location. The good news is that many hotel chains are realizing the benefits of courting canine travelers. For sure bets, see *Chain Hotels* in the *Resources* chapter of this book.

Unless you know it's a large facility with plenty of availability, call ahead to reserve a dog room and always get prior approval to bring your pets to bed-and-breakfasts and private inns. Listed rates for accommodations are for double rooms, unless otherwise noted. They do not include AARP, AAA, or other discounts you may be entitled to. Always ask about discounts and specials. Likewise, pet fees listed are nonrefundable, per pet, per night unless we say otherwise. The places that don't charge a pet fee are few and far between, but where we haven't listed one, you can assume there's no canine upcharge unless damage is done.

Natural Troubles

Chances are your adventuring will go without a hitch, but you should always be prepared to deal with trouble. Know the basics of animal first aid before you embark on a long journey with your dog.

The more common woes—ticks, burrs, poison oak and ivy, and skunks—can make life with a traveling dog a somewhat trying experience. Ticks are hard to avoid in parts of Oregon. Although Lyme disease is rarely reported here, you should check yourself and your dog all over after a day in the country. Don't forget to check ears and between the toes. If you see an attached tick, grasp it with tweezers as close to your dog's skin as possible and pull straight out, gently but steadily, or twist counterclockwise as you pull. Disinfect before and after removing the pest.

The tiny deer ticks that carry Lyme disease are difficult to find. Consult your veterinarian if your dog is lethargic for a few days, has a fever, loses her appetite, or becomes lame. These symptoms could indicate Lyme disease. Some vets recommend a new vaccine that is supposed to prevent the onset of the disease. If you spend serious time in the woods, we suggest you carry a tick collar and have your dog vaccinated.

As for mosquitoes, although a few cases of the West Nile virus have been reported in Oregon since 2006, it is very rare for humans to get infected in our area and scientists at Washington State University's animal disease lab have no confirmed cases in dogs. Your best bet is a good DEET repellant for yourself.

Burrs and seeds—those pieces of nature that attach to your socks, your sweater, and your dog—are an everyday annoyance. In rare cases, they can be lethal. They may stick in your dog's eyes, nose, ears, or mouth and work their way in. Check every nook and cranny of your dog after a walk in dry fields.

Poison oak and ivy are very common menaces in our woods. Get familiar with them through a friend who knows nature or through a guided walk.

Dogs don't generally have reactions, but they easily pass the oils on to people. If you think your dog has made contact with some poison plant, avoid petting her until you can get home and bathe her (preferably with rubber gloves). If you do pet her before you can wash her, don't touch your eyes and be sure to wash your hands immediately. There are several good products on the market specifically for removing poison oak and ivy oils.

If your dog loses a contest with a skunk (and he always will), rinse his eyes first with plain warm water, then bathe him with dog shampoo. Towel him off, then apply tomato juice. If you can't get tomato juice, try using a solution of one pint of vinegar per gallon of water to decrease the stink instead.

Sea water may not seem sinister, but a dog who isn't accustomed to it may not restrain himself from gulping down a few gallons, which makes him sick as a dog, usually all over your car. Keep him hydrated to avoid temptation, and when you arrive at the beach, don't let him race to the sea and drink.

The Price of Freedom

Most state parks and national forests require daily parking fees unless you are also camping overnight. A $30 annual Northwest Forest Pass is good for all United States Forest Service (USFS) sites except a few with private concessions. They are available online at www.discovernw.org or at ranger stations. Only 26 of Oregon's nearly 200 parks charge a $3 day-use fee. Oregon's annual pass is $25 ($40 for a two-year pass), available with a credit card by phone at 800/551-6949. Various Army Corps of Engineers sites, Bureau of Land Management (BLM) sites, and Fish and Wildlife locations may charge $1 to $10 per day for parking and/or camping.

For fishing, shellfish harvesting, and hunting licenses in Oregon, go to www.dfw.state.or.us and click the Licensing and Regulations link.

A Dog in Need

If you don't currently have a dog but could provide a good home for one, we'd like to make a plea on behalf of all the unwanted dogs who will be euthanized tomorrow—and the day after that and the day after that. Cooper came from a rescue organization and Isis from previous owners who knew they couldn't give her the personal attention she deserved. In their extended family, Coop 'n' Isis have a grandmother with two more dachshunds and a terrier, an uncle with a boxer, and an aunt with a corgi mix, all rescued. Animal shelters and humane organizations are overflowing with dogs who would devote their lives to being your best buddy, your faithful traveling companion, and a dedicated listener to all your tales. We also strongly support efforts to control the existing dog population—spay or neuter your dogs! In the immortal words of *Nike*, just do it.

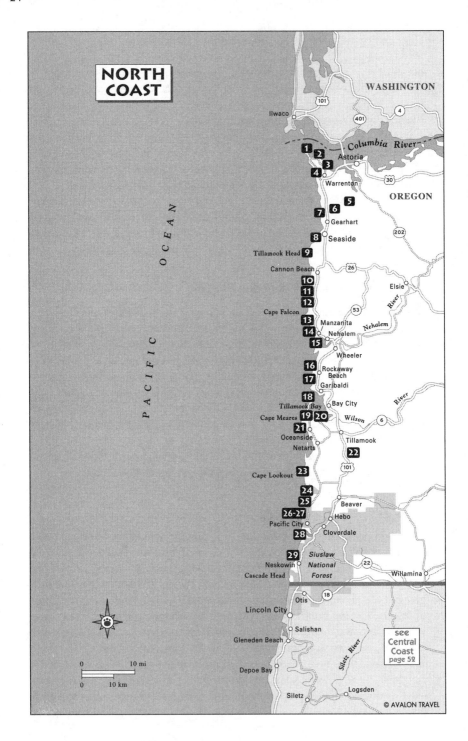

CHAPTER 1

North Coast

Though they are die-hard Washingtonians, Isis and Cooper will be the first to admit that Oregon's coast is a beautiful place to play near big water. To keep the shores looking their best, more than 5,000 residents gather twice a year for massive beach cleanup work parties. Go to www.solv.org for more information if you'd like to participate in the Great Beach Cleanup.

There are so many fun parks and beach access points that the coast had to be split into three chapters. Even then, the dogs had an agonizing time choosing only the best. Basically, you can't lift a leg along the coast and miss a state park or public beach. Access to them may be limited in areas where uplands are private property, but once you are on the sand, there's nothing to stop you other than high tides, cliffs, and rocks. Well, that and the snowy plover. The tiny bird is on the endangered species list, and because it makes its nest in the soft, dry sand, your dog's freedom may be restricted in marked areas March–September.

PICK OF THE LITTER—NORTH COAST

BEST PARKS
Ecola State Park, Cannon Beach (page 34)
Cape Lookout, Netarts (page 47)

BEST BEACHES
Neah-Kah-Nie Beach, Manzanita (page 38)
Manhattan Beach, Rockaway Beach (page 42)

BEST EVENT
Dog Show at the Beach, Cannon Beach (page 34)

BEST PLACES TO EAT
Cranky Sue's, Cannon Beach (page 36)
Bread and Ocean, Manzanita (page 38)

BEST PLACES TO STAY
Cannery Pier Hotel, Astoria (page 30)
Inn at Cannon Beach, Cannon Beach (page 37)
The Studio and **The Lighthouse,** Manzanita (page 41)
Inn at Cape Kiwanda, Pacific City (page 50)

You don't have to wait until summer to enjoy the quintessential coast experience. Lodging rates are much cheaper in the off-season. Winter storms produce shows of power and drama. Rare finds, such as Japanese glass floats and agates, are more likely to wash ashore during these turbulent times. If you get chilled, it is legal to have campfires on Oregon beaches unless a fire restriction is posted. You should be prepared for wet weather and ocean squalls at any time. Oregon's average coastal rainfall is higher than Seattle's, if you can believe that. Also, call ahead and keep in mind that business hours change dramatically with the seasons, and some shops and restaurants come and go with the ebb and flow of the economic tides.

Old-fashioned seaside resorts, working fishing ports, photographic natural landmarks, and the final destination of Lewis and Clark's great adventure— all of these await visitors to Oregon's coast. Of the 11 lighthouses on the coast, nine are on the National Register of Historic Places, seven of them open for public viewing and tours. Two are privately built and individually owned, open to the public only as sneak peaks from roadside viewpoints.

Astoria-Warrenton

Astoria is rich in history as the oldest settlement west of the Rocky Mountains. In 1792, explorer Robert Gray entered the mouth of the Columbia River, naming it after his ship, the *Columbia Rediviva*. It was here, in 1805, that the Lewis and Clark Expedition wintered at Fort Clatsop, waiting out the rain and preparing for their return journey. In 1811, American John Jacob Astor financed a trading post in what is now Astoria. As you walk through town, you can see the past in more buildings per square foot on the National Historic Register than any other Oregon location.

The Astoria Sunday Market along 12th Street, 10 A.M.–3 P.M. Mother's Day– October, has a long-standing reputation as a dog-friendly event (503/325-1010, www.astoriasundaymarket.com).

PARKS, BEACHES, AND RECREATION AREAS

◼ Fort Stevens
🐾🐾🐾 (See North Coast map on page 24)

At the tip of the Oregon Coast, this state park starts things off with a bang. Constructed during the Civil War, it remained an active military post until after World War II. Eight concrete gun batteries are the focal point of a self-guided tour of the abandoned fort, the tip of the iceberg in this 3,700-acre park.

There are five major parking areas to reach miles of windswept beach. Parking Lot A is primarily for equestrian access, Lot C has an excellent long-range viewing platform for watching the kiteboarders and surfers, and Lot D reaches the most protected area around the bend where the Columbia River meets the ocean. It's the lot without a letter, however, that's the most popular. The southernmost access point takes you to the wreck of the *Peter Iredale*. The rusting hulk of this English sailing ship remains onshore, a hundred years after it ran aground.

For some, the beach is too windy and exposed. Take to the six miles of hiking trails in the park instead, especially the two-mile, hikers-only loop around Coffenbury Lake. Locals also recommend the Columbia River Beach, where there's typically fewer people and more dogs.

Take U.S. Highway 101 four miles south of Astoria. Turn west on Warrenton Road and follow the signs another five miles to the park. Parking is $3. 503/861-1671.

◼ Carruthers Dog Park
🐾🐾🐕 (See North Coast map on page 24)

Contractor delays, a toppling giant spruce, and an errant car crashing into the fence did not stop Warrenton's determined dog owners from opening this off-leash area in 2008. Thanks to their perseverance, there's a new place for

NATURE HIKES AND URBAN WALKS

The **Fort Clatsop National Memorial** is a national park where dogs *are* allowed, except in the buildings. According to the park ranger, you may keep your traveling companion with you on the trails and grounds because Meriwether Lewis was never far from Seaman, his faithful Newfoundland, on his journey.

Together, you can walk the grounds and peek into the cramped spaces of this life-size replica shared by the 31 men, Sacagawea, and her papoose, from December 7, 1805 until March 23, 1806. The fort was re-created according to exact specifications described in Lewis's journals. At a site in nearby Seaside, the men made salt to preserve meats for the return journey, hunted, sewed moccasins, and traded frequently with Chinook and Clatsop Native Americans.

Open 9 A.M.–5 P.M. Entrance is $3 per person. Pets are free. 92343 Fort Clatsop Rd.; 503/861-2471; www.nps.gov/lewi.

dogs to run free on the coast. It's almost an acre of natural surroundings with shade trees. Separate, five-foot fenced areas for small and large rabble rousers allow free play. It remains to be seen how long the strong grass will last. Niceties include drinking water, an enclosed cement dog wash station, scattered benches, and pet waste disposal stations.

From downtown Astoria, head south on Highway 101 toward Seaside, across the Youngs Bay Bridge. Turn right on Harbor Street (State Route 104). You'll go straight at the stop sign as Harbor Drive becomes N. Main Avenue, and bear left at the fork in the road when it becomes N.W. Warrenton Drive on the way. It's three miles from the turnoff to the park, which comes up with little warning on the right. Open 6 A.M.–10 P.M. 503/861-2233; www.ci.warrenton.or.us.

3 Cathedral Tree Trail

(See North Coast map on page 24)

From 28th Street and Irving in downtown Astoria, you and your pup can climb up past lofty Cathedral Tree to Coxcomb Hill and the Astoria Column. Or, you can start and the top and wander down into town. Where you start depends on whether you want to go uphill first or last, and if you have someone to pick you up at either end. It is a pleasant, manageable walk, 1.5 miles one-way. There are stairs and boardwalks for the steep parts, and plenty of benches for resting along the way. The tree is about halfway through; you can shorten the trip using it as a turnaround. Or, to lengthen your excursion, additional short trails spur off to the sides.

Street parking is very limited in town. You'll have better luck if you pay the buck to park at Astoria Column.

4 Astoria Column

 (See North Coast map on page 24)

The park is called Astor Park, but it is known by its main feature, the 125-foot-tall Astoria Column, patterned after Rome's Trajan Column and Paris' Vendome. The bas-relief art of the column combines paint and plaster carvings to tell the story of Astoria's early white explorers and settlers.

Visitors crowd the column, leaving more room on the hillsides where your dog may better enjoy himself at view picnic tables and benches. The view from Coxcomb Hill, where the column sits, has always been stunning. It encompasses the wide mouth of the Columbia River, the grand Astoria-Megler Bridge, and the start of the Pacific Coast Scenic Highway, U.S. Highway 101. Naturally, it is the best place in town to watch sunsets.

From U.S. Highway 30, Marine Drive in town, turn north on 16th Street and follow the stencils of the column on the road. Parking is a $1 donation. Open daylight–10 P.M.

5 Youngs River Falls

 (See North Coast map on page 24)

Captain Patrick Gass of Lewis and Clark's Corps of Discovery recorded happening upon these 65-foot falls during a hunting expedition in March 1806. Today, this county park is an undeveloped picnic area with a gravel road and a few steps down to the bottom of the falls on the western fork of the Youngs River. Dogs can splash right into this local swimming hole and do some light hiking up and around the top of the cascade.

From U.S. Highway 30 in Astoria, take State Route 202 10 miles to Olney and turn south on Youngs River Falls Loop Road for another 3.8 miles.

PLACES TO EAT

Blue Scorcher: Kudos to Carlee and Jeff, the Dachsies' honorary Aunt and Uncle, for discovering this delectable bakery for breakfast, lunch, and beautiful breads. Being big on humane treatment for all beings, Coop 'n' Isis are happy to include this all-vegetarian and vegan hangout. The owners have turned a former auto body shop into a cool space where you simply want to hang out and eat your way to health and happiness. 1493 Duane St.; 503/338-7473; www.bluescorcher.com.

Bow Picker Fish and Chips: Order a half or full order of fish and chips right off the boat, only this 1956 wooden boat is moored in a field at the corner of 17th and Duane, across from the Maritime Museum. They serve seasonally, usually May–October, with a couple of picnic tables under a tree and beverages in a cooler. Cash only. 503/791-2942.

Wet Dog Café: Astoria Brewing Company's brewpub dishes up a massive menu of mondo burgers, including many involving seafood innards like catfish, swordfish, cod, and tuna. Okay, let's get real, you're here for the beer. Your dog's here because the patio is a party from Memorial Day until the rain blasts the siding off the walls. We couldn't pass up the Poop Deck Porter nor could we resist buying a Wet Dog hoodie. 144 11th St.; 503/325-6975.

PLACES TO STAY

Cannery Pier Hotel: Isis loves the three pet-friendly rooms at the glam CPH, opened in 2008, from its rooms with private, river view decks to the complimentary Finnish-inspired breakfast. She may have been swayed by the extensive pet goodie basket, which included treats and a squeaky toy. Isis' mom might also have been influenced by the claw foot tub, gas fireplace, complimentary wine happy hour and breakfast... oh, and the Finnish sauna. A single $40 charge applies to all pet stays. Rates range $170–300 for king and queen rooms; up to $350 for the suite. No. 10 Basin St.; 503/325-4996; www.cannerypierhotel.com.

Clementine's Bed and Breakfast: Judith welcomes dogs, has three of her own, and is happy to go with you on daily dog walks around town and lead you to the secret spots in the woods nearby. Her only request is that your dogs don't pee on her beautiful flowers; there's a park a few blocks away. Pets are allowed in the Riverview Loft ($135–165) and the two suites of the Moose Temple Lodge, next door to the main inn ($110–140 each, may be combined), plus a $25 cleaning fee per stay. 847 Exchange St.; 503/325-2005; www.clementines-bb.com.

Crest Motel: There are no pet fees at this Scandinavian-themed motel, and the only rules are that you keep your pets leashed on the property and don't leave them unattended in the rooms. Rates range from $60 for non-view queens to $115 for a view suite. 5366 Leif Erickson Dr.; 503/325-3141 or 800/421-3141; www.astoriacrestmotel.com.

Fort Stevens Campground: This campground is a city with 174 full-hookup, 302 electrical, and 19 tent sites in 14 loops. Rates are $13–22. Believe it or not, sites go fast in the summer. You'll need reservations. 100 Peter Iredale Rd.; 800/452-5687; www.reserveamerica.com.

More Accommodations: Please look under *Chain Hotels* in the *Resources* section for additional places to stay in this area.

Gearhart

Golf is the biggest attraction in this otherwise sleepy town, a tasteful and quiet oceanfront community that has been compared to old Cape Cod. There's a great lawn and beach access at the west end of Pacific Way, Gearhart's main street.

PARKS, BEACHES, AND RECREATION AREAS

6 Fort to Sea Trail

🐾🐾🐾 (See North Coast map on page 24)

At 6.5 miles one-way, this is a biggie, tracing the route that Lewis and Clark's men took from Fort Clatsop to the Pacific Ocean. It starts at Fort Clatsop visitors center and ends at Sunset Beach. In the summer, a shuttle will pick you up at either end and take you back. Otherwise, may we suggest breaking it into bite-sized pieces? For example, the one-mile round-trip down to Sunset Beach and back was definitely doable by the Dachsies. There's another one-mile loop that goes out and back from the fort side of things.

The fort and trail have seen some rough times, but they've prevailed. The replica of the fort burned to the ground in an accidental fire on October 3, 2005, and was completely rebuilt with safer materials and re-opened December 9, 2006. Then the trail was closed after extensive damage caused by a storm on December 3, 2007. It took eight months to clear away the debris and saw through the tree fall to recreate the trail, which reopened in August 2008. Come see what all the hard work has preserved.

From Highway 101, turn inland at the sign for Fort Clatsop, or turn west at the sign for Sunset Beach Lane, at milepost 13, south of Warrenton. Parking is $3 at the visitors center. www.forttosea.org.

7 Del Rey Beach

🐾🐾🐾 (See North Coast map on page 24)

At this State Recreation Site, you can experience the wonderful feeling of watching the rest of the world disappear. Once you climb over the sand dune that hides the parking lot, the only sight before you is the ocean and miles of flat, pristine beach. Light fog often obscures the town of Seaside and Tillamook Head, and even though cars are allowed on the wide, hard-packed sand, you'll watch the few that pass by shrink and fade in the distance. When the rest of the world seems too crowded and noisy, come to Del Rey to expand your horizons. Dogs appreciate the blissful simplicity of Del Rey's empty beach in the same way they can chase a single slobbery tennis ball until they drop.

From U.S. Highway 101, two miles north of Gearhart, turn west on Highlands Lane and continue straight onto the beach, or follow the left fork in the road until it dead-ends in the parking lot. There are no facilities at this beach.

PLACES TO STAY

Gearhart Ocean Inn: The cottage units at this 1941 restored inn are cool, crisp, and refreshing. The prices, ranging $100–165, are equally refreshing, only five blocks to the nearest beach. A maximum of two pets are allowed in units #3–5, 7, and 8, for $15 per pet per night. 67 N. Cottage Ave.; 503/738-7373; www.gearhartoceaninn.com.

Seaside

This beach city has attracted visitors for 150 years, and the antics of the seals at Seaside's famous aquarium have entertained people for more than 60 of those years. You get a glimpse of the old-time, carnival flavor of Oregon's first resort town along Broadway, a crowded arcade street with bumper cars, a restored carousel, and kitschy souvenir shops, ice cream parlors, and cotton candy and elephant ear vendors. Beach Books across from the Carousel Mall is a good find. Pop in for a lounge chair read and give Oz the cat a scratch behind the ears (37 N. Edgewood; 503/738-3500).

Sunset Boulevard, immediately south of downtown, is an aptly named place to park and watch the day descend into twilight, along a rocky, driftwood-scattered section of the beach. While in Seaside, your canine companion might enjoy a side trip to Oregon's largest tree, a 750-year-old Sitka spruce. The pullout is on U.S. Highway 26, 1.5 miles east of the junction with U.S. Highway 101.

PARKS, BEACHES, AND RECREATION AREAS

🖪 Seaside Promenade

 (See North Coast map on page 24)

The city's famous sidewalk promenade has been an institution since 1908. "The Prom" original was a boardwalk, replaced with a wide concrete structure in 1920. The aquarium marks the north end, and on the south you'll pass the site of Lewis and Clark's Salt Camp, with a historic re-creation of the seawater boiling operation. In the middle is an automobile turnaround commemorating the end of the Lewis and Clark Trail. There are excellent views of crashing waves all along the 1.5-mile one-way walk. Many resident and visiting canines cruise The Prom, along with walkers, joggers, bikers, and skaters. You can get down onto the beach at the turnaround.

Downtown public parking is easiest to find in the Trend West Tower at the intersection of 1st Avenue and Columbia Street. A one-block walk from there to the beach puts you right at the halfway point.

PLACES TO EAT

Big Foot Pub 'n' Grub: Patio dining at this bar and grill requires an extra level of vigilance. No matter how well-mannered, any canine culprit is going to be tempted to do a grab-and-dash, taking off with the juicy slab of prime rib that Big Foot is deservedly famous for serving. 2427 S. Roosevelt Dr.; 503/738-7009.

The Buzz: The Wonder Wieners bet you a box of chocolate-covered Twinkies that this is the most amazing candy store you'll ever see. Inside this magical emporium—home of the aforementioned confection—is floor to ceiling candy, from highbrow organic chocolates to giant lollipops in colors not found in nature. Don't count calories or dental fillings. Prefer to sip your sugar? Buzz carries 200 kinds of old-fashioned soda pop. Not enough for your sweet tooth? Next door is Chez Scoop, the ice cream shop. 406 Broadway; 503/717-8808.

Pirate's Cove General Store: Piracy is popular on the coast these days, and there's none more fun than this highway stop north of Seaside decked out as subtly as a theme park. The dessert and sundae list is longer than the main menu of burgers, salads, and sandwiches. Bring the whole family in for a Swiss Roast Beef Robinson and Pirate's Pig Out double banana split. There's outdoor seating under a covered patio at tables made from what just might be empty rum barrels washed ashore at nearby Fort Stevens. 90334 Hwy. 101; 503/861-7400.

PLACES TO STAY

Rivertide Suites: For those of you who prefer that new carpet smell to the odor of wet dog, this property, opened in 2008, is for you. You'll stay in designer condos, complete with kitchens fit for entertaining, gas fireplaces, big tubs, and flat-screen TVs mounted everywhere. Two dogs up to 75 pounds each are allowed, but it ain't cheap at $25 per pet per night. There's a pet goodie bag in the deal for you and a fenced relief area out back. Rates include four people, starting at $95–195 for studios, to $245–480 for 2-bedroom suites. 102 N. Holladay; 503/717-1100; www.rivertidesuites.com.

Sandy Cove Inn: An ambitious young couple has taken a derelict property in a brilliant location and turned it into a neat little beachside motel with charm and class. It's across from a pub, a block from a coffee shop, and two blocks to The Prom and Surfer's Cove. Eight ground-floor, pet-friendly rooms are furnished with antiques that you can buy out from under yourself. They openly welcome pets with a gift basket that includes treats and a gift certificate to a nearby pet boutique. Most of all, proprietors Mike and Betsy are down to earth, wonderfully friendly, and they've got their act together. Their affordable rates challenge the local Motel 6, ranging $45–130, plus a $10 pet fee. 241 Ave. U; 503/738-7473; www.sandycoveinn.biz.

More Accommodations: Please look under *Chain Hotels* in the *Resources* section for additional places to stay in this area.

Cannon Beach

Named for a cannon washed ashore in 1846 from the wreck of the schooner *Shark*, this booming community is the busiest destination on the North Coast. It has a reputation for its dramatic sea-stack rock formations, first-class lodging, and art from more than two dozen galleries and studio artists. The town bulges at the seams in the summer from the pressure of visitors and a growing number of permanent residents. For outdoor recreation with your dogs in and around Cannon Beach, the Dachshund Duo recommends the quiet season, October–April.

PARKS, BEACHES, AND RECREATION AREAS

🛛 Ecola State Park

🐾🐾🐾🐾 🐾➤ (See North Coast map on page 24)

Ecola smelled like a four-paw park from the moment Coop 'n' Isis drove through its 1,300 acres of forest, climbing up Tillamook Head to emerge at the first of many parking viewpoints at Ecola Point. The whole shebang is nine miles of ocean frontage, from Cannon Beach to Indian Head, following the coastal exploratory routes of Lewis and Clark.

The first hike you might want to try extends 1.5 miles from Ecola Point to Indian Head Beach, alternating between forests of mythical proportions and cliffside ocean views. You can also drive straight to Indian Head Beach to save your strength for more hiking.

The Clatsop Loop Interpretive Trail heads two miles north from Indian Head, with a brochure that traces the tale of a whale, where the Corps of Discovery, led by Lewis and Sacagawea, came upon Clatsop Indians carving and rendering whale blubber. At 1.5 miles, there is a hikers' camp, with primitive three-sided bunk cabins, a fire ring, water, and restrooms. Beyond the camp, the trail leads to the Tillamook Rock Lighthouse Viewpoint. All of the trails have areas of steep cliffs; leashes are a must.

Twelve miles out to sea, Tillamook Rock is the coast's most unusual lighthouse. The poor lightkeepers in this precarious spot were so battered by waves that the sentinel earned the nickname Terrible Tilly. It is the only registered historical lighthouse to be privately owned and it serves the unique purpose of being a Columbarium, a storage place for ashes of the deceased.

From U.S. Highway 101, turn off at the north Cannon Beach Loop exit onto

🐾 DOG-EAR YOUR CALENDAR

Your darling doesn't have to be a purebred to participate in the **Dog Show at the Beach** in Cannon Beach on the second Saturday in October. Pedigree isn't the point at this event, which features 1st-, 2nd-, and 3rd-place ribbons in more than 20 categories, everything from biggest ears to best tail wag. The event is sponsored by the Surfsand Resort, among others. There's no fee to enter, and any donations you wish to make will go to the Clatsop County Animal Shelter. Buy lots of raffle tickets! Find more information or make a donation at 800/547-6100 or www.cannonbeach.org.

Sunset Boulevard, bear right on 5th Street for a few blocks signs to turn off on Fir Street into the park. Parking is $3. O|
503/436-2844.

🔟 Tolovana Beach Wayside

😺😺😺🐾 (See North Coast map on page 24)

This State Recreation Site is the largest beach access point in the city, giving beach walkers an entry point for a seven-mile stretch of active waterfront. Your dog can pal around with the *many* other dogs who'll be on the beach.

Haystack Rock, the universal symbol of Cannon Beach, sits onshore. The 235-foot monolith is a National Wildlife Refuge, home to a large colony of bright tufted puffins. You'll need to stay off the rocks, but you can investigate the tidepools around the other sea stacks, called the Needles.

There's a lot of action at Tolovana Beach. You can grab a cup of chowder at Mo's or catch a game of pickup volleyball. Strong winds make for good kite flying; in fact, you can tie a kite to your lawn chair and it'll fly itself. Although Cannon Beach city municipal code states that dogs are only required to be under good voice control, crowds may necessitate the dreaded leash.

From U.S. Highway 101, turn west on Hemlock Street, also called the Cannon Beach Loop. After 0.4 mile, turn left into the wayside parking lot. Open 5 A.M.–10 P.M.

🔟 Arcadia Beach

😺😺 (See North Coast map on page 24)

From the gravel lot, you can park and sit and look at the ocean through the trees, for starters. After a short walk and a few wooden steps, your dog will love feeling the soft sand in his paws and the water lapping at his forelegs in this pretty cove. You might as well leave your shoes in the car, too. The odd sandal or sock left on the sand is a frequent sight, evidence of the irresistible urge to let loose on the beach and leave your cares behind. The waves crashing against offshore rocks have a hypnotic effect, inducing deep states of relaxation.

There is a restroom and a picnic table on a patch of lawn at this day-use-only State Recreation Site, three miles south of Cannon Beach on U.S. Highway 101. Open 6 A.M.–10 P.M.

🔟 Hug Point

😺😺😺 (See North Coast map on page 24)

You can trace the remnants of a treacherous stagecoach route carved into the cliffs that hugs the point on the north end of this glistening beach. You're free to walk along the historic roadbed, explore a couple of caves, and hike to a waterfall around the headland, but only at ebb tide. It's critical to know the tide table for the day, available free at the visitors center or most merchants town, or you could find yourself stranded on the rocks as travelers of old often were.

The highway parking lot has drinking water and a vault toilet. This State Recreation Site is 4.3 miles south of Cannon Beach on U.S. Highway 101. Open 6 A.M.–10 P.M.

1️⃣3️⃣ Oswald West

🐾🐾🐾🐾 🐾➤ (See North Coast map on page 24)

Oswald West, Oregon's governor from 1911 to 1915, is the man responsible for designating all of the state's beaches as public lands, preserving the coastal playground for all to enjoy. This 2,474-acre state park does him proud by honoring his memory and foresight.

As you drive into the park on U.S. Highway 101, there are a series of viewpoints as the road winds up and around Neah-Kah-Nie Mountain. From the southern parking lot, a 0.5-mile spur trail leads you down to Short Sands Beach, tucked into lush Smugglers Cove, a highly prized destination for surfers and boogie boarders chasing endless summer. The multiple waterways of Kerwin, Necarney, and Short Sands Creeks splash down the hillsides of Neah-Kah-Nie Mountain and Cape Falcon, the two headlands protecting the crescent beach. High-rise old-growth cedars, hemlocks, spruce, and firs hide a tent city of 30 hike-in sites; you can pass within feet of the campground and not see it.

From Manzanita to Arch Cape, a 13-mile stretch of the Oregon Coast Trail traverses the park. For you and your pup, two excellent trail sections break off from the beach spur. Cape Falcon is the easier trail, rising 300 feet in two miles to the tip of the headland to view the spectacle of the ocean below. The Neahkahnie Mountain Trail starts across a woozy suspension bridge, climbs switchbacks to a meadow, then crosses the highway on the way up to the summit at 1,631 feet. Up in this rarified air, every few footsteps lead you to another ocean vista.

Trail maps, wheelbarrows to transport camping gear, restrooms, and a drinking fountain are located in the larger parking lot on the east side of the highway. Oswald West is on U.S. Highway 101, 10 miles south of Cannon Beach. 503/368-3575.

PLACES TO EAT

Cranky Sue's: We don't know about Sue, but her famous "very crabby cakes," stuffed to the gills with succulent, sweet blue crab, put us in a fabulous mood. Seafood lovers, this corner café has to be on your "bucket list" of things to do before you die. Tables on the lawn out front are usually full, so take your cakes across the street to tables along Ecola Creek Park. Sue's dogs Cork and Rudy provide hilarious menu reviews. 308 Fir St.; 503/436-0301; www.crankysues.com.

Ye Olde Driftwood Inn: A kiss and a hug, apple pie á la mode, a dog and

his human, seafood and steaks... there are some perfect pairs sim
go together. Enjoy them whenever you can. Especially when they i
cocktail bar, and a railing on the porch to latch your pal to while imbibing. 179
N. Hemlock St.; 503/436-2439; www.driftwoodcannonbeach.com.

PLACES TO STAY

Arch Cape House: Dogs are usually permitted only in the Provence Room,
an intimate suite on the garden level with its own entrance through elegant
French doors. It's the only room at the inn with a terrace and a whirlpool tub.
Darn. The rate is $200–220 per night; the pet fee is $35. 31970 E. Ocean Rd.;
503/436-2800; www.archcapehouse.com.

Inn at Arch Cape: This intimate retreat is perfectly placed between Hug
Point and Oswald West. Rooms recall an earlier, gracious era when the well-
to-do summered at the coast. Each has tongue-and-groove pine interiors and
beach rock fireplaces, with wood provided. Two dogs are allowed in rooms
#3–6, for $15 per pet per night. Rates vary $95–205 seasonally. 79340 Hwy.
101; 503/738-7373 or 800/352-8034; www.innatarchcape.com.

Inn at Cannon Beach: There's something to be said for staying at a private
inn owned by savvy people with really good taste in things like HDTVs, gas
fireplaces, big windows, and two-person jetted tubs. A welcome basket for pet
guests includes linens, towels, bags, and biscuits. Of the 40 units, 16 allow a
maximum of two pets. Guest pets will appreciate the doors opening onto a
central courtyard with a pond and native plants. For the ultimate in luxury,
inquire about oceanfront rooms at their sister property, the Ocean Lodge.
Rates of $100–250 include a light buffet breakfast. The pet fee is $10 per pet
per night. 3215 S. Hemlock St.; 800/321-6304; www.innatcannonbeach.com
and www.theoceanlodge.com.

Lands End Motel: People book years in advance to return to "their" rooms at
this property, owned by the same couple since the 1970s. The owners update the
rooms frequently; when we checked in, it looked untouched and meticulously
clean. The dogs love the friendly staff, the beach location can't be beat, and
there's a wide choice of rooms. Rates range $140–295, plus a $15 one-time pet
fee. Two-dog maximum. 263 2nd St.; 503/436-2264; www.landsendmotel.com

Shaw's Oceanfront Bed and Breakfast: From the back deck at Shaw's, you
and your dog can step into the fenced backyard, through the gate, and onto
the beach. This casual home includes a separate bedroom, living room, and
kitchen for preparing meals and snacks, except for breakfast, which is made
for you. The entire two-bedroom suite is yours for $200 a night, $185 per night
for two or more nights. Pets are an additional $25 per stay. 79924 Cannon Rd.;
503/426-1422 or 888/269-4483; www.shawsoceanfrontbb.com.

Surfsand Resort: This large, cheerful family resort openly brags about
their pet-friendliness by sponsoring Cannon Beach's annual Dog Show on
the Beach. Dogs are welcome in all types of rooms except waterfront hot tub

suites, for a $15 pet fee. Pet-friendly condos and vacation rental homes are available as well. Your dog will receive a basket of goodies at the front desk and there are "walking" papers everywhere for your convenience. Room rates range widely from $150–360; see the website for home selection and pricing. 147 W. Gower; 800/547-6100; www.surfsand.com.

Oswald West Campground: For a more pristine camping experience, try one of 30 walk-in tent sites. It's about a third of a mile down to the campground, and you can borrow a wheelbarrow for no charge. There are restrooms and drinking water, but no showers. Rates are $10–14. Open March–October on a first-come, first-served basis. 503/368-3575.

Manzanita

This smaller beach community at the foot of Neah-Kah-Nie Mountain is so popular with the canine crowd, it has earned the flattering nickname Muttzanita. One hotel owner quoted a 30 percent occupancy rate in the area, just for the dogs! There are a few choice shops, eateries, funky bookstores, and a lovely beach on a loop off the beaten highway. In Cooper's humble opinion, it's a resort town perfected.

PARKS, BEACHES, AND RECREATION AREAS

14 Neah-Kah-Nie Beach

🐾🐾🐾🐾 (See North Coast map on page 24)

With a beach this good, you only need one. Manzanita's city park goes on seemingly forever, seven miles actually, and has enough going on to keep you busy for a week. There are tales of buried treasure, of a Spanish galleon strayed off course and wrecked at the foot of the mountain. No one has unearthed gleaming gold bullion, but artifacts such as a wine cup and a beeswax candle prove the story. As for beach treasures, the early dog gets the best pick of seashells, agates, and driftwood, seaweed, flotsam, and jetsam. Beachcombers are allowed to take the treasures they find, unless in a protected refuge area or marked signs indicate otherwise. Let us know if you find galleons.

From U.S. Highway 101, turn west on Laneda Avenue through town, and turn onto Ocean Road. Park at any one of several roadside areas and walk straight onto the beach. Take advantage of the doggie bag dispensers and garbage cans at several beach entrance points. No parking 11 P.M.–5 A.M.

PLACES TO EAT

Bread and Ocean: A beautiful hand-carved picnic table on the lawn in front welcomes you to this bakery and deli, a harbinger of more good things to come. The display case is filled with artisan breads and bowls of couscous, wild rice, roasted beets, and caprese salads. Isis nearly died and went to heaven

DIVERSIONS

While in Astoria, pop into **LaDeDog!** (120 10th St.; 503/325-8337; www.ladedog.net), a dog boutique around the corner from the River-walk, where you can bring your bud to sample some delicious treats. Bring a photo of your pup for their album, and check their website for yappy hour events.

The pet boutique in Cannon Beach is called **Puppy Love by the Sea** (271 N. Hemlock; 503/436-9800). It's petite, but well stocked. While there, grab the local pet informer, the *Bow Wow* dog newspaper (bowwowdognews.com).

In 2008, perfect Manzanita got even better with the opening of the dog boutique **Four Paws on the Beach** (144 Laneda; 503/368-3436; www.fourpawsonthebeach.com). The large collection of practical, outdoor gear from RuffWear is most impressive.

when allowed a bite of grilled panini with Serrano ham, Manchego cheese, quince paste, and arugula. She loves saying the word arugula. 387 Laneda; 503/368-5823; www.breadandocean.com.

Left Coast Siesta: The Siesta puts together Southwest-Mex like the board game *Clue:* It was tequila lime chicken, smothered by burrito sauce, finished off with black olives and sunflower seeds, wrapped in a red chili tortilla, to be polished off on the deck. Get it to go, and take your game to the beach, as the patio is too crowded to allow pets. 288 Laneda; 503/368-7997.

Manzanita News and Espresso: Get informed while sipping your daily fix at this fixture in the center of town. This joint win's Cooper's vote for best coffee on the coast and the most interesting locals with whom to chat. Savories include quiches, Mediterranean gyros, and chicken sandwiches. No dogs on deck, and on leash only please, using the hitching post provided for the purpose. 500 Laneda Ave.; 503/368-7450.

Manzanita Seafood and Chowderhouse: To go, they have the largest fresh seafood market on the North Coast. To stay, we love their multi-level brick patio with its large, round, family-style tables. Steamed clams, whole crab, and fried oysters taste better in the sea air. For less adventurous kids, they'll make a fluffernutter sandwich (peanut butter and marshmallow cream) or grilled cheese. No credit cards. 519 Laneda; 503/368-2722.

PLACES TO STAY

Coast Cabins: Isis would like to hire the interior decorator and landscaper for these exceptional cabins, which would be right at home in the pages of *Metropolitan Home* magazine. A package of goodies await your pet, who is allowed in all five cabins. The property is a few blocks from the beach, luxury worth the walk. Rates range $125–375. A nightly $25 per pet fee buys you greenies and a squeaky toy, towels, bowls, and a pet bed. There is also a $30 one-time, deep cleaning fee. 635 Laneda Ave.; 503/368-7113; www.coastcabins.com.

OceanEdge Specialty Rentals: Dogs are accepted in half a dozen rental homes. They phone interview potential renters and ask them to sign a reasonable doggie contract, and, based on your needs, they find the perfect home for you. Because a cleaning fee is charged, these rentals are most economical for stays of at least a week. 503/368-3343; www.manzanitavacation.com.

Ocean Inn: It's out the door and onto the beach for you if you stay at these perky, airy oceanfront cottages, which allow a maximum of two pets in units 2, 3, and 4. Rates are really decent for oceanfront, ranging $135–165, plus $15 per pet per night. 32 Laneda Ave.; 503/368-7701 or 866/368-7701; www.oceaninnatmanzanita.com.

Manzanita Rental Company: This agency rents 38 pet-friendly vacation homes with a wide variety of capacities and rates. Each listing on its website clearly states whether or not pets are allowed. There's a $15 per pet nightly charge, and some have limits on the number of pets. It's easiest to call and discuss your desires and dog situation with an agent. Homes have a one-week minimum stay requirement in July and August. 686 Manzanita Ave.; 503/368-6797 or 800/579-9801; www.manzanitarentals.com.

San Dune Inn: Props to AlanBob™ (yes, he's trademarked his name) and his pup Popcorn for finding such a refreshing and inexpensive motel with honest character and warm hospitality, that's still well maintained and clean. A few blocks off the beach will save you and your dog some dough. All six standard rooms ($65–100) and eight suites ($75–140) welcome pets warmly. Perks for pets include treats, bags, and Frisbees; for humans, it's a complimentary VCR library, books, games, bicycles, and beach chairs. There is a one-time $10 pet fee. 428 Dorcas Ln.; 888/368-5163; www.sandune-inn-manzanita.com.

The Studio and **The Lighthouse:** Thanks to Stephanie and her pals Riley and Lola for turning us on to these rental properties, two little pieces of heaven across the street from the beach. Just for couples, these bright, sunny spaces have unbelievable ocean views. The Lighthouse is a loft with a romantic alcove bed. The two-story Studio was designed by an artist. One look at their pictures on the web and you'll fall in love. They run $130–150 each, plus a $10 per pet per night fee. In the lighthouse, you can add a downstairs room for an extra charge. Call for directions. Neither building is ADA accessible. 503/593-1736; www.the-studio-lighthouse.com.

Nehalem

There's little here other than any and all activities involving the beach or bay. You might want to visit the Nehalem Bay Winery, a couple of miles inland (34965 Highway 53, 503/368-9463, www.nehalembaywinery.com). For dining, there are many fabulous choices two miles north in Manzanita.

PARKS, BEACHES, AND RECREATION AREAS

15 Nehalem Bay

🐾🐾🐾 (See North Coast map on page 24)

It's easy to get to this ultra-popular State Park, and there's plenty to do once you've arrived. On the four-mile spit enclosing Nehalem Bay, there's a landing strip for fly-in campers, six miles of horse trails and a separate camp for equestrians, and two miles of paved, wheelchair-accessible trails for pedestrians and cyclists. If beachcombing isn't your thing, the waters are quieter on the east side of the spit. A boat ramp provides access to kayaking, crabbing, and fishing in the bay.

Any noise from the airstrip and the hectic campground fades away completely once you've climbed over a substantial dune to the ocean. Four miles of soft white sand and ocean views stretch along the Nehalem Spit to the south, and Neah-Kah-Nie Mountain towers overhead. Small dog warning: Winds here are strong. A kite tied to a collar will fly itself and Toto just might get whisked off to Kansas.

From U.S. Highway 101, the turnoff to the park is 0.8 mile northwest of the center of town in Nehalem (from the south, take a left at the blinking light), and another 1.2 miles to the entrance, marked with an unmistakable timber archway. Parking is $3. Open 6:30 A.M.–10 P.M. 503/368-5154.

PLACES TO EAT

The Bunkhouse Restaurant: The owners are relaxed about allowing dogs on the porches while you eat. At worst, if someone on the front porch would rather not eat with a dog nearby, they may ask you to move to the back porch.

After you're finished with your heaping plate of comfort food, you won't feel like moving anywhere. If you like caramels, you cannot live another moment without a box of Sarah Jo's, made next door. 36315 Hwy. 101; 503/368-5424.

PLACES TO STAY

Nehalem Bay Campground: This campground is a parking lot of 267 electrical sites, one big block party with a changing cast of characters. Pets of every breed abound. Sites are $16–20, and summer reservations are a necessity. 800/452-5687; www.reserveamerica.com.

Rockaway Beach

This resort community emerged as a getaway for Portlanders in the 1920s, focused entirely on the seven miles of sandy beach accessible from the center of town.

PARKS, BEACHES, AND RECREATION AREAS

16 Manhattan Beach

🐾🐾🐾🐾 (See North Coast map on page 24)

This State Recreation Site is thoroughly relaxing. The Wonder Wieners prefer this type of beach wayside, one without an attached campground and not in a city center. The beach is secluded, the parking lot is protected from the highway, and the picnic tables are tucked away from the wind in groves of shore pine. There are restrooms and one main path of about 50 feet to the beach. Once onshore, there's no development on the hill behind you, and nothing to interrupt the glorious view before you.

Turn west on Beach Street from U.S. Highway 101, two miles north of Rockaway Beach, and immediately turn left onto the park access road.

17 Rockaway Beach City Wayside

🐾🐾 (See North Coast map on page 24)

This city park provides beach access, pure and simple. There's a parking lot with room for about 50 cars, although it's not well protected from traffic. Amenities include a drinking fountain and restroom, outdoor shower, volleyball beach setup, and a few picnic tables and viewing benches in the parking lot area. The beach extends for seven miles along the homes, hotels, shops, and restaurants of town.

From U.S. Highway 101, turn west on S. First Street into the park.

PLACES TO EAT

Dragonfly Sisters Café: Dogs and kids love this place, with its fenced lawn, sandbox, and picnic tables crammed out back in the alley behind the store.

They only offer treats and baked goods, espresso and ice cream. For real food, they recommend takeout from Rick's Roadhouse across the street to bring back to the picnic tables. 127 Miller St.; 503/355-2300.

PLACES TO STAY

Tradewinds Motel: Gone is the trademark stucco siding of 15 years, replaced by hardy wood planking. Gone is the lawn, swallowed by the sand. What remains are big rooms with even bigger views. Two pets max are allowed per room, in six of the oceanfront suites. Rates range $95–160, plus $15 per night for your dog, up to a maximum of $40 per stay. There are picnic tables and barbecue grills by the beach in back. 523 N. Pacific St.; 503/355-2112 or 800/824-0938; www.tradewinds-motel.com.

Garibaldi

Captain Robert Gray was the first known U.S. explorer to spend time in this area on what is now Tillamook Bay. His crew of 12 men arrived on the sloop *Lady Washington* in 1778 and left hastily in a week after a skirmish with Native Americans onshore. A replica of his tall ship moors and sails from harbor in Aberdeen, Washington.

The pace of life is calm in this fishing and oystering village. The Boat Basin at the mouth of the Miami River is the primary hive of activity, for commercial and sport anglers. To see the boats in the harbor, and get some fresh fish or crab for dinner, turn west on 7th from U.S. Highway 101 to Mooring Basin Road.

PARKS, BEACHES, AND RECREATION AREAS

18 Barview Jetty County Park

 (See North Coast map on page 24)

The Barview Jetty protects the boats entering and exiting Tillamook Bay, a rich estuary nicknamed the Ghost Hole. One local said the nickname comes from the ghost shrimp harvested in the bay; another told us a tale of an elusive 1,000-pound sturgeon who lurks out of reach of anglers' lines; a brochure said it's haunted by the spirit of a disgruntled settler, crushed to death by a log he moved on the hillside. We think it's a tradition for each local to make up a different story to tell unsuspecting tourists. You decide.

It's fun to watch the waves crash against the jetty wall and the boats entering and exiting the harbor while your dog sniffs around the beach extending north. You'll have to time your beach walks for low tide, although you can meander through the sand dunes and campground anytime. 503/322-3477.

PLACES TO STAY

Barview Jetty Campground: The brave windblown trees on this beach jetty provide a decent amount of privacy in this 290-site county campground with hot showers and heated restrooms. Tent sites are $20, RV hookups are $25, and pull-through sites are $30. For reservations, call and leave a message at 503/322-3522 with your name, address, phone number, site request, and dates. P.S.: The manager gets grouchy when he sees dogs off leash. In this wild area, it really is for their safety.

Cape Meares

Separating from Highway 101 in Tillamook, the Three Capes Scenic Loop—to Cape Meares, Cape Lookout, and Cape Kiwanda—presents a quieter side of the Oregon Coast. Rush hour might be the morning launch of the dory fishing boats into the surf, and traffic congestion probably means there are cows blocking the road. This is life in the slow lane, where you can pull over to the side of the road to watch a blue heron nabbing fish in Netarts Bay or an oysterman hauling nets out of the sludge.

PARKS, BEACHES, AND RECREATION AREAS

19 Bay Ocean Spit

🐾🐾 (See North Coast map on page 24)

Hike the dike, with binoculars in hand, for a birding extravaganza. This sand spit is a migration stop that nature periodically builds and then takes away. Little trails shoot off in several directions through thick dune grass. For smaller dogs, it's like going on safari. In the early 1900s, eager developers tried to create "the next Atlantic City" on this spit. Over time, the ocean consumed all of the homes, a bowling alley, a natatorium, and, most likely, several saloons and brothels, although the historical sign doesn't confess to as much.

Turn west at 3rd Street in Tillamook and drive three miles to Bayocean Spit. Turn right onto the one-way dirt road and go 1.5 miles to the parking area.

20 Cape Meares State Scenic Viewpoint

🐾🐾🐾 (See North Coast map on page 24)

Each of this cape's unique attractions are like small plates at a *tapas* bar, situated on a bluff 200 feet above the ocean. The paved path to the lighthouse is a quick 0.2-mile roundtrip. Next, a 0.4-mile out-and-back gravel loop leads to the Octopus Tree, a many-trunked Sitka spruce. Immediately to the north of the entrance is a 0.25-mile quickie that loops around another giant Sitka in a protected coastal old-growth forest. Then there's a picnic meadow to the south of the parking area, a neat surprise tucked between a rock alcove and the well-protected, fenced bluff. Many bird species nest in Cape Meares National Wildlife Refuge to the north and on the rock formations at sea, including peregrine falcons, a species slowly recovering from near extinction.

If all the sightseeing hasn't filled you up, there's a moderately difficult, two-mile trail down to a deserted beach that takes you through and under fallen old growth. For your dog's enjoyment, we can practically guarantee that this path will be muddy and plastered with giant banana slugs.

The Cape Meares Lighthouse is puny by most standards, only 38 feet tall. It was illuminated in 1890 and wasn't replaced with an automatic beacon until 1963. It has a gift shop and is open for tours April–October. Call 503/842-2244.

From the intersection of State Route 6 and U.S. Highway 101 in Tillamook, follow the signs for the Three Capes Scenic Loop, which begins on Netarts Highway. You'll bear right at Bayocean Road and travel four miles, then left on Cape Meares Loop for another two miles.

Oceanside

Look up! It's a bird... it's a plane... it's—actually, it's probably a hang glider, riding the wind currents down from this hillside to the beach below. In this quiet community, the most strenuous activities are usually hang gliding, paragliding, and kite flying.

PARKS, BEACHES, AND RECREATION AREAS

21 Oceanside Beach

🐾🐾 (See North Coast map on page 24)

Located in town, this State Recreation Site offers some of the best agate-hunting on the coast in the winter storm season when outgoing currents strip away the sand. Agates are colorful gemstones, rounded by the sea and tossed onto the sand. They can be opaque in white, carnelian, red, blue-black, and

dark green. Many are translucent, and crystal formations can be seen inside when they are held up to the sun. Look for them in loose gravel at the tide line.

The beach has great views of the Three Arch Rocks National Wildlife Refuge. These offshore rock formations support Oregon's largest colony of tufted puffins and the largest colony of common murres outside of Alaska. The barking you'll hear isn't from dogs, but from the Oregon Coast's only breeding grounds for Stellar sea lions. The beach extends about a mile and a half in either direction. There are two parking levels, restrooms, and a hillside picnic table.

Oceanside is 11 miles west of Tillamook on the Three Capes Scenic Loop. You can approach from the south on Netarts Bay Road or from the north on Bayocean Road. Parking open 5 A.M.–11 P.M.

Tillamook

At Tillamook, the Pacific Coast Scenic Highway drifts inland for a short detour through rich dairy valleys, through countless cows to the Tillamook Cheese Factory, the Pacific Northwest's most famous purveyor of all things dairy.

PARKS, BEACHES, AND RECREATION AREAS

22 Munson Creek Falls

 (See North Coast map on page 24)

It's an easy 0.5-mile out-and-back trot through ancient Sitka spruce and western red cedar to see the 319-foot falls, the highest in the Coastal Range. You'll follow rippling Munson Creek and pass by the world's second-largest recorded spruce, 260 feet tall and eight feet in diameter. It's a beautiful walk through this State Natural Site. Cooper only wishes it was longer.

From U.S. Highway 101, six miles south of Tillamook, turn west on Munson Creek Road. After 0.7 mile, the road becomes gravel, and you'll follow the signs to take first a left fork in the road, then a right, to reach the circular driveway at 1.5 miles.

PLACES TO EAT

Blue Heron French Cheese Company: The hens, roosters, turkeys, and pheasants are running amok in Tillamook, all over the grounds of this farmstead converted into a fantastic deli and gourmet food store. You can put together an amazing picnic basket full of food to go or eat in their picnic area, but keep your pet leashed to prevent him from chasing his own dinner. Kids like to buy oats in the store to feed the farm animals. 2001 Blue Heron Dr.; 503/842-8281; www.blueheronoregon.com.

Farmhouse Café at the Tillamook Cheese Factory: Although she would dearly love to join you, your dog will have to wait outside while you take the self-guided tour through the factory, but you'll be forgiven instantly if you sneak a couple of cheese curd samples into your pocket for her. There's a gourmet gift shop, ice cream counter, and deli in the factory, and you can share a meal together after the tour on the lawn of the visitors center next door. 4175 Hwy. 101; 503/815-1300; www.tillamookcheese.com.

PLACES TO STAY

In this area, chain hotels listed in the *Resources* section offer the best choices for dogs and their owners.

Netarts

Bring cash and cocktail sauce. Look out for hand-pain
Oysters" or "Live Crab" signs, and you've got yourself an insta-
at Cape Lookout.

48 THE DOG L

PARKS, BEACHES, AND RECREATION AREAS

23 Cape Lookout

🐾🐾🐾🐾 (See North Coast map on page 24)

Of the three trails available from the Cape Lookout Trailhead, the moderate,
2.5-mile Cape Trail is the most popular. For a nice change of pace, the trail
starts at the highest point and gradually descends 400 feet to the tip of the
cape, rambling through a coastal forest. When you reach the ocean, your grand
view encompasses the ocean to the horizon, Cape Kiwanda to the south, and
Cape Meares to the north. The South Trail is steeper, winding 1.8 miles down
to a secluded beach south of the cape, and the 2.3-mile North Trail leads to the
campground and the beach at Netarts Bay. There are steep drop-offs on all of
the trails. Distances listed are one-way. Protect your dog by keeping her on a
short leash at this stunning, 2000-acre state park.

If your dog would rather head right for the water, continue north of the
trailhead entrance to the campground. There's a large day-use parking area,
sheltered and viewpoint picnic tables, and a gorgeous beach.

From Sand Lake Road on the Three Capes Scenic Loop, turn onto Cape
Lookout Road for 3.5 miles to the trailhead parking lot and another 2.5 miles
to the campground. Parking is $3. Open 7 A.M.–9 P.M. 503/842-4981.

PLACES TO EAT

Schooner Oyster House and Lounge: Follow the locals if you know what's
good for you, like chicken-fried steak trucker breakfasts, light and crunchy
wood-fired mushroom pizza for lunch, or Cornish game hen for dinner. The
place looks like a dive, the food tastes like a dream. Peek inside for a look at
the beautiful bar carved out of maple. Hang with Radar, the owners' golden
retriever, at the picnic tables on the paved lot, and enjoy his shenanigans.
2065 Netarts Bay Rd.; 503/815-9900.

PLACES TO STAY

Cape Lookout Campground: At this state park, sites closer to the sea are more
open, in trees stripped bare of leaves by rough shore breezes. For privacy and
peace, head to loops C and D. There are 38 RV and 173 tent sites, for $12–20.
Reservations are wise in summer. 800/452-5687; www.reserveamerica.com.

acific City

Imagine a fishing village without docks, marinas, piers, or a wharf. On the south end of the Three Capes Loop, Pacific City is the home of the oceangoing dory fishing fleet, flat-bottomed boats that launch directly into the surf. When they've caught their load for the day, they return by running the boats full-throttle onto shore to a sand-slide stop. They have right-of-way, so you and your pooch better watch out!

Your dog will get a kick out of Pacific City's large population of domestic bunnies who have taken to the wild, hopping all over town. Kids can buy bunny food at the inn to feed them.

PARKS, BEACHES, AND RECREATION AREAS

24 Sand Lake

 (See North Coast map on page 24)

Sand Lake is a playground for all-terrain vehicles (ATVs), spinning and spitting their way through the sand dunes at the East Dunes and West Winds sites on the northwest side of the lake. For quiet dune hikes with your dog and playtime in the water, turn to the left as you enter the recreation area to the Fisherman Day-Use Area, where ATVs are not allowed. At high tide, there really is a lake, but when the tide is out, you can fool around on the mushy lake of sand and walk 0.75 mile out to the ocean. From Sand Lake Road on the Three Capes Scenic Loop, turn southwest on Galloway Road for 2.3 miles.

25 Clay Myers

 (See North Coast map on page 24)

The 180 acres of Whalen Island became a state park in 2000, one of the most significant additions to State Natural Areas in 30 years. From a small, gravel parking loop, you can walk straight to a bayfront beach or estuary and wetland overlooks on short, wheelchair-accessible trails. Cooper recommends going the long way around on an easy, level, wood-chip trail that loops 1.4 miles through Sitka spruce, shore pine, and salal dripping with moss. At low tide, you can dig for sand shrimp or walk 0.75 mile along the tidelands to the ocean. In this pristine ecosystem, you can watch the salmon returning to spawn in the fall and the salmon smolts struggling back to the ocean in the spring. Whether or not you are a fan of state lotteries, you can thank the people of Oregon for voting to use lottery funds to purchase this public treasure.

The site is maintained simply, with a vault toilet and trail map. From Pacific City, follow the Three Capes Scenic Route north on Sand Lake Road for 5.5 miles and turn left at the sign for Whalen Island–Clay Myers.

26 Tierra del Mar Beach

 (See North Coast map on page 24)

Sometimes there's a bit too much going on at Cape Kiwanda, with the dory boats crashing on shore and cars driving on the beach, so families and picnickers come the tiniest bit north to this beach access point to escape the ruckus. The beach is wide and windy here.

Vehicles are prohibited on the beach to the north May–September, and on weekends and holidays all year. Tierra del Mar is on Kiwanda Drive about a mile north of Cape Kiwanda.

27 Cape Kiwanda

 (See North Coast map on page 24)

The golden, wave-carved sandstone cliff of Cape Kiwanda, jutting a half mile out to sea, is of one Oregon's most frequently photographed natural wonders. It is the smallest of the three capes, yet it's usually the most exciting. Heading north from the parking area, carefully climb to the top of the dune. From this perch, you can get a better view of the haystack rock and watch the surfers, boogie boarders, and dory boats launching into the ocean. At low tide, the beach extends four miles south to the tip of Nestucca Spit. Beachcombers on the cape can come away with a great selection of sand dollars.

At this State Natural Area, Tillamook County maintains the parking lot, a restroom, and a wheelchair-accessible ocean viewing deck. Cars are allowed on the beach during certain times of the year.

From U.S. Highway 101, take the Pacific City exit at Brooten Road. Follow it for 2.8 miles into town, and turn left on Pacific Avenue across the bridge. Turn right at the stop sign onto Cape Kiwanda Drive, and follow it another mile.

28 Bob Straub State Park

 (See North Coast map on page 24)

This undisturbed beach on the Nestucca River sand spit is a wonderful spot for a scenic beach walk. To the south, you can see Porter Point and Cannery Hill, behind you are the uninterrupted dunes you climbed over to reach the beach, and to the north is a haystack rock formation with good potential for watching wave action and nesting birds. On the bay side of the spit, the Nestucca River is the stuff of fishing legend, where it's not unheard of to hook a 50-pound Chinook salmon.

From Pacific City, turn west at the only four-way stop in town on Pacific Avenue, go straight through the next intersection, over the bridge, and immediately into the park. The park has restrooms and a drinking fountain.

PLACES TO EAT

Pelican Pub and Brewery: Burgers and pizza wash down nice and easy with cream ales, pales, stouts, or darks at this large, airy, and popular pub. If you want to get fancy, Isis recommends the crab cakes paired with the Scottish ale. Breakfast includes haystack burritos, stuffed French toast, and beer battered pancakes. It's gotta be noon somewhere. Just beyond the patio are posts for tying up, on the soft sand within view of the surf. You can't miss it—on the beach next to Cape Kiwanda. 503/965-7007; www.pelicanbrewery.com.

Village Coffee Shoppe: If Pacific Northwesterners weren't so obsessed with coffee, this restaurant might have a more descriptive name, such as the Village Home of the World's Largest Chicken-Fried Steak. At patio picnic tables, dogs are treated to free toast scraps while they wait for the leftovers from your large portions of steak and eggs or clam chowder. 34910 Brooten Rd.; 503/965-7635.

PLACES TO STAY

Inn at Cape Kiwanda: Every warm, light-filled room at the inn has an ocean-view balcony and a gas fireplace. In the hot tub rooms, the view is from the tub! The beach and the pub are right across the street, Stimulus espresso café is downstairs, and there's a bag dispenser, washing station, and dog walk on the north side of the building. Treats and extra blankets are provided at check-in. Room rates range $130–230, up to $280 for hot tub rooms. The pet fee is $20. A three-bedroom cottage is also available for rental. 33105 Cape Kiwanda Dr.; 503/965-7001 or 888/965-7001; www.innatcapekiwanda.com.

Sea View Vacation Rentals: This pet-friendly agency has an excellent, easy-to-navigate website that clearly lists which properties in Pacific City, Tierra Del Mar, and Neskowin allow pets. 6340 Pacific Ave.; 503/965-7888 or 888/701-1023; www.seaview4u.com.

Shorepine Village Rentals: Pets are welcomed with treats and towels at 18 very recent, individually-owned and decorated beach homes, each sleeping 4–10 people. They're fully outfitted and a few have fenced yards. There's a two-night minimum in the off-season, three-night minimum all summer, and you're going to want to stay longer, because the community's dune ramp to the beach is simply amazing. Go in with friends or extended family to cover the costs of $130–250 per night, plus a $65–85 cleaning fee and an additional $20 per pet per night surcharge (some leniency for longer stays). 5975 Shorepine Dr.; 503/965-5776; www.shorepinerentals.com

Whalen Island Campground: All 30 county park sites are beachfront, on the quiet estuary of this park adjacent to Clay Myers State Natural Area. This primitive campground with vault toilets is appropriate for small RVs or tents only on a first-come, first-served basis. Sits are $10–15 per night; closed in winter if no camp host is available.

Neskowin

After heading inland through Tillamook, the Pacific Coast Scenic Highway 101 meets up with the ocean again in this tiny town with posh cottages, two golf courses, a general store, and a restaurant. Slightly north, you can canoe and kayak in Nestucca Bay's estuary waters through strands of spruce and ocean views. It's a beautiful spot that escapes the tourist frenzy.

PARKS, BEACHES, AND RECREATION AREAS

2.9 Neskowin Beach

🐾🐾🐾 (See North Coast map on page 24)

The beach cove at Neskowin is dominated by the island known as Proposal Rock. The history of the island's name is vague, as it seems that no one remembers whether it was an Indian Chief's daughter, a sea captain's lover, or an early postmaster's daughter who received a proposal here. There's no forgetting the profile of the rock, half onshore and half in the water, topped with a hairdo of tall spruce trees.

After crossing the parking lot, which has a couple of picnic tables and a restroom, and carefully walking across Hawk Street, you'll walk to the beach on a sidewalk that starts out paved and rapidly becomes engulfed in the deep, silky sand. You'll share the tidepools and surf with local dogs who wander about and people from the nearby inn, but few others.

Turn west at the sign for Neskowin Beach Wayside on Hawk Street from U.S. Highway 101 in Neskowin.

PLACES TO EAT

Hawk Creek Café: Although the post in the front yard says No Pets, the owners will make exceptions for respectful, leashed dogs who can relax on the lawn and chat with local dogs who wander by. You can tuck into harvest potatoes and pancakes or lunch sandwich-and-salad plates at a nearby picnic table as well. The homespun food is great, so it's worth behaving to be allowed to hang out. 4505 Salem Ave.; 503/392-3838.

PLACES TO STAY

Proposal Rock Inn: Each room or suite is individually owned and decorated at this inn. Some have fireplaces, most have kitchens, and what they all have in common are balconies and patios with views of Hawk Creek or the ocean and the rock. A bridge crosses the creek to the beach. Room rates are fabulous, only $60–140; up to $175 for suites that sleep six. The best oceanfront prices on the coast get even better with two-for-one return-customer discounts. There's a one-time pet fee of $15, two pet limit. 48988 Hwy. 101 S.; 503/392-3115; www.proposalrockneskowin.com.

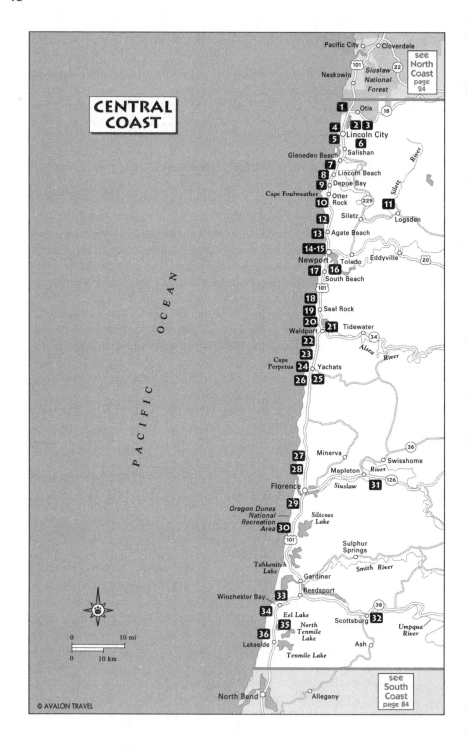

CENTRAL COAST

see North Coast page 24

Pacific City
Cloverdale
Neskowin
Siuslaw National Forest
101
22

1 Otis
18
2 3
4 Lincoln City
5
6
Salishan
7 Salishan
Gleneden Beach
8 Lincoln Beach
9 Depoe Bay
Cape Foulweather
10 Otter Rock
229
11 Logsden
12 Siletz
13 Agate Beach
14-15
Newport Toledo Eddyville
17 16 20
South Beach
101
18
19 Seal Rock
20
21 Tidewater
Waldport
22 34
23 Alsea River
Cape Perpetua 24 Yachats
26 25

PACIFIC OCEAN

Siletz River

36
27 Minerva
Swisshome
28 Mapleton River
Florence 126
Siuslaw
31
29
Oregon Dunes National Recreation Area 30
Siltcoos Lake
101
Sulphur Springs
Tahkenitch Lake
Smith River
Gardiner
Winchester Bay 33 Reedsport
38
34 Eel Lake
35 North Tenmile Lake
Scottsburg 32
Umpqua River
36
Lakeside
Ash
Tenmile Lake

0   10 mi
0   10 km

North Bend
Allegany

see South Coast page 84

© AVALON TRAVEL

CHAPTER 2

Central Coast

Oregon's central coast is all about more—more lodging options, beachfront parks, tourists, and infinitely more sand in the Oregon Dunes, an ever-changing landscape at the whim of the winds and tides. This section of the coast begins with dramatic capes and cliffs to the north that give way to the graceful dunes.

Even the surf is higher, and more dangerous, causing nine wrecks of significant historical record from 1852 to 1912. Four of Oregon's nine historic lighthouses cling to the rocks along Central Oregon, the sentinels to protect other mariners from similar fates. Two of them are in Newport at Yaquina Head and Yaquina Bay, one at Reedsport's Umpqua River, and the most famous at Heceta Head north of Florence.

If you want more of the coast, you have to stay longer, and for that, the Dachsies recommend finding a private rental. For more than 30 pet-friendly properties for rent in Yachats, Waldport, Seal Rock, and other Central Coast locations, contact **Ocean Odyssey**. Pets are an additional $30 per pet per stay with a maximum of two pets. Cleaning up after your pets is especially vital,

PICK OF THE LITTER—CENTRAL COAST

BEST PARKS
Fogarty Creek, Lincoln Beach (page 60)
Oregon Dunes Overlook, Florence (page 78)

BEST TRAILS
Siuslaw National Forest–Drift Creek Falls Trail,
Lincoln City (page 58)
Cummins Creek Loop Trail, Yachats (page 73)

BEST BEACHES
Ona Beach, Seal Rock (page 69)
Driftwood Beach, Waldport (page 70)

BEST EVENT
Mutt Masters Dog Show and Olympics, Lincoln City
(page 57)

BEST PLACES TO EAT
Waldport Seafood Company, Waldport (page 71)
Grand Occasions Gourmet Deli, Yachats (page 74)
Grape Leaf Wine Shop and Bistro, Florence (page 78)

BEST PLACES TO STAY
Looking Glass Inn, Lincoln City (page 59)
Agate Beach Oceanfront Motel, Newport (page 68)
Fireside Motel, Yachats (page 75)

as these are private homes. The office is in Clark's Market Plaza, 261 Hwy. 101, Yachats; 800/800-1915; www.ocean-odyssey.com (look for the pet icon on listings).

NATIONAL FORESTS AND RECREATION AREAS

Siuslaw National Forest

The Siuslaw (Sigh-OOH-slaw) covers 630,000 acres from Tillamook to Coos Bay, bordered east–west by the Willamette Valley and the Pacific Ocean. Hardy Sitka spruce grow in the coastal zone, able to withstand ocean winds and dense fog. Inland, western hemlock grow under a thick canopy of Douglas fir. The "Trip Planning" section of the forest website, www.fs.fed.us/r6/siuslaw/recreation, is an excellent way to find trails, campgrounds, swimming, and horseback riding opportunities. Hebo Ranger District: 503/392-5100.

Oregon Dunes National Recreation Area (ODNRA)
🐾🐾

The U.S. Forest Service manages a 47-mile sandbox between Florence and Coos Bay. While many use the dunes as a playground for off-highway vehicles (OHVs) or all-terrain vehicles (ATVs), approximately 27,200 of the park's 31,500 acres are reserved for people, dogs, and horses. The ODNRA Ranger Station is in Reedsport (Junction of Hwy. 101 and Hwy. 38; 541/271-3495 or 800/247-2155; www.reedsportcc.org).

Lincoln City

This coastal city is in the middle of everything. It's the halfway point between California and Washington, and it's on the 45th Parallel, the dividing line between the equator and the North Pole.

Lincoln City welcomes pets with open arms and good information about where to stay and local dog-oriented businesses. Call ahead for the Pet Friendly Vacation Guide, available at the visitors center (801 S.W. Hwy. 101; 541/996-1274; www.oregoncoast.org). You'll also want to grab a city map for 15 public beach access points along 14 miles of pristine beaches. The historic Taft District along S.W. 51st Street is a lively strip in town with the best outdoor food. Coop likes to practice his "arrgghh" at Captain Dan's Pirate Pastry Shop (5070 S.E. Hwy. 101 S.; 541/996-4600), while Isis prefers to "hang 20" for sunset barbecue at Tiki's (1005 S.W. 51st St.; 541/996-4200).

PARKS, BEACHES, AND RECREATION AREAS

1 Road's End
🐾🐾🐾 (See Central Coast map on page 52)

If you are on a mission to get to the beach, a couple of logs and some polished creek stones are all that separate you from the sand where the sidewalk ends. Then you're there, with the long-necked cormorants and sailboarders, on 14 miles of ocean stretching south through Lincoln City. There's only one catch: You have to fight for the right to park on busy summer weekends. A few picnic tables are placed in the parking lot, functional as opposed to scenic.

This State Recreation Site commemorates the end of the road for the Old Elk Trail, a route used by Native Americans for thousands of years to reach summer fishing grounds on the Pacific Ocean. From U.S. Highway 101, turn west on Logan Road and go to the end of the road. Open 6 A.M.–10 P.M.

 **DIVERSION**

A little absence now and then can make the heart grow fonder. Renew your puppy love by giving you and her a break at the **Critter Cottage** in Lincoln City. Doggy day care is $15 per pup for 1–5 hours, and only $20 for up to 10 hours 8 A.M.–6 P.M., seven days a week and holidays. Overnight boarding is similarly well priced, and if she stays more than four days, they'll give your Bedlington a bath. You can also inquire about at-home pet sitting from Neskowin to Depoe Bay. Methods of payment are check with ID or cash only. 960 S.E. Hwy. 101; 541/996-7434; www.crittercomfortncare.com.

② Sand Point Park

 (See Central Coast map on page 52)

Isis would be hard-pressed to choose a lakefront park when the ocean is so close, but this city park is a lovely place to enjoy the shores of Devil's Lake. There's a shady lawn—which you won't find on the beach—plus one picnic table in the sun and one in the shade. A wheelchair-accessible ramp leads down to a smidge of sand and a shallow swimming area. There's just enough room to launch a raft or do some dog paddling.

From U.S. Highway 101, turn at the north entrance to E. Devil's Lake Road and turn right onto Loop Road.

③ Spring Lake Trail

 (See Central Coast map on page 52)

About a mile's worth of hiking trails with spurs give your dog a hop, skip, and a jump through the woods around a pond in this open space. On your jaunt through a strand of birch trees with mossy limbs, you'll come to a sagging footbridge across the water and a few stairs. A portion of the trail goes up the ridgeline, too muddy and steep to tackle on the spring day we visited. All in all, just enough of a walk for the highway noise to die down.

Turn east on N.E. 14th Street from Highway 101. The trail marker is a quarter mile in on the north side, as 14th becomes West Devil's Lake Road, just west of Indian Shores and Regatta Grounds Park. There's pullout parking available for maybe three cars. Keep a tight leash for a few yards to get from the roadside to the trail.

④ D River

 (See Central Coast map on page 52)

At 120 feet, the shortest river in the Guinness Book of World Records doesn't need more than a single letter to name it. D River connects Devil's Lake to

DOG-EAR YOUR CALENDAR

Lincoln City's **Mutt Masters Dog Show and Olympics** celebrates our companions in ways that we can appreciate everyday, without having to worry about coiffure or conformation. Contests include best singing dog, tail wag champ, biggest ears, fastest eater, kid-dog look-alikes, and the sweetest smoocher. Come, sit, and stay in Lincoln City and strut your mutt at Mutt Masters. Usually held in late April or early May. It's a measly $2 per dog, $2 per parent, kids under 12 free. 541/996-1274 or 800/452-2151; www.oregoncoast.org.

the ocean at this tremendously popular city beach. The parking lot is akin to the mall at the holiday season, with cars jockeying for position. There's so little room off the sand that people hold impromptu tailgate picnics out of their car trunks.

If you are looking for some action, this state wayside is your beach. There are kites flying, beach volleyball games, families, kids squealing and running in the surf, boogie boarding, bubble blowing, you name it. D River is so reliably windy that the world's largest kite festivals are held here every spring and fall. It is a fun place, one you can escape a little bit by walking up to seven miles in either direction. People are very good about having their dogs on leash in this unpredictable environment.

The "D" is on U.S. Highway 101 in the middle of Lincoln City.

5 Siletz Bay

🐾🐾🐾 (See Central Coast map on page 52)

This city park is another people-packed destination. The gentle waters are protected by a sand spit, making them ideal for light canoeing, or for little tykes to toddle around in. Tough dogs can always walk around the bend to the north to reach the serious waves. It gets pretty muddy at low tide.

If you are lucky enough to find a spot, you can park along 51st Street, a popular restaurant and shopping strip paralleling the north side of the bay. That way, you can grab some chowder at Mo's or an ice cream cone at Eleanor's Undertow. There is a tiny patch of lawn and a covered picnic table in the city park at the entrance to 51st Street.

The Siletz Bay National Wildlife Refuge extends nearly the entire length of the bay along the east side of the highway. Trails, viewing platforms, and other opportunities for public use are in the planning stages. In the meantime, you can enjoy views of the salt grasses and brackish marsh from the road.

6 Siuslaw National Forest–Drift Creek Falls Trail

🐾 🐾 🐾 🐾 (See Central Coast map on page 52)

Chipmunks, scurry for your life, 'cause Cooper's coming! Everyone we talked to in town recommended this 1.5-mile trail as a great dog walk. The hike packs a big punch for little effort. It's the pride and joy of the Hebo Ranger District, well maintained with gravel and hard-pack. A mild slope takes you down to a 240-foot suspension bridge looking out over a 75-foot, free-flowing waterfall. Your dogs will love the journey and you'll appreciate the reward at the trail's destination.

The drive to get there takes all the work, along 10 miles of twisty, one-lane road. At least it's paved. From U.S. Highway 101, 0.25 mile south of Lincoln City, turn west on Drift Creek Road. At the next intersection, bear right to stay on Drift Creek, then, for the next 11 miles, turn or bear left at every intersection and Y in the road to stay on Forest Road 17 until you see the large parking lot, vault toilet, and trailhead. Parking is $5. 503/392-3161.

PLACES TO EAT

Beach Dog Café: This joint serves dressed-up dogs to humans and human-shaped treats to dogs. Build your own bratwurst, kielbasa, kosher, and veggie dogs and chat with the owner who sidelines as the local paper's food and wine critic. Beach dog breakfasts feature specialty house potatoes, omelets, and pancakes. 1226 S.W. 50th St.; 541/996-3647.

Eleanor's Undertow: This café and ice cream parlor is hard to miss, with its bright pink building, 20-foot-tall candy canes, and mermaid fountain. The list of indulgences is long, including quarter-pound chocolate chip cookies, saltwater taffy, and anything you can make with ice cream. 869 S.W. 51st St.; 541/996-3800.

McMenamins Lighthouse Brewpub: The four tables on the lower deck only, which is basically the smoking section on the sidewalk out front, is one of your few dinner choices in town if you've got a dog in tow. Luckily, the Lighthouse serves up decent chow featuring hot sandwiches and pizza, famous brews, and Edgefield wines. Now that's the spirit. Colorable kid menu with crayons provided for the under-21 set. 4157 N. Hwy. 101; 541/994-7238; www.mcmenamins.com.

Sun Garden Café and Cyber Garden: Two restaurants in one, with soothing atmospheres to counteract the caffeine and the hum of the computers in the cyber section. The café side of the house serves fresh, vegetarian-only dishes. There is a tiny garden out back and abundant outdoor seating in front. 1816 and 1826 N.E. Hwy. 101; coffee house: 541/994-3067, café: 541/557-1800.

PLACES TO STAY

Coast Inn Bed and Breakfast: Pets, at least those who can remain off the furniture, are allowed in the Cordova Cottage Suite of this restored 1930s

Craftsman-style home. The room, with a private entrance from the front lawn, embraces the beach theme, with light periwinkle walls, a ceiling fan, and a tropical scene painted on the wall. It's $135 per night, with a refundable $25 cleaning deposit. 4507 S.W. Coast Ave.; 541/994-7932 or 888/994-7932; www.oregoncoastinn.com.

Ester Lee Motel: Each vintage 1940s unit is unique at this homespun property that proudly advertises its pet-friendliness as far away as Portland. Up to two pets are allowed, in the cottages only, for $9 per pet per night. Each unit has the comforts of a kitchen, gas fireplace, and fantastic views. Most have showers; ask for one with a tub if you want it. Prices range from a low season $55 studio rate up to a two-bedroom for $160 in the summer. 3803 S.W. Hwy. 101; 888/996-3606; www.esterlee.com.

Looking Glass Inn: The wood-shingled buildings, gazebo, and outdoor picnic area lend this little inn a warm, breezy feeling, matched by the exceedingly pet-friendly staff. Dogs are given a basket with extra towels, bones, and a monogrammed bowl that you can keep for $5. Spacious rooms are a block from Siletz Bay in the lively Historic Taft District. Room rates are $80–140 (plus a gorgeous suite for up to $240); the dog fee is $10. 861 S.W. 51st St.; 541/996-3996 or 800/843-4940; www.lookingglass-inn.com.

Sea Horse Lodging and Vacation Rentals: If the fabulous views and feel-good comfort of the Sea Horse Motel don't do it for you, rent one of the private vacation homes with ocean views and/or private backyards. Motel rates are $90–200, less mid-week during winter; pets stay free in select rooms. Homes that sleep four to six people are described on the website along with restrictions and rates. Pets are $10 extra. 1301 N.W. 21st St.; 541/994-2101 or 800/662-2101; www.seahorsemotel.com.

More Accommodations: Please look under *Chain Hotels* in the *Resources* section for additional places to stay in this area.

Gleneden Beach

Gleneden is pronounced as though it were two words, Glen Eden, the latter the same as the garden of Adam and Eve. It is a fitting name for an idyllic ocean village and its pretty beach. On the north end of the Gleneden Beach loop, turn west on Laurel Street to the end to find a public beach access point with a couple of parking spaces.

PARKS, BEACHES, AND RECREATION AREAS

⁊ Gleneden Beach

😸😸😸 (See Central Coast map on page 52)

Wet-suited surfers come out in the morning to catch the best waves at this State Recreation Site with a quieter, more serious reputation, a 10-minute

ɔm the craziness of Lincoln City. The surf is strong and the
...ıto the water is fairly steep. Joggers and their dogs take to the
,el, coarse sand above the high-tide line. Seals bob in and out of the surf,
searching for supper. Cascade Head looms to the north and flanking you on
either side of the beach are ochre sandstone cliffs, a fitting backdrop for a
foggy morning beach walk or lovely evening sunset. There's a big parking lot
with restrooms and picnic tables on a fenced hillside and landscaped lawns.
Cooper prefers this reflective solitude, reached by a paved path through a
grove of shore pines.

From U.S. Highway 101 seven miles south of Lincoln City, turn west on
Wessler Street, the Gleneden Beach Loop, and follow the signs.

PLACES TO STAY

Salishan Lodge: A luxury golf resort and spa, Salishan captures that particular Northwest flair for cedar and stone and muted colors that complement the
lush green of the links and surrounding forest. It's a lovely setting, if a bit large
and impersonal. Traditional rooms range $200–250 and deluxe rooms with gas
fireplaces and private balconies are $250–275. Pets, who are $25 each per stay,
receive a letter with treats, beds, bowls, a generous roll of bags, and a guide to
the running loops, beach access points, and nature trails on the 350-acre property. 7760 Hwy. 101 N.; 541/764-2371 or 800/452-2300; www.salishan.com.

Lincoln Beach

PARKS, BEACHES, AND RECREATION AREAS

🐾 Fogarty Creek

🐾🐾🐾🐾 (See Central Coast map on page 52)

A dog can learn to love this State Recreation Area, with acres of grass to sink
his claws into and an abundance of bunny rabbits to chase. We like the large,
protected areas of grouped picnic tables, places to get together with family,
set up day camp, talk, and eat. The trouble with many other oceanfront parks
is that there are no decent places to have a meal without getting sand in your
food and other places we won't mention. You can reach these picnic areas from
two parking lots, over the creek on wooden footbridges, through the Sitka
spruce and Western hemlock.

To top it all off, there is a trail to an ocean cove, where the creek meets the
sea. The beach is famous for bird-watching and observing tide pools, and it
has the allure of steep headlands on either side and offshore rock formations.
There can be lots of seaweed onshore, which you may not adore, but will keep
your saluki's snoot occupied for hours.

Turn east off U.S. Highway 101 into either the north or south parking lots,
two miles north of Depoe Bay. Parking is $3. Open 6 A.M.–10 P.M.

PLACES TO STAY

Pana Sea Ah Bed and Breakfast: The accessible downstairs Cozy Suite allows pets at this multilevel contemporary home across the street from Lincoln Beach. The interior is refined, and sunsets through banks of windows in the drawing room are divine. The fee is $120–150, plus a $25 fee per stay. There's hot and cold water outside the front door, use of beach towels, and easy access to a beautiful three-mile-long beach. 4028 Lincoln Ave.; 541/764-3368; www.panaseah.com.

Depoe Bay

The main beach access points are four miles north and south, so this seaside resort plays up the fact that you can watch migrating whales from vantage points along the city sidewalk on a rocky cliff above the ocean. Sure enough, Cooper and Isis saw their first gray whale nearby at Boiler Bay. In addition to gray whales that travel between summers in Alaska and winters in California, there are several hundred that hang out around the Oregon Coast year-round, not bothering to migrate.

Depoe Bay brags about having the smallest navigable port in the world, spouting water horns that shoot water geysers above the seawall promenade, and a street full of boutique shopping.

PARKS, BEACHES, AND RECREATION AREAS

🔟 Boiler Bay

🐾🐾🐾 (See Central Coast map on page 52)

The rusting hulk of a boiler that lends its name to this State Scenic Viewpoint can be seen at low tide, where it rests after the 1910 explosion of the steam schooner *J. Marhoffer.* Before U.S. Highway 101 cut through the cliffs, these steam ships transported people along the coastline.

Coop 'n' Isis saw their first gray whale from this bluff, trolling the bay for its shrimp dinner. Averaging 45 feet long and 35 tons in weight, a gray is a baleen whale, with fringed plates in its mouth to gather and filter its food from the mud, sand, and water. The whale slurps up an area of the seafloor about the size of a desk, filters out the junk, and scoops the amphipods off the roof of its mouth with its tongue, much in the same way your dog sucks peanut butter off the roof of his mouth. If you train your binoculars to the north for a moment, you'll see Lincoln City.

Boiler Bay has restrooms, a sunny picnic meadow, and a loop parking lot. Off U.S. Highway 101 a mile north of Depoe Bay.

PLACES TO EAT

Bay Station Café: Ready-to-serve breakfast is what the folks at Bay Station call their specialty; Coop 'n' Isis call it the best of the brunch buffet to go. Choose from eggs, biscuits and gravy, bacon and sausage, Belgian waffles, hash browns and country potatoes, cinnamon rolls and coffee cake, all until 10:30 A.M. For lunch, switch over to daily soups, chili, and salads. If it's any indication, and it usually is, the place is always packed with locals. Sorry, no outdoor seating. 433 N. Hwy. 101; 541/765-3430; www.baystationcafe.com.

Java Bean Espresso: The scones are unbelievably good, the coffee is hot, and the club is a major dog hangout. Help yourself to the water bowl and jar of dog biscuits by the door and get your dog's picture taken for the Mutt Mug bulletin board. 26 N.E. Hwy. 101; 541/765-3023.

PLACES TO STAY

Inn at Arch Rock: Rooms at the inn are crisp and suitably beachy with light woods and wicker. The setting is superb, perched above the ocean and rock formations. Rooms 6–8 allow pets; rates range $120–140 per night, plus a $10 pet fee. It's a good price that includes a continental breakfast, ocean views, and wooden deck chairs on the lawn overlooking the bay. 70 Sunset N.W.; 541/765-2560; www.innatarchrock.com.

Trollers Lodge: At this bright hotel, each suite has a different personality, looking more like mini–summer homes than rooms. They accept pets in three oceanfront cottages and in all suites except numbers 8, 9, and 11; and three oceanfront cottages. Pets are $10 extra in rooms, $15 in oceanfront homes. Call ahead to find out which suite is appropriate for your size and number of pets. Room rates are $65–100. 355 S.W. Hwy. 101; 541/765-2287; www.trollerslodge.com.

Otter Rock and Cape Foulweather

Mother Nature was having a bit of a spat on March 7, 1778, when English explorer Captain James Cook rounded the headland and named it Cape Foulweather. His published accounts aroused interest in the area, and the fur trade came soon after. Now, everyone refers to this area by its most prominent offshore formation.

PARKS, BEACHES, AND RECREATION AREAS

🔟 Devil's Punch Bowl

🐾🐾 (See Central Coast map on page 52)

The various parts of this State Natural Area are spread out, offering more choices than are apparent at first glance. After turning onto Otter Crest Loop and then west on 1st Street, everyone heads to the overlook to see the geological formation that churns, swirls, and foams with sea water during high tide. From the windblown picnic tables above, you can also catch the action of the surfers to the south on Beverly Beach. Across the street are Mo's Chowder House, a local winery tasting room, and an ice cream truck.

Once you've filled your stomach and absorbed the views, take your dog to the beach and tide pools. Turn right onto C Avenue before the viewpoint, and park at the lot at 2nd Street and C Avenue to find a paved path and stairs to the Marine Garden. At low tide, you can climb over the rocks into the Punchbowl, where there are all kinds of sea creatures clinging to the rocks at dog nose level. A small lawn and restrooms are located on 1st Street between B and C Avenues.

From U.S. Highway 101, you can turn onto Otter Crest Loop from the north or south, approximately eight miles north of Newport.

PLACES TO EAT

Mo's West: People have been chowing down on Mo's clam chowder since the late 1960s. Today, the chain produces 500,000 gallons a year for various locations and grocery stores. Cups of the famous concoction come with every shrimp and oyster sandwich or dinner platter. Elbow your way through, get your food to go, and take your chowder hound across the street to Devil's Punchbowl picnic tables. 122 1st St.; 541/765-2442; www.moschowder.com.

Siletz

Pronounced with a soft "I," as in windowsill, this small community of about 1,500 people is the home of the Confederated Tribes of Siletz Indians.

PARKS, BEACHES, AND RECREATION AREAS

11 Moonshine Park

🐾🐾 (See Central Coast map on page 52)

For those times when the ocean is just too windy or noisy or cold or wet or whatever, come inland to escape. At this county park on the Upper Siletz River, tent sites with fireplaces and picnic tables are scattered on an 18-acre site, around a couple of decent open spaces for games of fetch. There's a boat launch and restroom facilities with drinkable water. Spend some quality time snooping around the area for the many swimming and fishing holes along this stretch of freshwater.

To reach this secluded spot, take Highway 229 to Siletz. Turn east onto Logsden Road and drive 7.5 miles to the Logsden Store. Cross the bridge and turn left onto Moonshine Park Road, and go another four miles to the park gateway.

Newport

Newport is the largest and reputedly friendliest city in the area, home of the Oregon Coast Aquarium and the Hatfield Marine Science Center. As Newport grew into a major commercial center, the character of its original neighborhoods was preserved in the Nye Beach promenade, with its art galleries,

ng arts, and shops; and along the Historic Bayfront, which makes
___ ____ walk or drive, complete with unique shops and shamelessly cheesy
Ripley's Believe It or Not, the Wax Works, and an Undersea Garden tucked in
among legit seafood processing plants.

PARKS, BEACHES, AND RECREATION AREAS

12 Beverly Beach
🐾 🐾 🐾 🐾 (See Central Coast map on page 52)

This state park is a zoo, no doubt because it is such a great beach. First of all, it
is vast, extending from Yaquina Head to Otter Rock. The sand is soft and pli-
able for sandcastle building, the winds are strong and reliable for kite flying,
and, on the north end of the beach, the waves are prime for surfers and kiteboarders. On a typical day, entire clans set up camp above the high-tide line.

DIVERSIONS

Stop by these fine establishments so you can answer in the affir-
mative when your dog cocks her head and gives you that look that
says, "Did you bring me something?"

Paws on the Sand: Pets are welcome to shop with their people
at Patty's boutique, which has been in Lincoln City for decades. She
carries premium food lines as well as collars for every occasion, collar
charms, bumper stickers, and signs that declare your canine tenden-
cies to the world. 1640 N.E. Hwy. 101, Lincoln City; 541/996-6019.

Bella's Pet Boutique: Cashmere sweaters, beautiful necklaces,
health and beauty aids, furniture, boating and camping equipment . . . yes, we're talking about a pet store, one that carries anything your little doggy's heart desires, and many wonderful things she
never knew she desired. Bella's would be right at home on New York's
5th Avenue or L.A.'s Rodeo Drive. Lucky for you, it's on the beach.
1688 N. Hwy. 101, SeaTowne Courtyard, Newport; 541/574-8600.

Raindogs: Although mostly a people store, this great shop has a
few toys and treats for your best friend, which is as good an excuse
as any to come in for the unique jewelry, books, gifts, bath and
body products, and so on for yourself. Raindogs has accumulated
an eclectic selection that somehow just fits. 162 Beach St., Yachats;
541/547-3000; www.raindogsonline.com.

Reigning Cats and Dogs: This shop carries an unashamed
extravagance of pillows, towels, stationery, and anything you can
think of geared toward humans' celebration of their pets, and the
largest selection of breed-specific gifts. 1384 Bay St., Old Town Florence; 541/997-8982.

If your dog can handle all this added stimulus, camp in one of Beverly Beach's 277 tree-sheltered spots and stay a while.

The day-use parking lot is to the left, just north of the campground entrance. A few picnic tables are practically in the parking lot, intended mainly for gulping down a bologna and cheese sandwich before running back to the beach. For a change of pace, there is a 0.75-mile creek trail that starts behind the gift shop.

Beverly Beach is seven miles north of Newport on U.S. Highway 101. Open 6 A.M.–10 P.M. 198 N.E. 123rd St.; 541/265-9278.

13 Yaquina Head

🐾🐾🐾 (See Central Coast map on page 52)

Yaquina Head (Yah-KWIN-nah) is an Outstanding Natural Area. That's not how the dogs rate it, that's its official name. It was formed by flowing lava around 14 million years ago, and the lighthouse perched on its outermost point is the tallest on the Oregon Coast, at 93 feet tall and 162 feet above sea level. The light, now automated, aids navigation along the coast and into Yaquina Bay. Call 541/574-3100 for visiting information (without your pooch).

There are five trails exploring the wildlife preserve, and your $5 pass is good for three days, so you should be able to do them all, except for the one around the lighthouse, which is off-limits to dogs. The walks are short, each less than a mile, and the steepest ones reward your efforts with great views.

Yaquina is full of noisy life, especially the thousands of squawking birds nesting on Colony Rock and the barking harbor seals on Seal Island. Another unique sound is the water tossing and tumbling beach cobbles, polished fragments of boiling hot lava that exploded upon impact with the cold water. About the time the Wieners hit Yaquina Head, they realized a common thread among Oregon beaches: They are windy, very and often. Birds taking off into a headwind fly backwards.

Yaquina Head is about 3.5 miles north of Newport on U.S. Highway 101. Open dawn–dusk.

14 Don Davis Park

🐾🐾🐾 (See Central Coast map on page 52)

This city beach park was rated by *Sunset Magazine* as the most romantic on the coast. Dogs don't know much about that; after all, their idea of romance is having you rub their tummies. For strolling couples, there are thought-provoking sculptures and built-in viewing benches along a stone paver pathway and rock wall that arches gracefully down to the beach. It's lighted at night by a host of lamps embedded along the walkway, which was built in honor of Vietnam veterans.

The icing on the cake is an indoor ocean-viewing conservatory, with wall-to-wall windows and cozy benches safe from the spray and freezing rain. It's the only public one on the coast, a choice place to watch sunsets and winter storms. Quiet, reflective dogs may join you in the rotunda.

From U.S. Highway 101, turn west on Olive Street to the end.

15 Yaquina Bay

🐾🐾 (See Central Coast map on page 52)

This State Recreation Site is the place to come for views. Of course, there is the ocean, which you can see even from the loop drive and parking areas. From the viewing platform, you can watch sailboats, speed craft, and commercial vessels navigating a constructed jetty system at the outlet of the bay into the sea. Towering above you is the historic Yaquina Bay Bridge, built in 1936, and behind you on the top of the bluff is the lighthouse.

The Yaquina Bay Lighthouse was lit for a mere three years, from 1871 to 1874, before it was outshone by its brighter neighbor to the north, at Yaquina Head. It experienced a second life of fame in a *Pacific Monthly* story from 1899, when Lischen Miller wrote about resident ghost Muriel in "The Haunted Lighthouse." In years since, it has been called to service as a Coast Guard lifeboat station and is now open for tours. Call 541/574-3129 or visit ww.yaquinalights.org for information.

Getting to the beach is a workout, first down a steep hill with several flights of stairs, and then through deep sand mounds before you reach the easygoing, hard-packed sand at the tide line. The park also has a playground, one of the few on the central coast; a fishermen's memorial sanctuary; and picnic tables in forested spruce and pine.

The entrance is immediately north of the Bay Bridge. Open 6 A.M.–10 P.M.

16 Mike Miller Park

🐾🐾🐾 (See Central Coast map on page 52)

Between you, me, and the trees, Cooper gets tired of all these beautiful ocean beaches after a while. So, he'd like to thank the former parks commissioner Miller personally for such a great county park that packs a bunch of mini-ecosystems into a one-mile loop. The low-grade gravel path is an interpretive trail through a Sitka spruce forest, past old beaches, logging sites, and railway remains. While you read the brochure that corresponds to the numbered posts along the path, your dog will decipher the scent patterns left by local wildlife. In such a hustle-and-bustle beach town, this walk is a place of peace and quiet.

The educational trail is 1.2 miles south of the Yaquina Bay Bridge, at S.E. 50th Street on the east side of U.S. Highway 101. There's room for a couple of cars to park alongside the road.

17 South Beach

🐾🐾🐾🐾 (See Central Coast map on page 52)

This state park has a lot going on. At the north end of the park are horse trails, as well as surfing, scuba diving, and windsurfing for the very skilled. For $15 per person, kayak tours are booked at South Beach, launching five miles south at Ona Beach. The Oregon Coast Aquarium and Hatfield Marine Science Center are within walking distance of the park, and a hospitality store and information center are on the grounds, as well as a campground with 227 sites for RVers and seven primitive tent sites that are first come, first served for $9 per night.

In a dog's world, the best things in the park are free: miles of windswept beach and multiple park trails to explore. After a bit of a drive from the highway, turn left to reach the picnic area, restrooms, and beach. The Cooper Ridge Nature Trail is a 1.75-mile sandy loop around the perimeter of the campground, our Cooper's favorite because it's protected from high winds. The South Jetty Trail is an accessible, 10-foot-wide paved pathway that's two miles to the bay wall and back through the dunes. The Old Jetty trail is the least traveled, a wilder path that picks its way through shore pine and beach grasses. The trails are the best way to escape the park's summer crowds, especially the school buses that spit out dozens of summer camp kids primed to get rowdy.

South Beach is two miles south of Newport on U.S. Highway 101. 5580 S. Hwy. 101; 541/867-4715.

PLACES TO EAT

Café Stephanie: Three mini–picnic tables sit on the sidewalk outside a cute house on the quaint Historic Nye Beach loop. The lunch menu is consistently good with hot and cold sandwiches, fish tacos, and turkey wraps. Breakfast changes daily, featuring quiches, breakfast burritos, crepes, and homemade granola. 411 Coast St.; 541/265-8082.

Local Ocean Seafood: The LOS's sidewalk tables are perfect observation points for people and boat traffic going by. With all the things with fins, shells, and claws on ice in the case, you may be convinced that heaven is an underwater kingdom. Roasted garlic and lightly seared are adjectives to seek out on the daily fresh sheet. 213 S.E. Bay Blvd.; 541/574-7959; www.localocean.net.

Rogue Ales Public House: The vice president of this regionally famous brew pub is a black Lab named Brewer. Until the pub got called to the carpet by health inspectors, dogs were allowed everywhere. Now, your pal is limited to being hitched outside the beer garden fence. He'll still be treated as a special guest, with a personal water bowl and dog menu that includes pigs' ears, among other things. 748 S.W. Bay Blvd.; 541/265-3188; www.rogue.com.

South Beach Fish Market: Some of the best seafood you'll find anywhere is sold from this unassuming building attached to a convenience store, which is why it's hard to get a snout in edgewise at the white picnic tables on the parking lot patio. You'll sit next to the stew pots steaming with clams, oysters, mussels, and crabs. The market folks also smoke their own salmon, albacore, and oysters. If you want something waiting for you at home, they ship next-day to anywhere in the United States. 3640 S.W. Hwy. 101; 866/816-7716; www.southbeachfishmarket.com.

PLACES TO STAY

Agate Beach Oceanfront Motel: Owner Maynard calls his classic 1940s carport motel a little piece of paradise, with a $50,000 stairway to heaven down to the beach. It's a great discovery, with a protected lawn for room to run. Every unit welcomes one or two pets for an extra $10 per night. Says Maynard, "When people with pet allergies call, I simply apologize, because I can't turn down a friend with a pet in any of my rooms." Those rooms are lovingly restored and well kept, with ocean views, kitchens, and decks. Queen-size-bed rooms are $100–150, suites are $150–170. 175 N.W. Gilbert Way; 541/265-8746 or 800/755-5674; www.agatebeachmotel.com.

Driftwood Village Motel: Cooper and Isis fell in love with the owner of this motel, who obviously cares deeply about animals. He's added that friendly touch to this nine-room motel, where dogs are welcome everywhere. What it has are profoundly excellent oceanfront views at prices almost unheard of on the coast. What it doesn't have is glamour or pretense. Doesn't have? Stylish decor. Has? Private trail straight to the beach. Rates are $65 low end, topping out at $160; one-time $10 pet fee. 7947 N. Coast Hwy.; 541/265-5738; www.driftwoodvillagemotel.com.

Hallmark Resort: This super-sized, cheerful, oceanfront resort prefers to put dogs and their people in first-floor rooms with walk-out patios to the backyard and immediate access to the beach trail. Deluxe rooms (fireplace, spa, and kitchen) top out at $185; standard rooms at $140, plus a $15 dog fee. 744 S.W. Elizabeth; 888/448-4449; www.hallmarkinns.com.

Melva Company Vacation Rentals: Linda Lewis rents two absolutely stunning three-bedroom, two-bath vacation homes, one here in South Beach on a bluff, and another in Waldport directly on the beach. Both have fully fenced yards, and pets are welcome for a $200 fully refundable security deposit. Her business is too small to have a website, but if you call her, she'll mail you photographs, and we bet you'll be sold on them. Rates are $225 per night; ask about mid-week winter discounts. 503/678-1144.

Beverly Beach Campground: Sites are surprisingly private and quiet considering how huge the campground is, with an even split of 128 tent sites and 128 RV sites. Tent sites are in their own loops (C, D, and E) in the spruce to the east of the highway. Reservations well in advance are a must at this desirable park. Rates are $13–22; 800/452-5687; www.reserveamerica.com.

More Accommodations: Please look under *Chain Hotels* in the *Resources* section for additional places to stay in this area.

Seal Rock

The town of Seal Rock was platted in 1887, and a large hotel was built at the end of the Corvallis and Yaquina Bay Wagon Road, the first road to reach the coast from the Willamette Valley. None of the early development remains from land transferred over to the railroads in the 1890s and then by default to nature when the locomotives ceased their locomotion.

PARKS, BEACHES, AND RECREATION AREAS

18 Ona Beach

🐾🐾🐾🐾 (See Central Coast map on page 52)

Developed on a forested ocean flat around several tributaries of the Beaver Creek Estuary, this state park is a varied and interesting place to bring dogs. There's more room to relax than at most oceanfront spots. Pick your pleasure of the plentiful meadows under the protection of tall spruce trees, sheltered from the windy and wilder beach.

Ona has an accessible, paved trail to the ocean, ending in a wooden footbridge crossing above the creek. Where it empties into the river, the creek forms a shallow pool that's a good play place for younger children. Behind you and to the south are high sandstone cliffs.

Kayak tours of Beaver Creek are available. The boat launch is across the highway from the entrance to the park, on N. Beaver Creek Road. You can register and pay for the tours at South Beach State Park five miles north; call 541/867-4715.

Ona Beach is one mile north of Seal Rock on U.S. Highway 101.

19 Seal Rock

🐾🐾 (See Central Coast map on page 52)

There is no single rock formation that is Seal Rock; there is, however, one known as Elephant Rock, the largest of many interesting geological formations with exposed faults sitting offshore. There are plenty of live seals, sea lions, and sea birds; a great place to observe the active wildlife is the paved path along a high cliff of the shoreline and from two accessible viewing platforms.

Dogs get bored with watching, tending to tug you to the steep, switchback trail down to the beach. When the moon is full, pulling the tides farther out to sea, you can walk across the stones and driftwood to play among the rocks and get a closer look at the birds and the tide pool life. This is when the beach gets busier with people harvesting littleneck clams and seaweed, the good stuff that holds your sushi together. Otherwise, the slice of sand you can walk is somewhat cramped. The picnic area and restrooms are in a strand of shore pine, salal, and spruce.

Seal Rock is 10 miles south of Newport on U.S. Highway 101.

PLACES TO EAT

Kadi's Fudge: Get summer's four food groups here—caramel corn, ice cream, cookies, and homemade fudge—in a cute, tiny red building with seagull shutters and a couple of porch tables. Come on, you gotta have fudge. 10449 N.W. Pacific Hwy; 541/563-4918.

Waldport

South of busy Newport is this quieter, gentler town where it's easy to enjoy yourself for little or no money. Fishing and clamming are popular, and there is a free crabbing dock. Stop at the Alsea Bay Bridge Interpretive Center to learn about Conde B. McCullough, Oregon's most famous engineer. He designed and built many art-deco bridges along the coast in the 1930s. All are still in use, except the Alsea Bay Bridge in Waldport, which has been reconstructed true to his artistic vision.

PARKS, BEACHES, AND RECREATION AREAS

20 Driftwood Beach
🐾 🐾 🐾 🐾 (See Central Coast map on page 52)

If Cooper and Isis had to choose their favorite place to reach the beach between Waldport and Yachats, this would be the one, with its perfect combination of nature and nurture. The nature comes in the form of five miles of wide, flat, unspoiled beach from Seal Rock to Alsea Bay. Despite the name, there's not too much driftwood, just enough to find the ultimate fetch stick. Nurture is in the details: a wheelchair-accessible path to the beach, flush toilets with changing areas, a large parking lot set back from the road, and two view picnic tables. Even from the parking lot, you have an uninterrupted view of the ocean.

Driftwood Beach is three miles north of Waldport on U.S. Highway 101. Open 6 A.M.–9 P.M.

21 Robinson Park on Alsea Bay
🐾 (See Central Coast map on page 52)

Pop in to this little park at Alsea Port at low tide and you might get to see the shrimp suckers in action. For 30 years, Alsea Bay's tidal flats have been a premier source of ghost shrimp, used not for human consumption but as bait for steelhead and salmon fishing. It's fun to watch the suction pumps mine the mud for these fish-tempting delicacies. You also have a great view of the Alsea Bridge, the harbor seals, and the brown pelicans that call the bay home. The park, funded in part by the National Oceanic and Atmospheric Administration, has protected picnic tables and easy bay access.

Turn east on Route 34 from U.S. Highway 101 and look for the Port Area sign, turning north on Broadway and west on Port Street. The park is on the far west side of the port, past the ramp and boat trailer parking.

22 Governor Patterson Beach
🐾 🐾 🐾 (See Central Coast map on page 52)

The state has gone to the trouble of doing some landscaping at this Memorial State Recreation Site, providing your pal with a good-sized lawn to sniff if he gets bored with the beach. Follow your nose to find the hidden picnic tables, each tucked into a private grove of thick dune vegetation, and most with great sea views. Several rough, short walkways take you to another fabulous swath of sand, running south from Alsea Bay for miles. Our only beef is that some of the lawns are too close to the highway for comfort.

The Guv'nor is one mile south of Waldport on U.S. Highway 101. Open 6 A.M.–9 P.M.

PLACES TO EAT

Sea Dog Bakery and Café: After she ate the "mess-a-puh-tatas" (herb roasted potatoes, onions, red peppers, cheese, and eggs) at the Sea Dog, Isis felt full, and fully justified in her bias toward any place that mentions her species. The folks at Sea Dog insist that real food tastes better, using natural and organic ingredients when available. Try the homemade granola with raisins and apricots. Sadly, there's no outdoor seating, so get it to go, and go the Guv', Governor Patterson Park that is. 180 Hwy. 101 at Willow, 541/563-3621.

Waldport Seafood Company: Same-day fresh shrimp, crab, oysters, and clams take center stage in soups, stews, sandwiches, and salads with homemade cocktail sauce and hot garlic toast. The tables out front are close to highway traffic; take your spoils of the sea and your ice cream out back to Kealy City Wayside on the bay. It's a Wi-Fi Hotspot; 310 S.W. Arrow St. (Hwy. 101); 541/563-4107; www.waldport-seafood-co.com.

PLACES TO STAY

Bayshore Rentals: This vacation service has an excellent selection of pet-friendly rentals in Waldport, Yachats, and more, typically for stays of three days to a week or more. Click the "Dog Friendly" link on the website or call 541/563-3162; www.bayshore-rentals.com.

Edgewater Cottages: Talk about location, location, location. If these nine cottages were any closer to the edge of the water, they'd be in it. All have sliding glass doors opening onto wind-protected sun decks, ocean views, beach access, kitchens, and fireplaces. They range from a tiny studio for two for $85 to a house that sleeps 14 for $315 per night, and any combination of "kids, dogs, and well-behaved adults" in between. They're popular enough to require a two-night minimum stay in the winter, up to a seven-night minimum July–September. Pets are $5–15 depending on the reservation. No credit cards. 3978 S.W. Hwy. 101; 541/563-2240; www.edgewatercottages.com.

Blackberry Campground: Oregon is famous for fat, juicy blackberries in late July through August. At this campground, 18 miles east of Waldport on Route 34, the only place that isn't plastered with prickly berry bushes is the area cleared for the sites and the boat ramp. Campsites are $15; the day-use fee is $5 per car. Sites #15–30 are along the river. Make reservations and get maps at the Waldport Ranger Station, 1094 S.W. Hwy. 101; 541/563-3211.

Yachats

Yachats (YAH-hots) is a laid-back village of 600 or so full-time residents, recently developing a reputation as a hotbed for artists and craftspeople. There remains less big-time tourist influence, more intimate lodging options and tiny shops with friendly owners. This charming community calls itself the Gem of the Coast, and the dogs agree, although they might express it as the Beef Marrow Bone with Peanut Butter Filling of the Coast, perhaps. Mountain scenery is unspoiled by development along miles of uninterrupted beaches. The section of U.S. Highway 101 between Yachats and Florence to the south is full of cliff-hugging, jaw-dropping oceanfront vistas and multiple highway pullouts for stopping and taking it all in. While here, take the one-mile Yachats Ocean Road scenic loop, and also stop by the Strawberry Hill and Bob Creek viewpoints.

PARKS, BEACHES, AND RECREATION AREAS

23 Smelt Sands

🐾🐾🐾 (See Central Coast map on page 52)

This turbulent section of coastline is designed not for playing in the surf, but for watching the surf play among the rocks and headlands. There are multiple blowholes, where waves crash up through holes carved in the rocks by thousands of years of water action.

Your dog will be content to join you on a sightseeing tour along the 804 Trail, a 0.75-mile, fine gravel path that is accessible for all users. Concerned citizens saved this piece of the former Road #804 for public enjoyment, and enjoy it they do, in large numbers. It's mere feet away from the crashing surf, and your pooch will meet lots of other dogs walking their owners along the way. Viewing benches along the trail give you front-row seats for divine ocean sunsets.

This State Recreation Site hosts the annual Smelt Fry in July, when you can watch thousands of the small, silvery relatives of salmon called smelt jump into catcher's nets.

Turn west on Lemwick Lane from U.S. Highway 101 into the parking lot, on the north side of Yachats.

24 Cape Perpetua Scenic Area
🐾🐾🐾🐾 🐾 (See Central Coast map on page 52)

There are 11 scenic hiking trails in and around Cape Perpetua, from 0.25 mile to 10 miles long, with a little something for everyone. The Wonder Wieners recommend the one-mile round-trip Captain Cook Trail and the 0.4-mile Restless Waters Loop for great views of an ocean spouting horn and chasm wave action, as well as for exploring tide pools. About the only thing you can't do at the cape is get to miles of sandy beach, but you only need to go 0.25 mile south to Neptune for that.

The guide at the interpretive center, open 9 A.M.–5 P.M., recommends the longer 6.5-mile Cook's Ridge/Gwynn Creek Loop Trail to explore old growth Sitka, Douglas fir, and cedar trees. About 1.5 miles in on the trail is an area called the Dog Hair Forest, where the trees grow so close and thick it looks like the hair on a komondor's back.

The Cape Perpetua Overlook is the highest viewpoint on the coast, and the U.S. Forest Service brags that it's also the best. A 1930s stone shelter, built for scouting enemy ships and planes during WWII, is used as a whale-watching lookout.

The entrance to the visitors center is three miles south of Yachats; it and the other areas of the park are well marked along U.S. Highway 101. Parking is $5.

25 Cummins Creek Loop Trail
🐾🐾🐾🐾 🐾 (See Central Coast map on page 52)

The Cummins Creek Trail is a highlight of any journey down the coast. Dappled sunlight filters through mossy branches, presenting multiple opportunities for botanical photography. On a beautiful spring day on the level, gravel trail through a hushed forest, you might not meet up with anyone else, while the path you tread meets up with both the Oregon Coast Trail system and Cape Perpetua trails. It was only after making it to the visitors center that Cooper and Isis discovered that dogs are allowed off-leash on this one trail in the area. What a bonus!

It's 1.5 miles northbound to the Cape Perpetua visitors center from the trailhead. Along the way, you can break off to the east for a 6.25-mile loop. For even more exercise, walk as far as you want on the 10-mile loop that follows the ridgeline.

It's easy to reach the trailhead, 0.25 miles in on a dirt road with a clear sign off Highway 101 around mile 169, just north of the highway bridge between the two picnic areas of Neptune Beach. Even so close, there's no highway noise once you're on the trail.

26 Neptune Beach
🐾🐾🐾 (See Central Coast map on page 52)

Neptune North and Neptune South are one beach or two, depending on time and tide. At high tide, there are two slivers of sand to enjoy while you watch waves meet up with the reef. At low tide, which Isis prefers, you can walk from one beach to the other on firm, level sand, in and among the craggy formations. Just don't get caught in between as the tide is coming in.

The north parking lot of this State Scenic Viewpoint is not marked. It has one picnic table, a viewing bench, and a trail to the beach. The south parking lot is much larger, has restrooms, and stairs down to the sand. It is also set back farther from the highway and has a larger meadow for spreading out a blanket. Cummins Creek is a shallow stream that empties into the sea at the south beach.

Neptune is three miles south of Yachats on U.S. Highway 101.

PLACES TO EAT

Drift Inn: Order food to go from this restaurant and pub recommended by the folks at Fireside Motel. All the family dining staples are on hand for breakfast, lunch, and dinner. Live music, craft beers, and a full-service bar are available inside if you can score a dog-sitter. 124 Hwy. 101; 541/547-4477.

Grand Occasions Gourmet Deli: They must have perfected things on the catering side of the business and brought only the best into the café, and certainly the food tasted even better at outdoor wine barrel tables, overlooking the mouth of the Yachats River as it empties into the ocean. Coop can recommend the prosciutto on sourdough with mozzarella, greens, and vinaigrette. 84 Beach St.; 541/547-4409.

PLACES TO STAY

Ambrosia Gardens Bed and Breakfast: The Carriage House, up the stairs above the garage of this contemporary home, is a kid- and dog-friendly place with a full kitchen. Mary requests that there be no smoking, no pets in the bedding, and no peeing on the flowers. Her green thumb nurtures three acres of gardens around the house, and National Forest land is to the east and south for hiking. Take in the view of Sea Rose Beach across the highway from the outdoor hot tub. Rooms are $125 per night; no pet fee. 95435 Hwy. 101; 541/547-3013; www.ambrosia-gardens.com.

Fireside Motel: At this large motel, the rooms are predictable, yet it has many attributes which will impress the family pets. The buildings are set among a grove of trees with lawns and picnic tables. Steps from your patio door is the 804 walking trail with its tide pools and sandy ocean coves. The rocky coastline views are dramatic, with waves crashing into spray foam against giant boulders. The staff is ultra-friendly and the pet package includes towels and treats and pickup bags. Decent rates for view rooms range $90–140, non-view rooms start as low as $70, plus a $10 nightly fee per pet. 1881 Hwy. 101 N.; 800/336-3573; www.firesidemotel.com.

Shamrock Lodgettes: Pets are allowed in all of the seven vintage cozy cabins, in the modern Danish-influenced Sherwood House, all set in a four-acre park. Yachats Ocean Road Park is right outside your door along the bay. Prices start as low as $100 per night, up to $190, plus a $15 per pet per night fee; two-pet limit. 105 Hwy. 101 S.; 541/547-3312; www.shamrocklodgettes.com.

More Accommodations: Please look under *Chain Hotels* in the *Resources* section for additional places to stay in this area.

Florence

Florence is your spot for kitschy family fun. Break up the scenery with family bonding activities such as bumper boats, dune buggy rides, putt-putt golf, sea lion caves, and other goofy stuff. The Shell gas station in the center of town has buckets of dog biscuits next to the pumps. Head straight to Bay Street in Old Town Florence for the best local flavor, boutique shopping, and outdoor dining with dogs.

For more hikes and campgrounds than we have room to mention, stop by the Mapleton Ranger Station of the Siuslaw National Forest (4480 Hwy. 101; 541/902-8526). Avoid the Siltcoos Lake Recreation Area; when the dunes of this section aren't overrun by ATVs, they're off-limits for rare bird nesting. The best dune hikes are south of Florence. Keep in mind that distances are deceiving on the beach, longer than they look. Drink up! The wind wicks the moisture right out of you and your pets.

PARKS, BEACHES, AND RECREATION AREAS

27 Carl G. Washburn

🐾🐾🐾 (See Central Coast map on page 52)

What can we say? This memorial state park is yet another awesome beach along this stretch of coastline, with 1,100 acres, a big parking lot, large restrooms with changing areas, and surprise picnic tables hidden in the stunted trees of the fore dunes. U.S. Highway 101 bisects the park, with the campground

NATURE HIKES AND URBAN WALKS

Up and down the Oregon Coast there are so many geological formations named after the devil that Cooper and Isis wondered why the god of the underworld is so popular in Oregon. They may never know for sure, but they did hear a highly plausible explanation. The Native American inhabitants of the region believed that many spirits, evil and good, inhabited the natural world around them. The European settlers who arrived and translated these native place names into their language had only one. So Beelzebub became the default spirit given credit for the wilder aspects of the coast. Here's a sample of the wicked places where you can walk your dog.

Devil's Churn, Yachats

Devil's Elbow, Florence

Devil's Kitchen, Bandon

Devil's Lake, Lincoln City

Devil's Punch Bowl, Otter Rock

Seven Devils State Park, Bandon

to the east and the picnic area to the west. This beach is often foggy, with wisps of clouds clinging to the tops of the trees like cotton at Heceta Head to the south. You can take the China Creek Trail from the campground, which joins up with the Hobbit Trail and then the Heceta Head Trail, to travel the three miles down to the lighthouse.

This state park is located 14 miles north of Florence on U.S. Highway 101. 93111 Hwy. 101 N.; 541/547-3416.

28 Heceta Head Lighthouse

🐾🐾 ◀● (See Central Coast map on page 52)

The Heceta (Huh-SEE-duh) Lighthouse is the most photographed structure on the coast. Operational in 1894, it is perched on the brink of a 205-foot outcropping on 1,000-foot-high headland. The former keeper's quarters are in an equally picture-perfect building below. Common murres lay their eggs directly on the rocks offshore, and gray whales and their calves pass close by in May on migrations to Alaska.

A half-mile trail, with a gradual uphill incline, takes you to the lighthouse. Halfway up is a gift shop and the quarters, with a viewing bench that is perfect for a rest stop. Tucked into Devil's Elbow, the curve of land below the landmark, is a tiny crescent beach. Get up with the sun for an early session of wave chasing; otherwise, expect to share the trail and the beach with throngs of people.

The lighthouse is often open for tours, without your pet partner; call

541/547-3416 for information. Local tip: Pop into the bar for a beverage at Driftwood Shores Resort after playing on the beach at Heceta Head.

On U.S. Highway 101, 12 miles north of Florence. South of the park on the highway are several pullouts that offer the choicest areas to capture snapshots of the famous maritime building. Parking is $3.

29 Jessie M. Honeyman
🐾🐾🐾 (See Central Coast map on page 52)

Jessie was a spunky Scottish woman, a tireless advocate for the protection of Oregon's natural resources. At her memorial state park, it's tough to choose between the two major lakes, Woahink and Cleawox, so you might as well stay longer and enjoy both. The dogs might vote for the East Woahink picnic area, with its huge, rolling lawns and lengthy beachfront access, plenty of room for a dog to be a dog. It can be crowded with water sport enthusiasts.

You might prefer the more scenic and quiet Cleawox Lake, to the west of U.S. Highway 101 near the campground. Picnic tables are shaded in the woods and surrounded by high sand dunes, two miles of them between the lake and the ocean. Kids grab plastic saucer slides and sand boards to ride the dunes. There's a foot-rinse station that doubles as a dog wash.

Honeyman is two miles south of Florence on U.S. Highway 101. Parking is $3. Open 8 A.M.–8 P.M. 84505 Hwy. 101 S.; 541/997-3641.

30 Oregon Dunes Overlook

😺 😺 😺 🐾 (See Central Coast map on page 52)

The first marvel at this roadside stop are elevated platforms, with wheelchair-accessible ramps, that provide you with bird's eye views of the dunes and the ocean beyond. From there, a three-mile loop trail takes you first up and over the dunes, and then through coastal woods to the beach. The first half mile of this trail is also paved for accessibility. On the sand, the sky is so blue it hurts; think sunscreen, sunglasses, and extra water. Until you reach the forested fore dune, the only way to know you're on the right path is to follow the posts topped with blue bands.

As little as a hundred years ago the area was nothing but sand, until settlers planted the aggressive European beach grass in the 1920s to stabilize the shifting landscape. This led to quick development of the other vegetation you see today. If you're not accustomed to hiking through sand, you might need some sports cream for your calves later.

The overlook and trailhead are 10 miles south of Florence on U.S. Highway 101. Parking is $5.

PLACES TO EAT

Grape Leaf Wine Shop and Bistro: The "and Bistro" part of this wine bar in trendy Old Town may interest your pooch more than the floor to ceiling racks of bottles from all over the world. A single fresh sheet of dinner specials changes weekly, with a regular lunch menu and Sunday brunch. Enjoy the signature grape leaf salad and perhaps some penne pasta with asparagus and a pinot gris as you people-watch from sidewalk tables. 1269 Bay St.; 541/997-1646.

Side Street Bistro: As sophisticated a restaurant as you'll find in a big city, the Side Street has a brick patio with seating around a fire pit as well as tables. The menu is divided into small plates and large plates, with ingredients sourced whenever possible from local and organic artisans. Isis points out that, ironically, small plates give you larger variety. 165 Maple Street; 541/997-1195.

Siuslaw River Coffee: This company is primarily a bean roaster that serves coffee and baked good, and not much else, with a busy location in Old Town and two outdoor tables overlooking the river for which it's named. 1240 Bay St.; 541/997-3443.

PLACES TO STAY

Ocean Breeze: This inexpensive motel in the historic Old Town area is a cut above, with small rooms that sparkle in a crisp white building that's a breath

of fresh air. Decorator touches and a lawn with a picnic table out front are very inviting for weary dune hikers. There are five pet rooms, all nonsmoking, for $50–120, with a $10 pet fee. 85165 Hwy. 101 S.; 541/997-2642 or 800/753-2642; www.oceanbreezemotel.com.

Park Motel and Cabins: Several tiny and tidy rooms and two of the luxury cabins open their doors to pets at this throwback 1950s lodge with genuine pine paneling on the walls and pine trees out back. A disposal can and shovel are provided at a designated dog lawn. Standard rooms are $50–135; cabins are $165. The pet fee is $10. 85034 Hwy. 101; 541/997-2634; www.parkmotel florence.com.

Mapleton

Slather on the citronella lotion and head into the deep woods for a breath of fresh Oregon mountain air. This tiny outpost makes for a nice change of pace from the salty shores.

PARKS, BEACHES, AND RECREATION AREAS

31 Siuslaw National Forest–Sweet Creek Falls

🐾🐾🐾🐾 (See Central Coast map on page 52)

At a little over two miles out and back, this trail is an easy one to hike. The 20-foot falls at the end are mostly hidden behind the rocks, but you won't care because there are dozens of rapids and falls in the gorge along the way. The whole trail is dazzling, and the elevated steel platforms, with bridges that cling to the hillside and carry you over the creek, are most exciting. It can be muddy, it can be buggy, and you must stay on the trail to avoid poison oak.

From Florence, travel 15 miles east to Mapleton on Highway 126. Shortly after town, you'll turn south on Sweet Creek Road and go another 10.2 miles to the marked trailhead. Bring your own drinking water; a latrine is available.

PLACES TO EAT

Alpha-bit: Books, gifts, and a health food café share a sunny space in a little strip of shops that are the center of town in Mapleton. Turkey and tuna are the only meats on the predominantly vegetarian and vegan menu. It's all light and delicious. Even the ice cream is light enough to float in a tall, frosted glass of IBC root beer. A tiny county park out back has a picnic table waiting for you. 10780 Highway 126; 541/268-4311.

Scottsburg

Highway 38 is a great road, paralleling the Umpqua River from I-5 out to the coast at Reedsport. Somewhere along the way, you'll pass the town of Scottsburg before you even know it, but don't miss the park, it's a good 'un.

PARKS, BEACHES, AND RECREATION AREAS

32 Scottsburg Park
🐾🐾🐾 (See Central Coast map on page 52)

The rare Myrtlewood tree flourishes along the south shore of the Umpqua River at this county park, one of five tracts of land designated to protect the northern boundary of the Myrtlewood habitat. The park, with its playground, restrooms, and big grass plot, is a beautiful and quiet setting for a break in your travels or a picnic. It's a popular fishing spot for coho and Chinook salmon; the anglers get up early to put in from the boat ramp and floating docks.

The park is just west of mile marker 16 on State Route 38, about 15 miles inland from Reedsport.

Reedsport and Winchester Bay

Reedsport is at the heart of the Oregon Dunes. If you come into town from State Route 38, pull into one of the Dean Creek elk viewing platforms, three miles east of Reedsport, to see if you can catch any of the reserve's 100 or so Roosevelt elk in action.

From the center of Winchester Bay, Salmon Harbor Drive takes you to aptly named Windy Cove, a marina packed with thousands of recreational vessels, lodging, multiple beach access points, and some of the best food on the central coast. A mile south of Winchester Bay is a wayfinding point pullout, the only spot between Port Orford and Florence where you can get an unobstructed view of the Pacific Ocean. You'll spy the top of the Umpqua Lighthouse and the Triangle Jetty, where oysters and mussels are cultivated.

PARKS, BEACHES, AND RECREATION AREAS

33 Umpqua Lighthouse

🐾🐾🐾 (See Central Coast map on page 52)

Cooper can think of three reasons to visit this state park—the lake trail, the lighthouse grounds, and the whale-watching station—all of which are wheelchair-accessible. The first is a fun, easy, one-mile trail around Lake Marie beneath a tall forest with huckleberry bushes. The east half of the trail is paved; the west is gravel and dirt.

Dogs are allowed on the grounds of the lighthouse and Coast Guard station, and you can hear its distinctive two-tone foghorn anywhere in the park. The present lighthouse was operational in 1894 and still uses the original lenses crafted in Paris in 1890. Tour guides will take you to the top Wednesday–Sunday, where visibility is 19 miles out to sea. Call 541/271-4631 for lighthouse museum and tour information.

Next to the lighthouse is a whale-watching station, with spotting scopes ($0.50 for five minutes). Whales migrate anywhere between December and May, and you can watch the ATVs crawl over the sand from this lookout year-round.

Off U.S. Highway 101, six miles south of Reedsport. Open 7 A.M.–9 P.M. 460 Lighthouse Rd.; 541/271-4118.

34 ODNRA–Umpqua Dunes Recreation Area

🐾🐾🐾 (See Central Coast map on page 52)

The beach at Umpqua stretches far and wide, with sand the pleasing texture of superfine sugar. There are three large parking lots with beach access 20 feet from the pavement. Parking at the first lot is free, so you might as well stay there. There is a $5 fee to park in the second and third lots, used as staging grounds for off-highway vehicles. The only reason to go to the second lot is for a barrier-free beach trail with two excellent, accessible viewing platforms. The third lot has flush toilets and a covered picnic shelter, amenities not available at the others. ATVs are allowed on the dunes to the east of the access road; they are not allowed on the beach to the west.

From U.S. Highway 101, turn west on Salmon Harbor Road. Follow the Umpqua Dunes and Beach Road sign, past the marina and Windy Cove. Watch out for ATVs on the side of the road. Open 10 A.M.–6 P.M., until sunset in the summertime.

35 William H. Tugman

🐾🐾 (See Central Coast map on page 52)

If the beach is too windy and cold, this memorial state park provides good stomping grounds along the sheltered shores of 350-acre Eel Lake. It has big, big, green lawns for fetch, big trees for naps in the shade, and a big lake you can paddle around in, in a big canoe. On the north side of the picnic area is a trail that wanders about a mile, with several handy places for your dog to at least get his paws wet. Flush toilets and changing rooms make it nice if you or the kids decide to go for a swim. Your view of the lake from the handicap-accessible fishing dock isn't spoiled by any development, and there's no day-use fee at this state park. Eel Lake fishing nets crappie, largemouth bass, stocked rainbow trout, and steelhead and coho salmon.

Off U.S. Highway 101, eight miles south of Reedsport. 72549 Hwy. 101; 541/759-3604.

36 ODNRA–John Dellenback Trail

🐾🐾🐾🐾 (See Central Coast map on page 52)

This one-mile loop trail takes you to the highest dunes in the park, 500 feet tall or more, named in honor of someone instrumental in establishing the dunes as a recreation area. Our little dog goddess fancied herself Isis of Arabia as she climbed up to the top and viewed the immensity before her. The northern half of the trail is through coastal woods, making the discovery of the dunes all the more exciting as you emerge from the trees. You continue through deep sand on the south to return.

For the ambitious and incredibly fit orienteer, there is a six-mile loop—2.5 miles to the beach, 0.5 mile on the beach, and back. It is marked by posts topped with blue bands, the only way to tell if you're on the right track. This is a very difficult hike, slogging through deep sand and over high hills. We were also told that the last part of the trail may be under a foot or so of water during the rainy season. If you attempt the longer trail, we recommend dog goggles and booties, gallons of water and sunscreen, and protective clothing for the sting of the sand whipped against your skin by the wind.

Watch for the entrance to trailhead parking on U.S. Highway 101, immediately north of the turnoff for Lakeside. Parking is $5.

PLACES TO EAT

Anchor Grill and Oyster Bar: Everybody brags about having the best chowder on the coast; Anchor's is right up there. Their garlic lime prawns, fettuccini, and "Tsunami" appetizer platter aren't too shabby either. 208 Bayfront Loop, Winchester Bay; 541/271-2104.

Kitty's Kitchen Is Christmas Forever: Dogs are welcome on the fantastic back patio of Kitty's, an eclectic diner and kitschy holiday gift shop. The cooks make whatever suits them that day, might be meatloaf, could be egg salad, and there's always chili dogs and homemade pies and cakes. 110 Bayfront Loop, Winchester Bay; 541/271-1919.

Pah Tong's Thai Food: When you are craving the taste of Thai, no other flavors will do. Try Pah Tong's to go for a change of pace from the seafood all over the place. 460 Beach Blvd., Winchester Bay; 541/271-1750.

Sportsmen's Cannery and Smokehouse: Not to be missed are summer barbecues Friday, Saturday, and Sunday nights from Memorial Day to Labor Day, hosted by this seafood market, filling the parking lot with picnic tables. Red snapper, crab, cod, and oysters share the grill with land-based meats. For the rest of the year, order shrimp and crab cocktails, smoked fish, and oysters to go for your beach fire pit. 182 Bayfront Loop, Winchester Bay; 541/271-3293.

Sugar Shack Bakery: We love a place that tells it like it is. Beyond enough baked goods, doughnuts, cookies, and fudge to send you into sugar shock, there are good deli sandwiches, daily soups, ubiquitous espresso drinks, and seasonal blackberry pies. Order to go from the counter. 145 N. 3rd, Reedsport; 541/271-3514.

PLACES TO STAY

Loon Lake Lodge: Half the joy of staying here is in the getting here (the other half in doing nothing once here). After 13 miles of driving along Highway 38 paralleling the Umpqua River, you'll turn south and travel another eight miles on a narrow, curvy road hugging Lake Creek to reach this full-service resort. The cabins, yurts, and cottages are rustic, bunk bed affairs, separate from the restroom and shower building. Rates start at $75, plus a one-time $25 pet fee; 30-pound limit. Additional lake access is available at a couple of BLM Recreation sites nearby. This destination wins our out-of-the-way award for the Central Coast, with few signs of humanity. You'll pass some excellent elk viewing stations along the way. 9011 Loon Lake Rd., 20 miles outside of Reedsport; 866/360-3116; www.loonlakerv.com.

Winchester Bay Inn: Pets are welcome to "be our guests" in all except four rooms of this bright, modern, squeaky-clean motel. There are a wide range of prices and room types, including kitchenette rooms, suites, and spa rooms. Rates range $50–80, plus a $5 pet charge. 390 Broadway, Winchester Bay; 541/271-4871 or 800/246-1462; www.winbayinn.com.

Umpqua Lighthouse State Park Campground: It may be a sand dune underneath, but it is a forest on top, enough to give each of the 24 tent sites and 24 hookup sites decent seclusion. Rates are $16–20. U.S. 101, six miles south of Reedsport; 800/452-5687; www.reserveamerica.com.

More Accommodations: Please look under *Chain Hotels* in the *Resources* section for additional places to stay in this area.

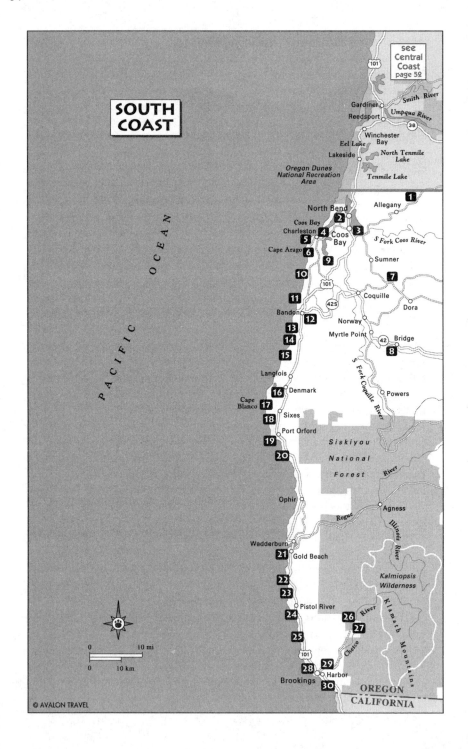

SOUTH COAST

see Central Coast page 52

CHAPTER 3

South Coast

The southern coast of Oregon is also called America's Wild Rivers Coast, where all of the major waterways that begin in the Cascades—Smith, Chetco, Pistol, Elk, Sixes, and mighty Rogue and Umpqua—empty into the sea, creating interesting lakes, estuaries, and Oregon's Bay Area, Coos Bay, along the way. The towns and recreation areas become less touristy the farther south you go. There's less saltwater taffy and more saltwater, exactly the kind of thing a dog pricks up her ears to hear.

In the forests south of the Umpqua River, your pet will have the pleasure of encountering the Oregon myrtlewood, a tree she's probably never smelled before. Famed for its multicolored burled wood and fragrant dark leaves that smell similar to bay, it grows only in this region of Oregon and the Holy Land in Israel.

If you travel in May and June, another exotic species your pup will meet is the *Vellela Vellela* (By the Wind Sailor), a member of the jellyfish family pushed ashore in massive numbers by west winds. Their fins are translucent, their

PICK OF THE LITTER—SOUTH COAST

BEST PARKS
Sunset Bay, Coos Bay (page 89)
Cape Blanco, Port Orford (page 97)

BEST BEACH
Seven Devils, Bandon (page 93)

BEST TRAIL
Oregon Redwood Nature Trail, Brookings-Harbor
(page 103)

BEST PLACE TO EAT
The Crazy Norwegian, Port Orford (page 98)

BEST PLACES TO STAY
Coos Bay Manor Bed and Breakfast, Coos Bay (page 90)
Tintagel by the Sea, Bandon (page 96)
Wild Rivers Motor Lodge, Brookings-Harbor (page 105)

bodies are cobalt blue, and, fortunately for curious wet noses, they don't have stingers or tentacles.

While the Dachsie Twins are not widely known for their hiking prowess, they recognize a great outdoor resource when they see one. They can therefore direct you to the Coos Regional Trails Partnership website at www.coostrails .com, and suggest you click the "Hiking Trails" link for a great clearinghouse of regional walks. Go ahead, knock yourself out.

Coos Bay

The Bay Area of Oregon refers to the city of Coos Bay and its suburbs North Bend and Charleston. Coos Bay is Oregon's largest bay, a significant commercial passage for coal at the turn of the 19th century, and later for lumber and seafood. The city is the coast's largest population center, and not a particularly memorable one, with a lumber mill and the Coquille Tribe's Mill Casino being the largest going concerns. A stroll along Coos Bay's boardwalk gives you the opportunity to gawk at the marina's working boats and pleasure craft.

Beyond that, the Dachshunds suggest you head straight through the city on Cape Arago Highway to Charleston, a fishing village that also serves as the gateway to three great beach parks, with their promontories and protected bays famous for blazing sunsets. Flower lovers come to the 743 acres of Shore Acres Botanical Gardens; however, this state park is off limits to dogs.

For a more scenic approach to Charleston from the south, leave Highway 101 and take W. Beaver Hill Road to Seven Devils Road through newly planted timberland.

PARKS, BEACHES, AND RECREATION AREAS

🞄 Golden and Silver Falls

🐾🐾 (See South Coast map on page 84)

Two trails, less than a half mile each, head off in opposite directions through an old-growth forest of maple, alder, Douglas fir, and myrtles to these cascades on Silver and Glenn Creeks. They are stunning, easy hikes. The 160-foot Silver Falls appears to rain straight out of the sky, and Golden Falls is only slightly less impressive. You've come all this way, so you might as well take to the 0.9-mile trail that climbs the edge of a steep cliff (leashes please) and gives you views of both falls. To reach the longer trail, head to the right from the parking lot, over a bridge, then left at the first trail junction.

The 24-mile drive inland from the coast to this State Natural Area is a roller coaster ride. From the Y intersection on the south end of Coos Bay, follow the sign to Allegany. Cross the bridge, turn north on 6th Avenue for 0.5 mile, and turn east on Coos River Road. The closer you get, the less of a road it is, and the last five miles are unpaved. Just when you're convinced that you can't possibly be on the right road, you'll see the sign to Glenn Creek Road indicating you have only three more miles to go. 541/888-3778.

🞄 Empire Lakes/John Topits Park

🐾🐾🐾 (See South Coast map on page 84)

These woodsy lakes are surrounded by strip malls and superstores, but you'd never know it from walking or fishing along the forested paths of their shores. Tourists usually miss this 120-acre destination, so the friendly dogs you meet and greet are probably locals. The 1.25-mile path around the lower lake is paved and wheelchair-accessible, and there are additional unpaved and primitive trails around Upper and Middle Empire. These bayous are full of what dogs think of as everything nice: bugs, frogs, birds, and "Gone fishin'" bumper stickers on trucks.

From Newmark Street, the main east–west thoroughfare in North Bend, turn north on Hull Road to find a parking lot, trailhead, and restrooms. 541/269-8918; www.coostrails.com/traildescriptions/empirelakes/empirelakes.htm

DOG-EAR YOUR CALENDAR

Didn't have time to make a float? Don't have a pet? No problem! Kids with pets—of the live or stuffed-animal variety but preferably *not* of the taxidermy kind—are encouraged to participate in the **July Jubilee Parade** in North Bend. Awards are given in various categories, and entries are generously "judged" on creativity and the inclusion of at least one animal in the theme. Parade entry forms and rules and regulations are available at the Coos Bay or North Bend visitors centers (www.oregonsbayarea.org).

The Pacific Cove Humane Society in Coos Bay holds their largest annual fundraiser in October each year. The **Bite of the Bay** features about 10 chefs, local wines, and silent and live auctions, hosted at the Mill Casino. Go to www.pacificcovehumane.org for information or call 541/756-6522.

❸ Mingus Park

🐾🐾 (See South Coast map on page 84)

Mingus is a truly lovely city park, with immaculate Japanese and rhododendron gardens surrounding a pond complete with water fountains (lighted from underneath at night), lily pads, and waterfowl. Even if you start out in a hurry, the peaceful grounds tempt you to stop to smell the flowers. The paved, accessible path around the pond is 0.4 mile, passing by viewing benches and crossing over a traditional arched bridge. There is a covered picnic gondola at the far end and a few minor wooded trails in an arboretum beyond.

From U.S. Highway 101, turn west onto Commercial Avenue and turn north on 10th Street. Pass the ball field and the skate park and cross the street to Chosi Gardens. 541/269-8918.

❹ Bastendorff Beach

🐾🐾🐾 (See South Coast map on page 84)

No pets are allowed in the picnic area of this county park and campground, and camping is nicer at Sunset Bay anyway, so Coop 'n' Isis suggest driving right past the county property straight to the beach. The sun rises early on these shores, which curve two miles around to the north and east. You can park steps away from the beach in multiple places along a mile of road below the Coos Head U.S. Naval Facility. Walk your dog on the superfine sand for miles, from the jetty access to Coos Bay at the north end on down.

Take Cape Arago Highway west from U.S. Highway 101 and turn right at the sign for the county park onto Coos Head Road. 541/888-5353.

5 Sunset Bay

🐾🐾🐾🐾 (See South Coast map on page 84)

Partially enclosed by high sandstone bluffs and a narrow sea passage, this state park once played safe haven to vessels during storms, and as local lore has it, pirate ships waiting to spring on unsuspecting ships passing in the night. Waves are gentle behind the protected breakwall, and the water is shallow, making it a great place to play. The tide pools send dogs' noses and kids' imaginations into overdrive checking out the hermit crabs, sea anemones, starfish, limpets, urchins, and so on (eyes only, no touching please).

For hiking, complete with ocean vistas, primal forests, and wildflowers, you can pick up a two-mile section of the Oregon Coast Trail between Sunset Bay and Shore Acres. The trail marker is tucked behind the right side of the restroom in the picnic area. The park meadow is big enough for a hot-air balloon, as proved by Malcolm Forbes in 1973 when he took off on his successful transcontinental flight.

On Cape Arago Highway, 12 miles southwest of Coos Bay. 541/888-4902.

6 Cape Arago

🐾🐾🐾 (See South Coast map on page 84)

It's rewarding to simply drive or walk the loop at the road's end, gawking at incredible views, explosive surf, and sunsets beyond compare from a wheelchair-accessible lookout. Your dog will certainly appreciate it if you look for the multiple pullouts and markers indicating trails that wind through this state park. The Pack Trail, for example, is a 2.25-mile trip that gains 400 feet in elevation past WWII bunkers to the end of the cape. From another trail, you can catch a glimpse of the Cape Arago Lighthouse perched on the edge of the cliffs and hear its unusual foghorn. A third, paved switchback trail leads down to the South Cove, a sliver of beach with lots of smelly detritus washed onshore. (Oh boy! Oh boy!) If your dog thinks his bark is loud, he ought to get a load of the chorus of pinnipeds—that's seals and sea lions to us lay dogs—along Simpson Reef. Hundreds to thousands of them haul out on the rocks of Shell Island Refuge offshore to bask, bark, and breed in the sun.

Think "'ere I go" to correctly pronounce Arago, and to get there, take the Cape Arago Highway west from U.S. Highway 101, and watch for signs that say Charleston–State Parks. Cape Arago is the end of the road, 14 miles southwest of Coos Bay. Open 7 A.M.–6 P.M., until 9 P.M. in the summer. 541/888-3778, ext. 26.

PLACES TO EAT

Blue Heron Bistro: This restaurant specializes in two distinctly different types of cuisine: seafood and German food. If the shrimp, bacon-wrapped oysters, or blackened salmon sandwiches don't tempt you, perhaps the bratwurst, knockwurst, and sauerkraut will. You can squeeze into one of a couple of tiny sidewalk tables for lunch or dinner. 100 Commercial Ave.; 541/267-3933; www.blueheronbistro.com.

Charleston Station Donuts and Bagels: … and ice cream, and espresso, and Laotian and Thai food. Odd combinations perhaps, but sometimes, out here in the boonies, you have to diversify to survive. Isis double-dog-dares you to order one of everything to go. 91120 Cape Arago Hwy., Charleston; 541/888-3306.

City Subs: A cut above any other sub shop we've encountered, City Subs in downtown Coos Bay par-bakes their own rolls daily, then finishes them when they make your sandwich, for pure fabulousness. Dustbuster (Dusty for short), the resident Bichon Frisee, says, "Order chef salads or low-carb wraps for the peeps if you must, but stick to the meatballs for the pups." For seating, a wide awning protects a row of café tables. 149 N. 4th St.; 541/269-9000.

Top Dog Espresso: With a name like that, of course this drive-through serves dog biscuits to canine backseat drivers. Try the espresso milkshake; it's good enough to growl for. 3636 Tremont (Hwy. 101 S.), North Bend; 541/756-6135.

PLACES TO STAY

Coos Bay Manor Bed and Breakfast: Innkeepers John and Felicia welcome mannerly dogs with open arms in all five rooms of their home, a stunning example of neo-Colonial architecture on the National Register of Historic Places. The original owner was a paper-pulp mill baron named Nerdrum, who settled in Coos Bay from Finland in 1912. Many famous families have since sheltered on the portico and front porch. Rooms are $135, combined suites are $220, and both include breakfast. 955 S. 5th St.; 800/269-1224; www.coosbaymanor.com.

Edgewater Inn: Coos Bay's only waterfront motel has big, rooms with sliding glass doors out to a nice strip of lawn by the range $90–135, plus a $10 pet fee. 275 E. Johnson Ave.; 800/233-04. .edgewater-inns.com.

Sunset Bay Campground: You'll need reservations for the 29 hookup, 36 electrical, and 66 tent sites in a sheltered cove, each with decent privacy thanks to tall trees and shrubbery. Spaces are $12–20, which includes free admission to nearby Shore Acres Botanical Gardens, where, alas, dogs are not allowed. 89526 Cape Arago Hwy.; 800/452-5687; www.reserveamerica.com.

More Accommodations: Please look under *Chain Hotels* in the *Resources* section for additional places to stay in this area.

Coquille and Myrtle Point

These two towns are off the radar, inland 20 miles from Bandon on the coast, and their combined population is probably less than 5,000. The countryside is serene, most notable for large groves of the exotic myrtle tree and the multiple winding forks of the Coquille River.

PARKS, BEACHES, AND RECREATION AREAS

7 LaVerne Park

🐾🐾🐾 (See South Coast map on page 84)

When it's time to leave behind the tourist frenzy on the beaches and escape into the countryside, come to this beautiful county park. A broad playfield is bordered by tall Douglas firs and myrtlewood trees set on the banks of the North Fork of the Coquille River. The park has been around a while and has matured nicely into a pleasant rural getaway. No dogs are allowed on the designated swimming beach, which isn't much to brag about anyway. There are other spots along the river where your dog could sneak in for a quick swim.

From State Route 42 in Coquille, follow the signs to turn on West Central Boulevard, and east on Fairview Road 14 miles to the Upper North Fork Road. 541/396-2344; www.co.coos.or.us/ccpark.

8 Sandy Creek Covered Bridge Wayside

🐾 (See South Coast map on page 84)

Just west of a town called Remote, 42 miles from Roseburg on State Route 42, is a covered bridge built in 1921 beside a circle of lawn, some good-sized pine trees, and a latrine. It may come in handy on the ride out to the coast if your backseat companion is giving you that special whine and you've got your legs crossed. You both can get out and stretch your legs while you look at the map of Coos County parks on display.

PLACES TO EAT

Figaro's Italian Kitchen and Sub Express: We bet your coonhound would happily serenade you with the famous refrain from the opera *Barber of Seville* for this Figaro's hot fajita or cool ranch chicken wrap. At the drive-through or on the wraparound porch, the restaurant's pizza, subs, calzones, ice cream, and frozen yogurt are tasty enough to entice your minstrel mutt to sing for his supper. 29 W. 1st St., Coquille; 541/396-5277.

PLACES TO STAY

LaVerne County Park Campground: The camping pads at LaVerne are gravel, and most sites have river views. It's first come, first served, and the park host recommends leaving the place to the locals on crowded Memorial Day and Labor Day weekends. Tent sites are $11, full hookups are $16; local checks only, so bring cash. 541/247-3719.

Bandon

The official name of this cute village is Bandon by the Sea. The first settlements were destroyed by fire in 1914 and again in 1936, and now, Old Town Bandon is generally what the place looked like after the latter, and hopefully last, fire. Bandon is also a sweet town, home of the best fudge on the coast (Big Wheel General Store; 130 Baltimore; 541/247-3719) and Cranberry Sweets, a company that makes a huge variety of jelly-fruit candies and gives out free samples.

Turn onto Beach Loop Drive, starting south of Bandon and ending in Old Town, for a scenic byway that winds you past most of the lodging and beach parks.

PARKS, BEACHES, AND RECREATION AREAS

🖸 South Slough National Estuarine Research Reserve

🐾🐾 (See South Coast map on page 84)

With a mouthful of a name that is easily shortened to South Slough, this 19,000-acre estuary is only a fraction of the larger 384,000 protected acres of the Coos Bay Estuary. An estuary is a rich wetlands environment where freshwater meets and mixes with saltwater, creating a biological stew perfect for infinite varieties of marine-, plant-, and birdlife. The 10-Minute Loop trail gives you a quick look at the local flora, labeled for easy identification. There are a variety of other trails and boardwalks, from 0.75 mile to three miles, for you and your curious pet to explore a variety of marshes full of frogs and snails and puppy dogs' tails (just kidding about that last one). They were all underwater when we visited; call ahead to the interpretive center for their status before you visit. 61907 Seven Devils Rd.; 541/888-5558; www .southsloughestuary.org.

🔟 Seven Devils

🐾🐾🐾🐾 (See South Coast map on page 84)

Seven is your gambling greyhound's lucky number. The Wonder Wieners give this beach wayside high marks for sticking to the KISS principle. You have instant access to the beach, the whole beach, and nothing but the beach, seven miles of it. A narrow strip of meadow is protected by cliffs that rise to either side, and a smattering of picnic tables have outstanding views. At seven miles off the highway, it doesn't get much action other than a few rockhounders looking for agates. Come up here and get away from the hubbub for a purist beach experience. Restrooms are available.

From U.S. Highway 101, 14 miles north of Bandon, turn west another seven miles onto Seven Devils Road. The approach to Seven Devils from the south is easier by far.

🔢 Bullards Beach

🐾🐾 (See South Coast map on page 84)

This state park has multiple picnic areas, parking lots, and campground loops along the wide mouth of the Coquille River as it dumps into the sea. The campground is a mile from the beach along a paved trail, and the three-mile Cut Creek Trail is a dirt track through flat grassland out to the Coquille River Lighthouse, built in 1896. The smallest lighthouse on the coast, it was officially

decommissioned in 1939 and restored in 1979 with a solar-powered light in the tower to re-create the visual effect.

The best access to Cut Creek is between corrals #7 and #8 in the horse camp. If you're not interested in hoofing it alongside the horses, a road with parking leads directly to the beach and lighthouse. The campground at Bullards Beach is designed for RVs and horse trailers rather than tent campers. The turnoff is two miles north of Bandon on U.S. Highway 101. 541/347-3501.

12 Bandon City Park

🐾🐾🐾 (See South Coast map on page 84)

The rules listed on the secure gate at this off-leash area include a notation that your dogs owe their thanks to Edith Leslie for her donation that made possible the designated and fenced play area. There are a couple of picnic tables, a water faucet, trash can, and bag dispenser in an uneven acre of meadow with a stand of trees in the middle. In short, the OLA is a little piece of dog delight.

The larger city park is an oval, and traffic is routed one-way westbound on the north, eastbound on the south. The OLA is on the south, eastbound side of the loop. From U.S. Highway 101, turn west on 11th Street, go past Jackson Avenue, make the loop around the park, and look to your right. The Russ Sommers Memorial Playground and the skate park are worth detours from the dog park (dogs on leash) if you have kids.

13 Face Rock Wayside

🐾🐾 (See South Coast map on page 84)

Don't be embarrassed if you can't see her face at first. It's like one of those Rorschach inkblots, where once someone points the picture out to you, you can't *not* see it. Nah-So-Mah Tribe legend says that the woman rising out of the water is Ewanua, a chief's daughter who swam into the sea and was turned to stone when she refused to look into the face of the spiteful god Seatka. When her faithful dog Komax swam out to rescue her, the monster petrified him as well (now that's evil), along with her cats and kittens, creating the string of rocks to the northwest.

The rock formations are viewed from a paved walkway above, and a long series of steps leads down to the beach proper. It's a favorite spot of joggers, beachcombers, and people who like to peer into the busy marine goings-on of tide pools.

From U.S. Highway 101, turn west on Beach Loop Road, one mile south of Bandon to this State Scenic Viewpoint.

14 Devil's Kitchen

🐾🐾🐾 (See South Coast map on page 84)

Bandon State Natural Area is this park's official name; Devil's Kitchen is the colloquialism. At the southernmost Beach Access Road, you have to cross an ankle-deep river to reach the ocean. The trail down to the beach is on the north end of the parking lot, hiding behind some rocks. The second wayside has a shady picnic meadow, but the beach is over a very steep dune, covered with prickly bushes and spiky trees. The dachshunds never made it, having been distracted by turquoise dragonflies.

Of the three waysides, the northernmost gives you the easiest path to the sand, by way of a partially paved trail and series of wooden steps. It's also the largest and most developed, with rolling meadows, restrooms, picnic tables, and fire pits. The rock formations include a haystack rock, but it is not *the* Haystack Rock everyone talks about, which is farther north in Cannon Beach.

From U.S. Highway 101, five miles south of Bandon, turn on Beach Loop Road and follow the signs to reach the three park waysides.

15 New River ACEC

🐾🐾🐾 (See South Coast map on page 84)

An ACEC is an Area of Critical Environmental Concern, land granted federal status for the protection of unique ecosystems and wildlife. In this park, a reserve for globally important birding, three miles of trails take you through a variety of habitats, across a meadow, past ponds, into a forest, along the sand, and among marsh grasses. The trail surface varies, but is always easy and clear, and a small portion is paved for wheelchair accessibility. The New River separates you from the ocean, but as you approach you can hear the surf pounding and catch a glimpse of it from the top of the boat ramp. Car and boat access is restricted March 15–September 15 to protect the snowy plover. Trails are open all year, along with the Ellen Warring Learning Center, where kids can touch and explore exhibits about the creatures that live in the park (dogs not allowed inside the center). Isis and Cooper saw a brace or two of birds but were more impressed by the abundance of bunnies.

From U.S. Highway 101, 8.5 miles south of Bandon, turn west on Croft Lake Lane for 1.7 miles down a somewhat bumpy dirt road, and bear right at the fork in the road marked by a small brown sign with binoculars to reach the Storm Ranch entrance. Trail maps are available at the center. Open sunrise–sunset. 541/756-0100.

PLACES TO EAT

Bandon Baking Co. and Deli: This excellent deli specializes in made-to-order sandwiches for lunch, which you may not need after picking and choosing from the rows of cakes and baked goods and loaves of bread to take home. Cooper spied fat homemade dog biscuits. Cash only, unless you order online with a credit card. 160 2nd St.; 541/347-9440; www.bandonbakingco.com.

Bandon Fish Market: The rockfish fish-and-chips baskets, fish tacos, and chowder in sourdough bread bowls somehow taste better than usual when you're seated at outdoor tables with spiffy blue-and-white checkered tablecloths. There's a dog dish outside, a bucket o' biscuits at the counter, and you could buy your best friend a $2 dried salmon stick for a splurge. "They feed you too much," said one patron, who obviously didn't have a dog to take the excess off of his hands. 249 1st St. S.E.; 541/347-4282; www.bandonfishmarket.com.

Old Town Pizza and Pasta: The name is self-explanatory and the outdoor tables on the sidewalk patio are as red as tomato sauce, perhaps to get you in the mood. For fettuccini Alfredo, Cooper would be willing to come back as an Italian greyhound in his next life. 395 2nd St.; 541/347-3911.

Port O' Call: Owners of the largest breeds may want to keep an eye out for the dangerous combination of curious noses and paws around the claws of the live lobsters and crabs in the tanks at this authentic seafood market. Order your crustaceans steamed or served up in tomato broth for a spicy cioppino soup, while you sit at the outdoor oyster bar and sip bottled beer and wines by the glass. 155 1st St.; 541/347-2875.

PLACES TO STAY

Sunset Oceanfront: In the trade, ocean view means you can catch a glimpse of the ocean from your window and oceanfront means you can reach the beach from your door. This motel has both, and both recently renovated and a bit dated rooms, all facing Face Rock. Oceanfront rooms range $90–160; ocean views are noticeably cheaper at $65–90; non-view rooms $50–70; all require a $10 pet fee. 1865 Beach Loop Dr. S.W.; 541/347-2453; www.sunsetmotel.com.

Tintagel by the Sea: Tintagel is named after a headland in Cornwall, England; this one is a great-looking rental house, with private beach access, and "in your face" ocean viewing sunrooms on each level. The lower unit is perfect for a couple, with a couple of pets max, going for a song at $105–135 a night, plus a $10 per pet fee. The main house is even juicier, with a private master bedroom and bath with clawfoot tub ($200–250). One-week summer minimum stay. Neither unit is ADA-accessible; you must be able to handle 57 steps to get there. 1430 Beach Loop Dr.; 800/868-2304; www.tintagel bythesea.com.

More Accommodations: Please look under *Chain Hotels* in the *Resources* section for additional places to stay in this area.

Port Orford

After much strife with the land's earlier inhabitants, this port became the oldest European settled town on the coast in 1851. The coast's oldest continuously operating lighthouse is at nearby Cape Blanco, commissioned in 1870 to aid the ships transporting gold and lumber from the region.

PARKS, BEACHES, AND RECREATION AREAS

16 Boice-Cope at Floras Lake

🐾🐾 (See South Coast map on page 84)

In 1910, there were about 400 people living here on a developer's promise to build a canal connecting the lake to the ocean to create a thriving sea port. When they discovered that the lake is at a slightly higher elevation, and thus would drain out into the ocean if linked, the plan dried up and so did the people. The windsurfers don't mind a bit, making the lake a favorite place to practice because winds are steady at 15–25 knots, it's shallow, and water temperature averages 68°F.

You can walk around the lake on a sandy trail, and up over a single dune to the ocean on the far side from the parking lot/campground. Campsites at this county park are all together in a big meadow, for $16 per night. Windsurfing, kite boarding, and kayak rentals and lessons are available on the lake. 541/348-9912; www.floraslake.com.

Turn onto Floras Lake Loop from U.S. Highway 101, west onto Floras Lake Road, and west again on Boice-Cope Road. Parking is $2 per day.

17 Cape Blanco

🐾🐾🐾🐾 (See South Coast map on page 84)

Among some pretty stiff competition, Cape Blanco manages to stand out as a superb state park, the tip of which sticks out as the westernmost spot in the contiguous 48 states. It's got everything a dog dreams of: beach access along the south, picnicking in fields along the Sixes River, and eight miles of trails through a wide variety of ecosystems, from forest to tall grass dunes. For the people in your party, the views of the ocean surrounding three sides of the landmass are unbeatable. History buffs will appreciate the tours of the 245-foot Cape Blanco Lighthouse, the Victorian Hughes House on the National Register of Historic Places, and the remains of the church and cemetery. The lighthouse is the southernmost in Oregon, and the first to have a Fresnel lens installed in 1870. Call 541/332-6774 for information about hours and tours for the lighthouse and Hughes House, both of which have wheelchair-accessible areas.

The easiest beach access point is through the campground, next to site #A32. You can drive or walk down a winding lane that eventually crumbles right onto the beach, with a few parking places just before the sidewalk ends.

From U.S. Highway 101, nine miles north of Port Orford, go west on Cape Blanco Road to the end. 39745 S. Hwy. 101.

18 Paradise Point

🐾🐾 (See South Coast map on page 84)

Paradise, in this instance, is a parking lot with access to a coarse sand beach that extends several miles from the Port Orford Heads to Cape Blanco. Look closely, and you'll see that the beach is actually billions of tiny pebbles that have yet to be ground to the fine texture of sand. In most places, it is a steep slope of sand down to the water, making it tricky to walk long distances without feeling lopsided.

Look for the turnoff to Paradise Point Road about one mile north of town. Don't let the Dead End signs scare you; the road dead-ends into the State Recreation Site.

19 Port Orford Heads

😺😺😺 (See South Coast map on page 84)

From 1934 to 1970, this state park was one of the busiest Coast Guard stations on a stretch of treacherous water. The heads are prominent landmasses jutting over the ocean, providing the best viewpoint for sighting ships in trouble on the rocks, or to give you some fantastic views. Trails in the park are well groomed in soft wood-mulch that's easy to walk. The half-mile Headland Trail leads out onto the edge of the bluff, and from there, you can connect to the 0.75-mile Loop Trail that takes you past the site of the former lookout tower and the boat house where rescuers launched into the rough seas. While you read the placards telling the stories of the search-and-rescue station and check out the restored lifeboat, your watchdog can keep his eyes peeled for the black-tailed deer common to the area. You can't reach the beach at the heads, but you can look out over it for miles in every direction.

From U.S. Highway 101, follow the signs to turn west on 9th Street, and then south on Coast Guard Road. Open 6 A.M.–8 P.M.

20 Humbug Mountain

😺😺😺 (See South Coast map on page 84)

Rottweilers, get ready to rumble. Pull out those paw booties and take on the challenge of Humbug Mountain, a six-mile loop trail that climbs from the beach up to the summit at 1,748 feet. As you rest along the way, your pal can sniff out the subtle differences between myrtle, maple, and old-growth Douglas firs. Those who make the trek are treated to a northward viewpoint of Redfish Rocks and Port Orford and another south to Gold Beach. Trailhead parking is just north of the campground entrance. Isis has a tricky back that wasn't quite up to the rigors of the trail, but she did enjoy herself on the park's coarse gravel beach, north of the mountain, accessible along the banks of a creek starting near campsite #C7. The waves crash against the base of the mountain, and the surf has a wicked undertow.

To the south of the mountain is a picnic area, with its own parking and a meadow the length of a football field that's fun to run around on. Walk down the paved pathway along the stream to find it.

This state park is unmistakable, even before you get there on U.S. Highway 101, six miles south of Port Orford. Open 6 A.M.–10 P.M. 39745 Hwy. 101; 541/332-6774.

PLACES TO EAT

The Crazy Norwegian: As honorary Norwegians (grandmother on their maternal side), Isis and Cooper can say with tongue firmly in cheek that putting "crazy" and "Norwegian" together is a bit redundant. The cook will make you some insanely good fish-and-chips, salads, homemade cookies, burgers, sandwiches, and chowder to go. While you wait, you can experience the dry

Scandinavian sense of humor, reading the menu and learning the various meanings of the expression "Uff Da," including "Waking yourself up in church with your own snoring." 259 6th St. (Hwy. 101); 541/332-8601.

PLACES TO STAY

Castaway by the Sea: The major selling point at this little 13-room motel is the private, enclosed sun porch/storm watching veranda. Fantastic views, plain and simple. Rooms still look good after renovations in 2004; a "no pets on the furniture" policy helps keep them that way. A variety of room sizes are priced at $65–155. Pets are $10 each per night, no more than two, please. 545 W. 5th St.; 541/332-4502; www.castawaybythesea.com.

Cape Blanco Campground: A few of the 53 electric/water sites at this state park have water views, but most are neatly hidden from the water, and each other, widely spaced among the thick woods. It's miles to the main road through farm country; the only sounds you'll hear are the other campers, neighing from the neighboring horse camp, and the surf. Rates are $12–16 for first-come, first-served sites. 39745 S. Hwy. 101; 541/332-6774.

Gold Beach

This coastal community is where Oregon's most famous river, the Rogue, meets the Pacific Ocean. Ocean fishing charters for salmon and steelhead are at your beck and call and Jerry's Rogue Jets will speed you upriver. Coop 'n' Isis claim that the beaches between Brookings and Gold Beach are the best and most accessible on the Southern Coast. South Park and Kissing Rock provide two wheelchair-accessible ocean viewpoints, the former on the far south end of town, and the latter a mile south, on the south side of Hunter Creek. Even the visitors center has beach access, a playground, and picnic tables at South Beach Park (541/247-7526; www.goldbeach.org).

Although the dogs wouldn't technically list it as a park, Ophir rest stop is nine miles north of Gold Beach on U.S. Highway 101, giving you instant access to miles of unspoiled sand between Nesika Beach and a spot known as Sisters Rocks. All that, plus a potty and picnic tables.

PARKS, BEACHES, AND RECREATION AREAS

21 Buffington Park

🐾 (See South Coast map on page 84)

While everyone else is getting sand in their muzzles on the beach, you can escape to this cute community park in the center of town, with clean restrooms, covered and open picnic tables, and a Kid Castle playground.

From Ellensburg Avenue in town, turn on E. Caughell at the sign pointing to the library and community park. Open sunrise–sunset.

22 Cape Sebastian

😊😊 (See South Coast map on page 84)

The cape is a cliff you can climb for the widest ocean, shore, and mountain panoramas on the lower coast. Views start from the two parking lots, 200 feet above sea level, 40 miles to the north and Humbug Mountain and 50 miles as far south as California. From the southern lot, there is a 1.5-mile trail leading to even more panoramic vistas. The first half mile is paved, a real treat for wheelchair patrons (just about the best accessible views on the coast), and then it settles into a softer, paw-pleasing dirt trail through Sitka spruce with frequent clearings. It's essential to keep your pal on leash to avoid him going over the edge in his enthusiasm.

This State Scenic Corridor is seven miles south of Gold Beach on U.S. Highway 101.

23 Myers Creek Beach

😊😊 (See South Coast map on page 84)

Immediately south of a small bridge, exactly at mile marker 337, is a very large gravel roadside pullout. On the north end of the lot is an easy and quick trail directly to a gorgeous beach where the creek meets the sea, complete with rock formations, upland driftwood to sniff around, and extensive, smooth sand. Despite its proximity to the highway, small bluffs protect your scouting party from the silly people in cars who aren't stopping to smell the seaweed and get in touch with their inner beach bums. There are no amenities here.

24 Pistol River Sand Dunes

😊😊😊 (See South Coast map on page 84)

In 1856, an infamous Native American–U.S. Army battle was fought here, and the park's name comes from a militia soldier rumored to have dropped his gun in the river in the heat of the fight. It'll be a slightly different park every time you visit. The sand dunes shift and grow in the summer, and the river has changed course several times in recent years. The big, bold surf is different every day, a boon for the many windsurfers. After a short climb over the sand dunes, you reach an open stretch of beach between Brookings and Gold Beach.

The pullout for parking is directly off U.S. Highway 101, 11 miles south of Gold Beach. There are no amenities at this State Scenic Viewpoint, only sand, sea, and sky.

PLACES TO EAT

The Cannery Building: This building is home to a bunch of options including the Coffee Dock (541/247-6158) for espresso, pastries, and fruit smoothies; Cone Amor (541/247-4270) for ice cream and sweets; Port Hole Café (541/247-7411) for family dining; and Fisherman's Direct Seafoods

DIVERSIONS

In the foyer at **Woof's Dog Bakery** in Gold Beach, treat samples are served at "Yappy Hour," 3–5 P.M. daily. At this divine doggy destination, two bakers work full time turning out treats that are far too beautiful for you-know-who to eat. More than a bakery, this is a full-service dog store featuring high-quality foods and an eye-popping selection of accessories and toys. 29525 Ellensburg Ave. (Hwy. 101); 541/247-6835; www.woofsdogbakery.com.

You ought to stop at **Dog Style Boutique's** "barkery," too, for treats and last-minute essentials when in Bandon. One of the owners of this pet boutique also makes and sells a raw food diet for animals at www.boneappetitrawfood.com. 95 S.W. 11th; 541/347-2504.

(541/247-9494), a cooperative of local boat operators offering live and cooked crab, shrimp cocktail, smoked salmon, and other fresh treasures from the sea. Outside, a few picnic tables are scattered around. 29975 S. Harbor Way.

Cutter and Co. BBQ Stand: Where's the beef? Call ahead to find out where the grill and picnic benches are parked this season, and order to share heaping plates of ribs, brisket, pork, and chicken from this authentic slow roaster of fine meats. Bring cash. 541/247-2271.

Rollin' 'n Dough Bakery and Bistro: The tiny white cottage with red trim looks humble, but locals say true gourmet food comes out of Patti's kitchen, but only 10:30 A.M.–3 P.M. daily, so time your visit accordingly. A Culinary Institute grad, Patti uses organic and local ingredients for artistic dishes such as pan-seared tuna or crab po'boys. Your pals can be secured to the back patio fence, or they can loll around on the lawn and make friends, human and canine. 94257 North Bank Road; 541/247-4438.

PLACES TO STAY

Ireland's Rustic Lodges: There's a surprising amount of room in the real log cabins, each one unique, with separate bedrooms and living rooms with fireplaces. Pets are allowed in cabins #1–8, but Cooper prefers the Hobbitish rooms out back (#24, #25, #26) because they have sliding glass doors that open onto a huge lawn and the beach trail. The price is more than right at $70–135 per night. Pets over 30 pounds are $10 per night; those under are $5. Their insurance prohibits Dobermans and pit bulls. In 2006, they added a sheltered hot tub deck (no dogs in tubs, please). 29330 Ellensburg Ave.; 541/247-7718; www.irelandsrusticlodges.com.

Turtle Rock Resort Cottages: Wipe your paws before entering these eight pet-friendly rentals. With carpets and furniture in tasteful neutral tones, the cottages look like shrunken town homes, nicely decked out with amenities in petite proportions. They're tightly grouped alongside the banks of Hunter Creek, or tucked up against a wooded hillside, which we prefer. They all have lofts, kitchens, and decks with barbecue grills; some have hot tubs and fireplaces. Rates range $140–180 per night, with a $15 fee per pet, two pet maximum. Check in the office for local restaurants that will deliver to the cottages. 28788 Hunter Creek Loop; 541/247-9203; www.turtlerockresorts.com.

Huntley Park Campground: This privately owned rustic campground is a super secret, seven miles up the Rogue River from Gold Beach. Spacious sites in a deep myrtle grove are only $10 a night. Bring quarters for the hot showers. Firewood and blocks of ice are also available for a small fee. Impromptu potlucks and sing-a-longs have been known to happen from time to time. No hookups. 96847 Jerry's Flat Rd.; 541/247-9377.

More Accommodations: Please look under *Chain Hotels* in the *Resources* section for additional places to stay in this area.

Brookings-Harbor

Only four miles north of the California border, Brookings benefits from weather patterns that give it the warmest average temperatures on the coast. The town is famous for its flowers, especially azaleas and Easter lilies, producing about 75 percent of all Easter lily bulbs grown in the United States. Vast fields of the tall white flowers are in full bloom in July, and the bulbs are shipped worldwide. You can reach this southernmost Oregon town only by coming down from U.S. Highway 101, or by dipping into California from Grants Pass and back up again on the famed Redwood Highway, U.S. Highway 199.

If the parks and trails listed here are too tame for your taste, there are literally hundreds of options in the **Kalmiopsis Wilderness,** with 197,000 acres of solitude and wildlife, 30 miles inland from Brookings. The Chetco Ranger Station in Brookings can give you all the details (539 Chetco Ave.; 541/412-6000; www.fs.fed.us/r6/rogue-siskiyou).

PARKS, BEACHES, AND RECREATION AREAS

🌊 Samuel H. Boardman

🐾 🐾 🐾 🐾 (See South Coast map on page 84)

Sam Boardman was Oregon's first Superintendent of Parks, a visionary who led the effort to build a phenomenal system of preserved public lands. The acquisition of this State Scenic Corridor named in his honor was successfully negotiated as his last triumph before retiring. It's not so much a park as an adventure, a 12-mile long forest on rugged cliffs punctuated by small beaches. As you drive through the park on U.S. Highway 101, there are viewpoints, picnic areas, 300-year-old Sitka spruce trees, and beach access. If you'd rather

explore the park on foot, 27 miles of the Oregon Coast Trail w
forests and along the coast.

The dynamic duo got a kick out of seeing how fast they could
humans, hopping in and out of the car at every viewpoint and w   ...the
1,471 acres. Of them all, the Whalehead Beach Trail is the paws-down winner.
A narrow path winds through thick brush for about a half mile (in the spring,
before feet have trampled down the brush, parts of the path are almost invis-
ible). Undaunted trailblazing bulldogs are rewarded with the largest, most
fabulous beach in the park.

You can't miss the park. U.S. Highway 101 drives straight through the
middle, beginning four miles north of Brookings. You'll see signs for stops,
including a good picnic area at Lone Ranch Beach and great viewpoints at
Cape Ferrelo, House Rock, and Indian Sands. On your way, you'll cross over
the tallest bridge in Oregon.

26 Oregon Redwood Nature Trail

🐾🐾🐾🐾 🦴 (See South Coast map on page 84)

This awe-inspiring one-mile trail takes you through the Pacific Coast's northernmost grove of redwood trees in the Siskiyou National Forest. You'll get a
crick in your neck as you wonder at these giants, estimated to be between 600
and 800 years old. The path is generally easy, with a few steep, rocky, and narrow sections. Your pooch may not appreciate the height of the trees, but she'll
certainly enjoy sniffing around their girth and in the equally large ferns on
the forest floor. Pick up an interpretive map at the trailhead, which leads you
counterclockwise around the trail.

From U.S. Highway 101, turn on the North Bank Chetco River Road and
follow the signs. Parking at the trailhead is $5 per day, but if you're up to it,
you can park free at Alfred A. Loeb State Park and take the 0.7-mile Riverview
Trail connecting to and from this trail.

27 Alfred A. Loeb

🐾🐾🐾 (See South Coast map on page 84)

If you've worked your way along the coast, overdosing on ocean vistas, this
state park in the deep woods is a welcome change of pace. Dozens of secluded
picnic areas are tucked into a 200-year-old myrtlewood grove, the fragrant
trees smelling like bay leaves. The meadows and trails and woods are next to
the banks of the Chetco River, here a swift-moving, shallow stream in a wide
bed of river rocks. Fish from the gravel bar for salmon and steelhead.

From the picnic area, the Riverview Trail travels 0.7 mile along the shore,
connecting you to the Redwood Trail. Cooper highly recommends camping
here in the peaceful forest by crystal-clear waters. Isis comes for the amazing
variety of birds living in the grove. Note to dogs: Don't eat or play with the
orange newts in the region, because their skin secretes a deadly toxin. Note to

...umans: Don't worry too much, as the newts are fast and can probably out-scamper your scamp.

From U.S. Highway 101, follow the signs to the state park, 10 miles in on the North Bank Chetco River Road. Open 7:30 A.M.–10 P.M. 541/469-2021.

28 Harris Beach

 (See South Coast map on page 84)

You begin to see the wonders of the ocean from the minute you drive into this state park. Unique rock formations loom from several pullout viewpoints, including Goat Island, the coast's largest offshore island. From this area, you can reach the first section of beach on the short Sunset Beach Trail.

Keep driving, and you'll pass the campground to reach the looped parking lot for the main picnic area and a second crescent of silky sand. Picnic tables are well placed for maximum views on a terraced hillside, wheelchair-accessible along a paved path. In between them is an outdoor shower where you and pup can rinse off after a frolic on the small beach. Cooper can't recommend camping here because the sawmill next door makes too much noise at night.

Harris Beach is directly off of U.S. Highway 101, just north of the main section of Brookings. Parking is $3 per day at the main lot. Open 8 A.M.–8 P.M. 541/469-2021.

29 Azalea Park

(See South Coast map on page 84)

This beautiful and unique city park is at its peak in mid-May, when the azaleas are in full bloom. Imagine the nuances a dog's nose must smell among 1,100 bushes of three species, some up to 300 years old. There are aspects of the park for you and your pets to appreciate all year: rolling hills, an accessible sidewalk and paths through the trees, sand-pit volleyball courts, viewing benches, and hidden picnic tables. Dogs are allowed to pull up a patch of lawn and enjoy summer concerts with you at the Stage Under the Stars and on the big playground called Kid Town. The fragrance from the riot of flowers is most heady in the center of the park, from the observation tower. There are no restrictions except to keep your pet on leash in the ball fields. Like Dorothy and her companions in the poppies, a drowsy afternoon here may lull you to sleep.

The park is easy to find by following the signs from U.S. Highway 101 just north of the Chetco River bridge.

30 McVay Rock

(See South Coast map on page 84)

This windy, brisk picnic spot is off the beaten path, a quieter place for your dog to explore the local flora and fauna while you take in the endless ocean views. From a gravel parking lot and a petite lawn, a very steep but short trail will take you down to the beach. It's mostly gravel, without water access because of the large rocks in the surf. The rock itself sits several stories tall behind you in someone's field of veggies.

There are no signs directing you to this state recreation site, so watch for Ocean View Drive on U.S. Highway 101, two miles south of Brookings. Turn left there, travel about a mile, and turn left again on Seagull Lane.

PLACES TO EAT

Boogie Board Bagels: Order one of 14 custom bagel sandwiches, or design your own, for breakfast and lunch. Jib Juice smoothies, green salads, and Sailin' Soups are made from scratch daily, just like the bagels. Call ahead to order and go through the drive-through, as there's no outdoor seating. 925 Chetco Ave.; 541/412-9050.

Slugs 'n' Stones 'n' Ice Cream Cones: Where there is moisture in the Northwest, there will be slugs, so why not celebrate them at an ice cream shop? Cooper says they can name themselves after giant Madagascar hissing cockroaches for all he cares, so long as they keep serving up free doggy cones, and big waffle cones of locally famous, more-than-31-flavors of hard scoop Umpqua ice cream. Open March–October. Lower Harbor Rd.; 541/469-7584.

Zola's Pizzeria at the Port: Please do not feed the birds from the patio or tables, asks the management. Feeding the dogs is up to you. Lots of folks in town recommended hanging out and feeding your face with buffalo wings, pizza pies, beer, and wine here at covered, heated, bright red picnic tables. 16362 Lower Harbor Rd.; 541/412-7100.

PLACES TO STAY

Wild Rivers Motor Lodge: The pet-friendliest place in town also happens to be a really excellent choice. Rooms in the newest wing, built in 2004, have granite countertops, big tubs, slate floors, and cherrywood furniture; but even the rooms in the 1970s wing and 1950s wing are great. The owners are a husband and wife team and their son takes care of maintenance. They believe in uncompromising cleanliness and superior customer service. It really shows. Second-floor rooms have distant ocean views. It's the best in town by a mile. At rates of $60–90, it's also a steal. A one-time $20 pet fee covers you for up to two pets and five days. 437 Chetco Ave.; 541/469-5361.

Alfred A. Loeb Campground: There are 48 electrical sites with water, flush toilets, and hot showers by the Chetco River in a grove of myrtlewood trees. Summer rates are $16 per site; in the off-season it's a measly $12. All sites are on a first-come, first-served basis. North Bank Chetco River Road, 10 miles northeast of Brookings. 541/469-2021.

More Accommodations: Please look under *Chain Hotels* in the *Resources* section for additional places to stay in this area.

CHAPTER 4

Greater Portland

It makes sense to be a dog lover in a metro area with 37,000 acres of parks and green spaces within city limits. Despite an annual rainfall that rivals Seattle's, Isis and Cooper can testify that Portlanders will tolerate wet dog smells and muddy paw prints to take advantage of the outdoors under *any* weather conditions. A total of 32 city parks have some off-leash opportunities. There are five full-time, fenced off-leash areas; the remaining 27 are unfenced open areas in specific city parks, and 19 of the 27 have seasonal or limited off-leash hours, some with annoyingly complicated schedules. These latter sites give dogs a place to exercise and play in open areas not designed for other uses. Look for the Exercising Your Pet Off-Leash sign. Good maps are also available at www.portlandonline.com/parks (under the "Recreation" tab, choose "Dogs") or call Portland Parks and Recreation's dog program hotline at 503/823-3647. The Wonder Wieners have included as many of these areas as reasonable, hoping you can find them and that there's at least some parking. They hope you'll go on a dog park tour of the city, exploring historic neighborhoods you might not see otherwise.

PICK OF THE LITTER—GREATER PORTLAND

BEST PARKS
Forest Park, Northwest Portland (page 117)
South Park Blocks, Downtown and Historic Waterfront
(page 123)

BEST DOG PARKS
Chimney Park, North Portland (page 110)
Gabriel Park, Southwest Portland (page 133)
Hondo Dog Park, Hillsboro (page 134)
Hazeldale Dog Park, Beaverton (page 135)
Luscher Farm Dog Park, Lake Oswego (page 139)

BEST EVENT
Dogtoberfest, Southeast Portland (page 127)

BEST PLACES TO EAT
Tin Shed Garden Café, Northeast Portland (page 116)
St. Honoré Boulangerie, Northwest Portland (page 118)
The Lucky Lab Brew Pub, Southeast Portland (page 131)

BEST PLACES TO STAY
Ace Hotel, Downtown and Historic Waterfront (page 125)
Hotel deLuxe, Downtown and Historic Waterfront (page 125)
Hotel Lucia, Downtown and Historic Waterfront (page 125)
Jupiter Hotel, Southeast Portland (page 131)

When not braving the elements, the city's diverse populations cluster in ever-present neighborhood coffee houses and bookstores, the greatest of which is Powell's City of Books, the country's largest independent bookseller (1005 W. Burnside; 503/228-0540 or 866/201-7601; www.powells.com). When not drowning in mud, Portland natives also like to drown their sorrows in one of the city's several dozen craft breweries.

If you live in PDX, as locals call their town by its airport designation, you're either an Eastsider or a Westsider, depending on what side of the Willamette River you live on. As a visitor, you get to be a Topsider and take it all in. If you're only in town for a day or two, we suggest you stick around Northwest Portland and Downtown.

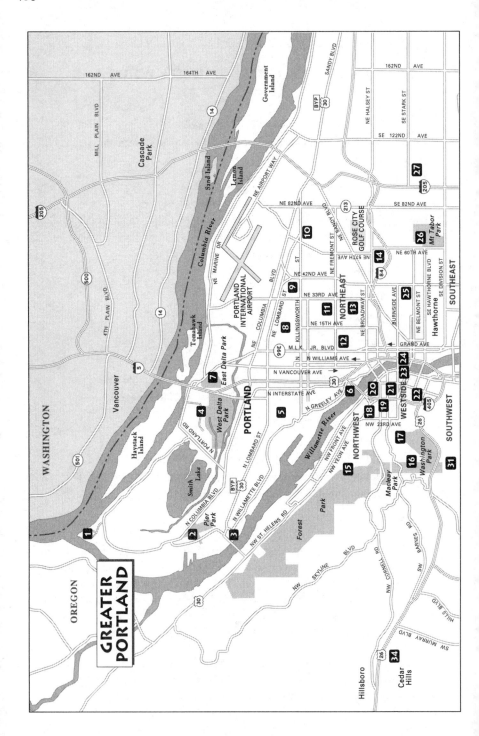

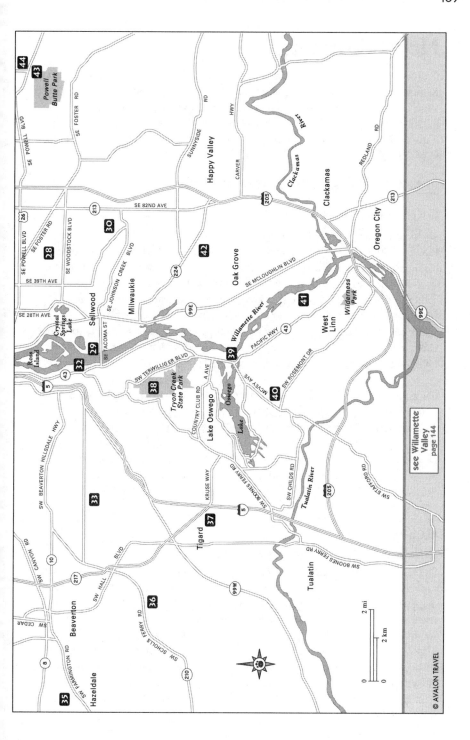

see Willamette
Valley
page 144

© AVALON TRAVEL

North Portland

Call it NoPo to sound like a local. North Portland is a heavy industrial area, with a couple of historic neighborhoods experiencing modest revitalization. With so few attractions to distract you, your dog hopes you'll have no alternative but to spend hours with her in the district's big off-leash areas, perhaps with a side trip to Tré Bone, a neat little dog shop (8326 N. Lombard; 971/255-0772).

PARKS, BEACHES, AND RECREATION AREAS

◼ Kelley Point Park
🐾🐾🐾 (See Greater Portland map on page 108)

Pioneer Hall Jackson Kelley spent most of his later life trying to gain attention for his discoveries in the Oregon Territory. You, on the other hand, can happily spend hours going unnoticed in his 104-acre namesake park, built upon river dredgings. If anything, some spots are a little too private; we were tempted to whistle or wear bear bells to avoid stumbling upon clandestine trysts.

Among heavy tree cover, Kelley Point has paved walkways, woodchip pathways, gravel and dirt trails, and open fields dotted with tiny daisies and clover. Narrow beach coves are strewn with a natural obstacle course of rotting pier posts and driftwood. With the exception of a close-cropped picnic meadow, the place is generally unkempt and overgrown and there are multiple chances to get into Columbia Slough. In short, it's a brilliant park for dogs.

Located on the very tip of Portland, Kelly Point has two large parking areas. First is the south lot, the only place you'll see a worn map for the lay of the land. Dogs may prefer the second, or north lot, for its quick beach access, more open terrain, and massive picnic meadow.

Take Exit 307 from I-5 and go west on N. Marine Drive for 4.5 miles. Turn right into the park. Open 6 A.M.–9 P.M. N. Marine Dr. and Lombard St.

◻ Chimney Park
🐾🐾🐾🐾🐕 (See Greater Portland map on page 108)

Dogs are having a field day at the city's largest fenced and gated off-leash area. It's only a four-mile trip from downtown to get to this full-time 16-acre dog park. Two separately enclosed and gated plots are dedicated to dogs from the crack of dawn until it's too dark to see. The north side is a well-groomed, gently sloping hill with large, mature shade trees. It's also the side with a picnic table, poop bag supplies, and a garbage can. The south side is an uneven field of wildflowers infrequently mowed over. The groomed side is occasionally closed to give the grass time to breathe. Don't look for a tall landmark to guide you; the city's incinerator smokestack that gave the park its name has been removed. Bring your own water.

From I-5 northbound, take exit 306A. Go east on N. Columbia Boulevard for 4.5 miles. Turn left at the sign for the Stanley Parr Archives and Records Center. There's plenty of gravel parking behind the building. Open 5 A.M.-midnight. 9360 N. Columbia.

🐾🐕 Cathedral Park

(See Greater Portland map on page 108)

Named after the graceful arches of the St. Johns Bridge overhead, this city park has an illustrious history as one of the camping sites for Lewis and Clark's men. Away from the boat launch and excessive boat trailer parking is a small, unsecured off-leash area, delineated by cable car tracks, the bridge, and Pittsburg Avenue. Cooper can't get excited about coming here for the OLA; he does, however, think the underside workings of the bridge are pretty keen, as are some interesting sculptures on park grounds. It's not too shabby as a picnic choice either, with its setting along the Willamette River and a dabbling of tables. Humans have a real restroom at the boat launch; poop bags and a can are stationed for dogs.

Exit 305B, go west on Lombard Avenue for four miles to the historic St. Johns neighborhood. Turn left on Baltimore and left on Crawford. Park along Crawford or turn right on Pittsburg and park on the street. Open 5 A.M.–midnight.

🐾🐕 Portland International Raceway

(See Greater Portland map on page 108)

This off-leash area, formerly known as West Delta Park, has definitely got some quirks. The grounds may flood in the rainy season, the area is used for overflow parking for raceway events, and the winter wild geese population can overrun the field, leaving a whole mess of poop behind. Last, and most bizarre, the place smells like stinky cheese on hot days. It's an empty, three-acre field of scrubby bush, protected by a fence on the north and separated only by a guardrail on the south. There are no amenities.

Why do we bother to mention it? One, the only other OLA in the immediate vicinity closes November–April. Two, it's usually not crowded. And three, even a bad day at a mediocre dog park is better than a good day at the office.

From I-5, take exit 306B and follow the signs to Portland International Raceway. From N. Expo Road, turn left onto N. Broadacre Street. Gravel parking is available along Broadacre. Open 5 A.M.–midnight; check the event schedule at www.portlandraceway.com before you go. 1940 N. Victory Blvd; 503/823-7223.

🐾🐕 Arbor Lodge

(See Greater Portland map on page 108)

As in many of the city's limited-hours off-leash sites, the dog area at Arbor Lodge is an unfenced, tree-filled section of a pretty city park. Although partially bounded by tennis courts, basketball courts, and paved pathways, you must have excellent voice control of your pet to protect him from residential traffic on all four sides. You'll need to provide bags and water for your dog. The people's potty is in the center.

From I-5, take Exit 304. Go west on N. Portland Boulevard 0.75 mile, turn right on N. Greeley Avenue and right on N. Bryant Street. The OLA is on the northwest corner of the park. Street parking is available on parts of Bryant. OLA hours are complicated and vary by the season; call 503/823-3647 or go to www.portlandonline.com/parks and select "Dogs" under the "Recreation" tab. N. Bryant St. and Delaware Ave.

6 Overlook Park

 (See Greater Portland map on page 108)

The off-leash area at this city park overlooks the industrial workings of a busy city port and rail yards, the Fremont Bridge, and the downtown skyline. More suited to people than pets, it's a tiny triangle at the south end of the park. The view is the upside; the downsides are scarce parking, an unenclosed area without amenities, and a busy medical center next door. It's a panoramic potty stop and not much more.

From I-5, take Exit 303 and turn right on N. Alberta Street. Turn left at the next light and continue south on N. Interstate Avenue for 0.7 mile. You can pass Overlook Boulevard and turn right on N. Fremont Street to park in the cul-de-sac next to the OLA, if you're lucky enough to score a spot. Or, you can turn right on Overlook Boulevard to find easier street parking and walk south on leash until you see the OLA sign. June 15–August 31, OLA hours are 5–10 A.M. and 7 P.M.–midnight; open 5 A.M.–midnight the rest of the year. N. Fremont St. and Interstate Ave.

PLACES TO EAT

Equinox Restaurant: Much like the perfect balance between light and dark, this much-acclaimed restaurant manages to create food that seems light, yet is somehow completely filling. Their mission is to serve food that's fresh, organic, local, and in season, from a natural harvest in tune with the environment. We call it high-falutin' food brought down to earth. Leashed pets will be greeted with a water bowl on the stonework patio. 830 N. Shaver St.; 503/460-3333; www.equinoxrestaurantpdx.com.

PLACES TO STAY

In this area, chain hotels listed in the *Resources* section offer the best choices for dogs and their owners.

Northeast Portland–Airport

Northeast Portland provides room for the large facilities that can't be crammed into the downtown core on the Westside, such as the Portland International Airport and the Convention Center. Lloyd Center, Oregon's largest shopping mall, has 200 retail stores encircling an indoor ice rink. Only a few blocks farther out, the historic neighborhoods of Northeast Portland have distinct personalities, from the blowsy Hollywood area to highly starched Laurelhurst. The many wonderful city parks in Northeast Portland also share a signature look of rolling hills, thick carpets of grass, and a treasure trove of stately, mature deciduous trees that have guarded the city since its infancy.

PARKS, BEACHES, AND RECREATION AREAS

7 East Delta Park

🐾🐾🦴 (See Greater Portland map on page 108)

Across the street from a massive sports complex, this five-acre off-leash area is fully fenced and reserved for unfettered romping. Unfortunately, this OLA site isn't really year-round. It's open only May–October because it tends to be a swamp the rest of the year. Three gates lead into the rectangular space that features rough grass, a few trees, scattered water bowls, and a couple of picnic tables in the shade.

DIVERSION

There are times, no matter how close you are to your canine, that you will need or want to hop on a plane without her. For such times, the **AirPet Hotel** is a stroke of genius. This dog day-care and boarding service is located five minutes from Portland International Airport and offers shuttle services to park-and-fly lots and the flight terminal. Board your dog, park your car, and board your flight. It's that easy.

For a reasonable $30 per day (20 percent discount for multiple dogs), your pet sleeps in a comfy indoor kennel overnight, and during the day she gets to play in a supervised indoor playpen with dogs of similar temperament and size, and she is taken outside for at least five 10-minute potty breaks. She'll fall asleep each night exhausted, well fed, and happy.

Although normal business hours are 6 A.M.–10 P.M., the facility is staffed 24 hours a day. You can arrange early or late drop-off and pickup times by appointment for those red-eye flights. For once, your pet might not mind being left behind. 6212 N.E. 78th Court; 503/255-1388; www.airpethotel.com.

Other areas of the large city park make for good sunbathing and picnicking, but dogs must be leashed, and they are not allowed in the playgrounds, on paved trails, or on the sports fields.

From I-5, take Exit 307 and follow signs to Delta Park and Marine Drive East. Take a left on N. Union Court. The dog park is on the left. Open 5 A.M.–midnight May–October. N. Denver and MLK Jr. Blvd.

8 Alberta Park

🐾🐾🐾 🐕 (See Greater Portland map on page 108)

The off-leash area at Alberta is comfortable and roomy. The lawn is soft, punctuated by big trees widely spaced apart. It's unsecured, with borders marked by park pathways along a fairly quiet side of the street. Restrooms, trash cans, water, and poop bag dispensers are available, although the latter are frequently empty. The sheltered basketball court and ball fields at Alberta get only moderate use, often leaving the park to the dogs.

From I-5, take Exit 303 and follow signs to N.E. Killingsworth Street. Go east a little more than a mile and turn left on N.E. 22nd Avenue. The OLA is on the east side of the park. Limited street parking is available alongside. Open 5 A.M.–midnight. N.E. 22nd Ave. and Killingsworth St.

9 Fernhill Park

🐾🐾🐾 🐕 (See Greater Portland map on page 108)

The off-leash area at Fernhill Park is a vague, amorphous blob in the center of a 24-acre green space. Your dog will have her choice between open, gently rolling hills and gently rolling hills lightly covered with venerable trees. She's likely to meet new friends among the large group of local dogs who come here. There are no boundaries or fences of any kind to mark the OLA. However, it is big enough to stay a safe distance from the residential streets and the school sports fields. There are restrooms, water fountains, and playground areas. Bring your own bags. Heck, always bring your own bags.

From I-5, take Exit 303 and follow signs to N.E. Killingsworth Street. Go east almost two miles, turn left on N.E. 42nd Avenue and left on N.E. Ainsworth Street. Street parking is available between Ainsworth Street and Ainsworth Court. Open 5 A.M.–midnight. N.E. 37th Ave. and Ainsworth St.

10 Sacajawea Park

🐾🐾 🐢 (See Greater Portland map on page 108)

Mornings and evenings, this lovely scratch pad of city greenery goes to the dogs, when kids are out of session at the neighboring head start center. Portland keeps its lawns in tip-top shape and this level plot adds a healthy set of mature trees to vary the funscape. The compact park is entered by a cul de sac and is further protected on two sides by fencing. A single can and a few straggly bags are there for your pick-up pleasure.

Take Exit 23B off I-205, going west on N.E. Killingsworth Street. Turn left on N.E. 82nd Avenue, right on Prescott Street, and right on 75th Avenue, which dead-ends at the park. OLA hours are complicated and vary by the season; call 503/823-3647 or go to www.portlandonline.com/parks and select "Dogs" under the "Recreation" tab. N.E. 75th and Roselawn St.

11 Wilshire Park

😸😸😸 🐾 (See Greater Portland map on page 108)

Portland's mature trees are alive and well in Wilshire Park in the off-leash area bordered by woodchip walkways, pleasing to the paws for leashed walks. Wilshire has the characteristic look of parks in this area: huge shade trees evenly spaced on lush lawns. The open area is a good size, on the northeast corner of the park bordered by Skidmore and 37th. It's near picnic tables and a children's play area. The nearby streets are not too busy, and the park doesn't seem to get heavy traffic from other users. You are on your own for water and bags, and the nearest garbage can is quite a walk away.

From I-5, take Exit 303. Go east on N.E. Killingsworth for 1.25 miles, turn right on N.E. 33rd Avenue, go 0.6 mile, turn left on N.E. Skidmore Street and right on N.E. 37th Avenue. Street parking is available. Open 5 A.M.–midnight. N.E. 33rd Ave. and Skidmore St.

12 Irving Park

😸😸🐢 (See Greater Portland map on page 108)

Irving Park is built on one of Portland's four defunct racetracks converted into city parks. Neighborhood dogs cut some racing tracks of their own on the park's hilly off-leash area, bordered by the horseshoe pits and the basketball courts on the west side of the park along 7th Street. Although not secured, the dog spot is a couple of blocks removed from the busiest side street. Irving is another park that is rich and green, sporting a healthy crop of tall trees. There are garbage cans and water fountains; as ever, bring poop bags.

From Highway 99E, go west on N.E. Fremont Street, right on N.E. 7th Avenue, and left on N.E. Siskiyou Street. The safest parking is available on N.E. 8th, 9th, and 10th Avenues, which dead-end into the south side of the park. June 15–September 1, off-leash hours are 5–10 A.M. and 6 P.M.–midnight, extended 4 P.M.–midnight the rest of the year. N.E. 7th Ave. and Fremont St.

13 Grant Park

😸🐢 (See Greater Portland map on page 108)

This park is named in honor of the 18th president of the United States, Ulysses S., who began his career at nearby Fort Vancouver and continued to visit the city throughout his presidency. A celebrity in its own right, the park's setting has inspired many scenes in Beverly Cleary's children's books. There are so many varied activities going on at this community centerpiece that there's not much room left over for the off-leash area. It occupies a tiny, unsecured sliver on the north end at 35th Avenue and Knott Street beyond the soccer fields. Coop 'n' Isis enjoyed a leashed stroll on the park's paved walkways more than spending time in the OLA.

From Highway 99E/Martin Luther King Jr. Boulevard, go east on N.E. Knott Street. Turn right on N.E. 35th Place and park along this dead-end; you'll be directly in front of the dog area. OLA hours are complicated and vary by the season; call 503/823-3647 or go to www.portlandonline.com/parks and select "Dogs" under the "Recreation" tab. N.E. 33rd Ave. and U.S. Grant Pl.

14 Normandale Park

🐾🐾🐾🐕 (See Greater Portland map on page 108)

Double your pleasure and double your fun at this city park's identical twin off-leash sites. The two separately gated and fenced areas are both open in the summer, and one side or the other will close periodically in the rainy season for "turf restoration." The re-greening of these high-traffic dog sites is a lost cause. Lately the city has resorted to dumping piles of sand and wood chips in an attempt to mitigate the mud. Messy conditions do nothing to dampen Normandale's popularity; it's the closest full-time OLA to the city center. These dog parks are a 50–50 balance of open areas and tall conifers, and the sites share water and garbage facilities just outside the front gates. Bring your beloved to bond and smell butts in a lively canine social circle and join in on the turf wars.

From I-84, take Exit 2 into the right-most lane to go west on N.E. Halsey Street. Turn south on 57th to the parking lot at the intersection of N.E. 57th Avenue and N.E. Hassalo Street. Open 5 A.M.–midnight.

PLACES TO EAT

Cup and Saucer: This neighborhood haunt has healthy and filling food concentrating on vegan and vegetarian dishes, not to mention the biggest bowl of dog biscuits the Dachsie Twins have ever seen. It has its own picnic tables and is near Alberta and Fernhill parks. 3000 N.E. Killingsworth; 503/287-4427.

The New Deal Café: A very kid-friendly spot near Normandale Park, The New Deal Café has a small selection of natural foods on one side, tables with a play space on the other, and two picnic tables out front for Frenchie. A chalkboard touts the big breakfast menu, and soups, scrambles, hash, and sandwiches are featured on a daily short list. In the evenings, it's time for burgers and build-your-own pizzas. 5250 N.E. Halsey St.; 503/546-1833; www.thenewdealcafe.com.

Tin Shed Garden Café: Everything on the menu is called Goodness— Stacked Goodness, Scrambled Goodness, Sandwich Goodness, etc.—and oh my goodness, they aren't lying. Get this: There's even a Pet Goodness menu of Kibbles 'n' Bacon Bits (free-range beef), Ham "Barker" Helper (a garden burger), or Paw Lickin' Good (chicken), each with brown rice and garlic. It truly is a big tin shed, with an immense patio, heated by a live fireplace and covered by an authentic wavy garden roof. Humans, don't miss the Belly Pleaser, rice porridge made with coconut milk, spiced with cinnamon, ginger, and vanilla, and topped with mango. 1438 N.E. Alberta; 503/288-6966; www.tinshedgardencafe.com.

PLACES TO STAY

Portlander Inn: This motel is primarily for long-haul truck drivers, but they're good dog people, too. It's a city unto itself. You get a room for great rates starting at $85 per night, and you have access to a movie theater, shoe repair, laundry facilities, deli, country and western bar, gift shop, visitors center, gas station, chiropractor, convenience store, medical clinic, and hair salon. The pet fee is $5 per night for up to two pets, no more than $40 per stay. 10350 N. Vancouver Way; 800/523-1193; www.portlanderinn.com.

More Accommodations: Please look under *Chain Hotels* in the *Resources* section for additional places to stay in this area.

Northwest Portland

In this metro quadrant, there is a city park so large that a man and his daughter lived quite well in its woods for four years before anyone noticed. For hounds who love to hike, the words "Forest Park" may earn a place in the dog linguistic hall of fame alongside treat, ball, car, dinner, and walk.

PARKS, BEACHES, AND RECREATION AREAS

15 Forest Park

🐾🐾🐾🐾 (See Greater Portland map on page 108)

As if the 5,400 acres of Forest Park weren't enough, its most popular hiking trail doesn't even start within its borders! The 28-mile hikers-only Wildwood Trail begins near Washington Park's rose garden and wanders up through Hoyt Arboretum before it enters the deep woods of this city wilderness. From the moment you step onto any of Forest Park's trails, Oregon's largest city might as well not exist. Total hiking mileage on developed trails tops out near 70 miles, not including the cross-country trekking people also enjoy in the park. Leif Erickson Drive is the former road that winds 11 miles through the center, providing the widest and most visible path. It rises gently uphill and has handy markers every 0.25 mile to let you know how far you've come. You'll have to share Leif Erickson Drive with mountain bikers; leashes are required and helpful. There's a trail map and a water fountain at the start of Leif Erickson Drive.

From I-405, take Exit 3 and follow the N.W. Vaughn Street exit ramp. Get in the second to the right lane and turn left on N.W. 23rd at the bottom of the exit. Go one block and turn right on N.W. Thurman Street and follow it 1.4 miles to the end. Limited angled parking is available in front of the trailhead gate. Your best resource for park maps is at www.friendsofforestpark.org.

16 Hoyt Arboretum

🐾🐾🐾 (See Greater Portland map on page 108)

The $2 fee is a small price to pay for the map that provides peace of mind in this 185-acre tree museum's maze of vaguely marked trails. Twelve miles of hiking opportunities wind through about 1,100 species of trees, grouped by horticultural family. Starting at the visitors center, where a water bowl is thoughtfully provided for pets, the wheelchair-accessible Overlook Trail will take you and your dog to the dogwood collection. The rest of the park's trails are soft surface. Cooper recommends a seasonal approach to the Hoyt, visiting tree families at their showiest times of the year.

From U.S. Highway 26, 1.8 miles west of downtown, take Exit 72. Turn right on S.W. Knights Boulevard, pass the zoo and the forestry center, and turn right on S.W. Fairview to the parking lot. Grounds are open 6 A.M.–10 P.M.; visitors center hours are 9 A.M.–4 P.M. 4000 S.W. Fairview Blvd.; 503/865-8733; www.hoytarboretum.org.

17 Washington Park–International Rose Test Garden

🐾🐾 🐾 (See Greater Portland map on page 108)

No proper visit to the City of Roses would be complete without a visit to the garden that started it all. Portland's International Rose Test Garden in Washington Park is one of the largest and oldest gardens in the country dedicated to the fragrant blooms of the romantic flower. At least 550 varieties are represented in 10,000 plantings on 4.5 acres, on a hilltop with city views. Picture-taking, stopping to smell the flowers, and walking on leash are encouraged, whereas pruning or digging is punishable by a $500 fine. There is a rose gift shop, and for the nose who thinks a rose by any other name wouldn't smell as sweet as a hot dog, there is a snack bar.

Beyond the rose garden, Washington Park includes many non-dog activities and sites, including the Oregon Zoo, the World Forestry Education Center, the Children's Museum (CM2), and a Japanese Botanical Garden.

Go west through downtown on W. Burnside Street. Although you'll see several signs to Washington Park, wait until S.W. Tichner Drive to make a sharp left-hand turn up the hill, then turn right on S.W. Kingston, following the more specific signs to the rose garden. 400 S.W. Kingston Ave.; 503/823-3636.

PLACES TO EAT

St. Honoré Boulangerie: The car turned, seemingly of its own will, toward this French café as we headed up to Forest Park. The soups, salads, and rows of éclairs and croissants are all stunning, and there's ample outdoor seating at umbrella-shaded tables. 2335 N.W. Thurman St.; 503/445-4342; www.sainthonorebakery.com.

Nob Hill

This high-profile neighborhood is also called the Northwest District or the Alphabet District, because the streets progress alphabetically north from Burnside. Its north–south avenues, especially 23rd and 21st, are full of trendy shops and a superb collection of outdoor eats. Your dog is sure to get extra pats and leftovers in this sophisticated and pet-perfect area to walk, window shop, and dine.

PARKS, BEACHES, AND RECREATION AREAS

18 Wallace Park

 (See Greater Portland map on page 108)

For years, Wallace Park has been known as the place to go for a pickup game of basketball. Since implementation of this park's off-leash area, a new breed of ball players are dribbling in the northeast corner, and the pickup action is equally hot. The whole park is only five acres, so the OLA is perhaps a tad larger than a regulation half-court. It has a chicken wire fence on three sides to protect it from busy side streets, and the fourth side is open to the interior of the park, with covered and open picnic tables for spectators. Bring your own bags; water and a trash can are provided.

Go west on W. Burnside Street, turn right on N.W. 23rd Avenue, left on N.W. Pettygrove Street, and right on N.W. 25th Avenue. The OLA is on the northeast corner at the intersection of 25th and Raleigh. Limited parking is available on side streets. OLA hours are 5–9 A.M. and 6 P.M.–midnight April–October, extended from 4 P.M. November–March. N.W. 25th Ave. and Raleigh St.

19 Couch Park

 (See Greater Portland map on page 108)

Rarely has so small a space received so much gleeful use by the four-legged patrons who call Couch Park home. And oh boy does it get muddy in the winter! The small, unsecured off-leash area is squished between a terraced play structure and a walkway on a slight slope on the north side on the park on Hoyt Street between the 19th and 20th Avenue blocks. It's hectic day and night in and around the park, across the street from a private school and only two blocks from one of the hottest street scenes in the city. Only the most civilized and completely voice-controlled dogs should be allowed off leash. Barking and street parking are at a premium in Couch Park.

Go west on W. Burnside Street, turn right on N.W. 21st Avenue and right

on N.W. Hoyt Street. OLA hours are complicated and vary by the season; call 503/823-3647 or go to www.portlandonline.com/parks and select "Dogs" under the "Recreation" tab. N.W. 19th Ave. and Glisan St.

PLACES TO EAT

Alotto Gelato: The only thing served at this storefront counter is gelato, up to 30 flavors of ice cream and sorbets, every day a little different. The line often goes around the block, and that's just the dogs. 931 N.W. 23rd Ave.; 503/228-1709.

McMenamins Blue Moon Tavern: People and their pets have been gathering at the sidewalk picnic tables of this hot spot since 1933 to drink pints of ale and down great burgers and fresh-cut fries. The Terminator Stout should impress even Guinness fans. 432 N.W. 21st Ave.; 503/223-3184; www.mcmenamins.com.

Papa Haydn: This sidewalk dessert bar is a Sunday brunch tradition. The small selection of lunch and dinner items is far outstripped by a menu of profanely rich cakes. Come for cake; the rest is an afterthought. 701 N.W. 23rd; 503/228-7317; www.papahaydn.com.

Yuki: This Japanese restaurant's menu is a struggle for the indecisive. The sushi menu alone takes up four pages, and that doesn't include the yakisoba noodles, teriyaki, tempura, and combinations of all of the above. Bento boxes are the perfect compromise, and they look like little works of art. 930 N.W. 23rd Ave.; 503/525-8807.

PLACES TO STAY

Park Lane Suites: This suites hotel is perfect for longer stays. Each unit is apartment-style, with full kitchens, living rooms with TV, onsite laundry, and business desks. One medium-sized dog per room is allowed for a $15 per night fee (negotiable for longer stays). It's in a desirable neighborhood surrounded by restored mansions, a block away from chic 23rd Street. Rates range $100–210. 809 S.W. King Ave.; 503/226-6288; www.parklanesuites.com.

More Accommodations: Please look under *Chain Hotels* in the *Resources* section for additional places to stay in this area.

Pearl District

Just north of downtown is the recently gentrified Pearl District, where industrial warehouses have been reborn into sleek loft apartments and galleries. To say that The Pearl is dog-friendly is to utter a profound understatement. Seemingly, life has been designed around the dog, including enough places to eat outdoors to fill four hollow legs. For in-city living and visiting, the Pearl is the cat's meow. Sorry dogs, it had to be said.

PARKS, BEACHES, AND RECREATION AREAS

20 "The Field" in the Pearl

🐾 🐕 (See Greater Portland map on page 108)

There's an unofficial off-leash area in The Pearl, and as this book went to press, it did exist, but there's no telling what'll happen in the future. The local condo construction company has been really cool about supporting The Pearl's extensive pet community, installing some benches, planting a few trees, and placing and maintaining several bag dispensers in the wide, open area. The ground cover consists of alternating patches of sand and grass, and there's

DIVERSIONS

Catering especially to petite canine clientele, **Lexidog** does it all. The boutique and social club hosts fashion shows, carries a high-end gift selection, has a bakery, and provides highly-supervised play groups. 416 N.W. 10th Ave.; 503/243-6200; lexidog.com. Feeling less than fresh? **D'Tails in the Pearl** next door will spiff you up with a pawdicure, body wrap, facial, or some soothing aromatherapy. 503/516-7387; dtailsdogsalon.com.

Dogstar is a big winner with long suffering, hard working pet parents, who can drop Darling off for daycare early and pick her up late when she's clean, tired, and happy to see you. Dogstar also charges only $10 for three hours of sitting from 6–9 P.M. on **First Thursday,** the Pearl District's popular art gallery walk. Check out explorethe pearl.com. 1313 N.W. Kearney; 503/227-0292; dogstar.us.

some fencing, but don't count on it for security. All we ask is that you be extra conscientious of your dog's behavior here, to improve the chances of any part of it becoming an official dog park. There's no shade; bring your own water.

Go to the corner of 11th Avenue and N.W. Overton Street, and then look to the northeast to find the field, past the construction fencing. You'll see the bag dispensers and garbage cans, the only clue you're in the right place. There's paid parking along side streets, but do not park inside construction areas.

21 North Park Blocks

🐾 🐾 (See Greater Portland map on page 108)

These six park squares in The Pearl are close to the majority of downtown's vintage hotels, a handy place to walk your dog. If you see dogs veering automatically to the west at the corner of N.W. Everett Street, it's because they know treats await them at Urban Fauna. Also in the North Blocks, Portland dogs have their very own Benson Bubbler, a bottomless brass bowl of water on the west side north of N.W. Davis Street, created by the famous dog photographer William Wegman. Coop thinks he should've made it in the shape of a toilet bowl.

The North Park Blocks are on Park Avenue between W. Burnside Street and N.W. Hoyt Street. Metered street parking is $1.50 for up to 90 minutes. Open 5 A.M.–10 P.M.

PLACES TO EAT

Blue Hour: Seattleites Stacya, David, and Chester the Dog frequent this gourmet Mediterranean nightspot when in Portland. They enjoy being pleasantly surprised by the menu, printed daily to use the freshest seasonal ingredients and to please the chef's whim. Repeat after Isis: "Five star elegance—when eating your own dung simply will not do." 250 N.W. 13th Ave.; 503/226-3394; www.bluehouronline.com.

Paragon Restaurant and Bar: Coop 'n' Isis' mom has two words for you: signature cocktails. Here's two more: house-made desserts. At Paragon, truly fine Americana food is served outdoors on a covered, elevated platform. The restaurant gives a former warehouse building with rolling garage doors a second life, while their infused vodkas, tequila, and rums will give you a second wind for being the life of the party. 1309 N.W. Hoyt; 503/833-5060; www.paragonrestaurant.com.

Pearl Bakery: This patisserie and bistro excels in the French tradition of foods that make the difficult look easy and taste simply delectable. Try their meltingly rich brioche, chiffon cake, and eggplant, red pepper, and mozzarella sandwiches. We did. 102 N.W. 9th Ave.; 503/827-0910; www.pearlbakery.com.

Pop Culture: This shop makes frozen, fat free, lactose free, live culture yogurt treats that are as good for dogs' digestive systems as they are for yours. Imagine, guilt-free goodness! The "Home of the Pearl Swirl," a yogurt and fresh fruit extravaganza, has sandwiches and soups as well, plus a couple of outdoor tables. 900 N.W. Lovejoy St.; 503/477-9172; www.pcyogurt.com.

Rogue Ales Distillery and Public House: How about a burger, fries, and a carob-frosted cupcake? No, silly, that's the dog's menu, not yours! Rogue has a full specialty menu for your pooch. You can have a beer and, okay, your own menu on the patio, when joining your dog for a night out. 1339 Flanders; 503/222-5910; www.rogue.com.

Downtown and Historic Waterfront

Downtown Portland is ideal for dog-walkers. Built on a European model, using half-size city blocks, the city encourages exploration on foot. Smaller lots have left more room for pocket parks, water gardens, plazas, and plenty of foliage. Drinking water, too, is plentiful downtown in Benson Bubblers, 20 elegant freshwater drinking fountains commissioned at the turn of the 19th century by wealthy lumber baron and teetotaler Simon Benson. Pet-friendly lodging is equally abundant downtown. It's difficult to find a hotel that's *not* pet-friendly.

Portland's enhanced status as a pedestrian city may be due partially to the fact that getting around by car can be complicated. With the Willamette River cutting a wide swath north–south, and the Columbia River dividing Oregon and Washington, going across town requires crossing one of the area's 17 major bridges.

To take in the city in a nutshell, hang out with your dog in Pioneer Courthouse Square, Portland's outdoor living room. Walk along the waterfront park for the Portland Saturday Market under the Burnside Bridge, for more than 250 crafts booths, food, and music on Saturday (and Sunday) March–December 24th.

PARKS, BEACHES, AND RECREATION AREAS

22 South Park Blocks

🐾🐾🐾 (See Greater Portland map on page 108)

Leave plenty of time for walks along the city's South Park Blocks, an even dozen lawn-carpeted squares lined with aged elms from Salmon Street to

DETOURS

PDX Pedicabs allows dogs for no extra charge. While you relax on the comfy bench in back, a driver pedals the tricycle along the length of the Riverplace Marina area, pointing out the many stops for outdoor wining and dining. Our driver Leeman gave us great tips on where to eat while he worked off his calories, if not yours. 503/733-4222; www.pdxpedicab.com.

Jackson Street on Park Avenue. You'll pass through Portland State University and the heart of the cultural district, including the Portland Center for the Performing Arts, Arlene Schnitzer Concert Hall ("The Schnitz"), classical Portland Art Museum, historic First Congregational Church, and the Oregon Historical Society, with its multi-story, elaborate *trompe l'oeil* mural. You'll see all walks of life, and many manners of breeds, on your perambulations.

If you're slaving away at the computer, but your dog is waiting at your feet with his leash in his mouth, make a compromise. Check your email or surf the Internet from any park bench in the South Blocks. The whole area is a free Wi-Fi hotspot.

Parking is practically nonexistent along the South Park Blocks. Find a long-term lot downtown and walk. Open 5 A.M.–10 P.M.

23 Governor Tom McCall Waterfront Park

 (See Greater Portland map on page 108)

Waterfront Park is a mile-long sidewalk promenade built on top of Portland Harbor Wall, the single most expensive piece of infrastructure built by the city. It replaced rotting docks and dilapidated pier buildings in the 1920s. Buried within is the first sewer system on the west side of the river. From 2003 to 2006, another 1.2 billion dollars was spent on the Big Pipe project, to update the sewer system to handle modern population pressures. A master plan currently in place proposes $45 million in park improvements over the next 25 years.

The park is well used and it shows. What once were lawns have taken a repeated beating from Saturday Market booths and frequent city festivals. Goose poop takes over on the south end, and transients sleep here and there. It's still a languid stroll among statues and fountains, sculptures, and the occasional garden. We recommend crossing at the Hawthorne or Steel Bridges to join up with the Eastbank Esplanade. The south end of Waterfront Park expands to a grassy slope down to the beach. North of the Burnside Bridge, the Japanese Historical Plaza deserves a quick look-see. From the north end, the Pearl District is close, as is Powell's City of Books.

Tom McCall Waterfront Park is on Naito Parkway, essentially between the Broadway Bridge and the Marquam Bridge. We can recommend parking in a Smart Park Lot between N.W. Davis and N.W. Everett Streets.

PLACES TO EAT

Carafe: With an owner from Paris, this French bistro is as authentic as it gets. It serves escargot, smelly cheeses, and confit of duck, and *pomme frites* come with mayo, not ketchup. The outdoor seating is also traditional European, with all seats facing out toward the park plaza to observe the pulse of the city. 200 S.W. Market St.; 503/248-0004; www.carafebistro.com.

Kenny and Zukes: Borscht and blintzes and bialys, oh my! A delicatessen in the Jewish tradition, Kenny and Zuke's is the place to get your fix for old-fashioned flavors such as pastrami, liver, and corned beef on sandwiches bigger than Cooper's head. 1038 S.W. Stark St.; 503/222-3354; www .kennyandzukes.com.

South Park: Reservations are a must for dinner at this seafood grill and wine bar in the midst of the cultural center of town. You and your well-mannered dog will compete for patio tables with crowds from the symphony, theater, and college. South Park combines fresh local produce and catch of the day in creative ways, paired with a lengthy list of wines by the glass. 901 S.W. Salmon St.; 503/326-1300; www.southparkseafood.com.

PLACES TO STAY

Ace Hotel: Our dear friend Andrea and her golden Ellie turned us onto this unique and über-cool (as in, as cool as it gets) locale. Designer touches include Pendleton wool blankets, natural latex bedding, iPod docks, and art in every room. The Ace is awesome for connoisseurs of the spare and modern. From rooms with shared bathrooms as low as $95 to penthouse suites at $250, the choice to be among the cognoscenti is yours. The Ace doesn't charge a pet fee. 1022 S.W. Stark St.; 503/228-2277; www.acehotel.com.

Heathman Hotel: *Condé Nast Traveler* and *Travel + Leisure* have rated this luxurious hotel among their top favorites in the world, perhaps because its list of services and amenities is longer than a Great Dane's legs. The Heathman is perhaps most famous for doormen dressed like the guy on the Beefeater Gin bottle. Pets are welcome on the third floor for a $35 per night pet fee. A park is right behind the hotel for necessary business. Rates range $190–300. 1001 S.W. Broadway; 503/241-4100; www.heathmanhotel.com.

Hotel deLuxe: This 1912 boutique hotel near the PGE Stadium has gone Hollywood, in a historic renovation of what used to be the beloved but worse for wear Hotel Mallory. The deLuxe pays homage to Hollywood's heyday, decorating all floors and rooms with more than 400 black-and-white movie stills from the 1930s to the 1950s. You can be relaxing in throwback glitz, tempered by modern conveniences such as iPod docks, Wi-Fi, and flat-screen HDTVs watched from the comfort of your downy bed. Your pet is as pampered as a starlet with bottled water, a bag of treats, and the Furry Friend's Room Service Menu. Rooms run $170–250, and there's a non-refundable $45 pet fee per stay. 729 S.W. 15th Ave.; 503/219-2094 or 800/228-8657; www.hoteldeluxe.com.

Hotel Lucia: Cooper and Isis get into a tiff when we travel to Portland, because he wants to stay at this modern masterpiece of serenity, while she prefers the Studio-era Hollywood glam of Hotel deLuxe. Although opposites in character, the hotels are owned by the same group, one that welcomes pets without restrictions. Hotel Lucia's art collection alone is worthy of a visit, including 679 photographs of Pulitzer Prize–winner David Hume Kennerly. The dog bowls are on loan only, but you may keep the Aveda products and the jazz CD from your room. Rates range $125–195. 400 S.W. Broadway; 503/225-1717; www.hotellucia.com.

Hotel Monaco: A part of the always super dog-friendly Kimpton Hotel group, this hotel is part exotic and part whimsical, with a style featuring rich colors and Anglo-Chinois furnishings and decor. It's got every amenity you can imagine, including Art, the golden lab who is Director of Pet Relations. There are treats, waste bags, and bottled water for pets; there are no pet deposits, weight restrictions, or limitations. Three woofs for Kimpton! Humans, never fret, you are also taken care of exceptionally well here. Rates range $150–260. 506 S.W. Washington St.; 503/222-0001; www.monaco-portland.com.

Hotel Vintage Plaza: Lovely and luxurious, this upscale hotel is cared for as though it were a well-loved antique. The ambience is inspired by a French vineyard, bright enough to make you thirsty for a sip of the grape, and relaxing enough for you to nap peacefully afterward. This is a Kimpton Hotel, where dogs are always treated as first-class citizens; for example, there's a pet honor bar in each room stocked with treats and goodies rivaling yours. Rates range $130–270; there is no fee for pets. 422 S.W. Broadway; 800/263-2305; www.vintageplaza.com.

Mark Spencer Hotel: The Spence was famous as a traveling artists' hotel from 1907 to the 1960s. It was converted to apartments and then back to a hotel again, with a rooftop garden, tiny appliances, and walk-in closets left over from its apartment era. The hotel's frumpy Bohemian air is favored by the arts and theater crowd. While a bit worn around the edges, it's one of the few affordably elegant choices downtown, with rates ranging $100–190, and a name your price option when availability allows. 409 S.W. 11th Ave.; 503/224-3293; www.markspencer.com.

RiverPlace Hotel: Isis never knew that the royal treatment—bottled water, porcelain bowls, dog biscuits, and personalized notes delivered on a tray to the room—is standard for all canine guests. Humans are equally spoiled. Request a riverside or courtyard room for the best views. All rooms are open to dogs without size restrictions, except for a 30-pound limit in 10 condo units. A Doggie Diner menu is available from room service. Waterfront Park is the hotel's backyard. Rates range from $210 for a deluxe room to $525 for the grand suite; there is a $50 nonrefundable pet cleaning fee. 1510 Southwest Harbor Way; 800/227-1333; www.riverplacehotel.com.

More Accommodations: Please look under *Chain Hotels* in the *Resources* section for additional places to stay in this area.

Southeast Portland

Southeast Portland is perhaps best described as bohemian, honoring the hippie more than the hip. Hawthorne Boulevard and Belmont Street are the places to find an eclectic mix of retro storefronts, dining, and avant-garde theater. If

DOG-EAR YOUR CALENDAR

It's a dog-eat-dog world at the Berlin Inn's annual **Barktober-fest,** where the pooch sausage-eating contest is about technique, not quantity. On the second weekend in September, this restaurant hosts dog events and activities all weekend, complete with beer and bratwurst for canine chaperones. Funds raised benefit the humane society, dog rescue, and no-kill shelters. 3131 S.E. 12th; 503/236-6761; www.berlininn.com.

Dogtoberfest, otherwise known as the dog wash at the Lucky Lab, celebrated its 15th year in 2009. The record is 600 dogs washed and $4,000 raised in one day to benefit local Dove Lewis Animal Hospital. Festivities include T-shirts, music, and a special brew, Dog Wash Pale Ale. Drink some suds while celebrity dog-washers suds up your pup. Usually held on a September weekend, it's just one of many annual events to support Dove Lewis, a pet hospital specializing in emergency and critical care, 365 days a year, 24 hours a day. Keep your eye on the events calendar for more fun, including DoveBowl, the Wet Nose Soiree, Pets in the Pearl, and Dine Out for Dove, at www.dovelewis.org or 503/535-3384.

you or your kids are science buffs, drop your pal at doggy daycare for a half day and visit the Oregon Museum of Science and Industry (OMSI). A stop into The Lucky Lab Brewing Co. is a must for dog lovers.

PARKS, BEACHES, AND RECREATION AREAS

∑4 Eastbank Esplanade

🐾🐾 (See Greater Portland map on page 108)

Located between the historic Hawthorne and Steel Bridges, this 1.5-mile waterfront promenade hugs the eastern banks of the Willamette River. It provides a superb unobstructed look at the city skyline and boasts a series of sculptures celebrating Portland's history. On the north end, a lower deck on the Steel Bridge provides bicycle and pedestrian access to Waterfront Park. The park's 1,200-foot floating dock is the longest in the United States, supported by 65 concrete pylons.

Your only hope for parking is on Carruthers Street, south of the Hawthorne Bridge. From I-5, take Exit 300 and get in the right lane to exit at OMSI/Central Eastside Industrial District. Turn right onto S.E. Water Street, go 0.7 mile, and turn right on S.E. Carruthers Street to the dead-end.

25 Laurelhurst Park

🐾🐾🐾🐾 ◀● (See Greater Portland map on page 108)

Laurelhurst is a city institution. Emanuel Mische of the famed Olmsted Brothers landscape firm created the park in 1912, the electric lights were lit for the first time in 1915, and, in 1919, it was named the most beautiful park on the West Coast. In 2001, it became the first city park to be listed on the National Register of Historic Places. The park is straight out of an impressionist painting, complete with parasol-shaded ladies and dapper gentlemen walking arm in arm under antique lighting fixtures. The pond has elegant swans and blue herons nesting under a weeping willow. The leaves fall gently as a yellow Lab runs screaming by after stealing a toy from his Doberman playmate. Yes, friends, as genteel as it may seem on the surface, Laurelhurst has had a regular base of boisterous canine clientele.

Dogs are fortunate to have an off-leash area in such a high-profile park. To help keep the privilege, it's critical that you and your dog respect the area's boundaries in the center on the south side, along Oak Street, defined by the walkways, and remain leashed while walking the rest of the park.

From Highway 99E, go east on E. Burnside Street to S.E. 39th Avenue, the eastern border of the park. Turn right on S.E. Oak Street. Parking is ad hoc, on the streets bordering the park perimeter. OLA hours vary by season and events; call 503/823-3647 or go to www.portlandonline.com/parks and select "Dogs" under the "Activities" tab. S.E. 39th Ave. and Stark St.

26 Mount Tabor Park

🐾🐾🐾🐾 (See Greater Portland map on page 108)

Mount Tabor is an extinct volcano, which probably hasn't been active for about 3 million years. The dog scene, on the other hand, is very active at this city park. Only a tiny sliver of the 196-acre mountain is designated as an off-leash area, and it isn't even where the crowds tend to congregate. The city is trying to discourage the impromptu sniffing social on the west side of the mountain, above the largest reservoir, because the grass gets torn up, leading to runoff problems. You can help by sticking to the official, partially fenced area, on the south side near the Harrison Street entrance.

You can join the cruising canines hanging out of car windows on the loop drive to the 643-foot summit. On Wednesdays, the park is car-free, transforming the roads into bigger trails. For buns of steel, you and your Bernese can try climbing the stairs, essentially straight up. Multiple dirt paths cross and climb the point, and you can make up a different route every time you go, past the park's three reservoirs, the bronze statue by Gutzon Borglum (of Mount Rushmore fame), through the Douglas fir, around the crater amphitheater, and so on. Mount Tabor is a gathering place in the heart of Southeast Portland, and your dog can make multiple friends while you take in the great city views.

From I-84, take Exit 5 and turn right at the stop sign at the bottom of the exit ramp. Go one block and turn left on S.E. 82nd Avenue, go 1.1 miles, turn right on S.E. Yamhill Street, turn left on S.E. 76th Avenue, go 0.5 mile and turn right on S.E. Harrison Street, and follow the signs into the park. There is angled parking. Open 7 A.M.–9 P.M., www.taborfriends.com.

27 Cherry Park

🐾🐾 🐕 (See Greater Portland map on page 108)

Cherry is long and skinny with a shaggy border—hey, like a Saluki! It's safely hemmed in on the two long sides by nice tall fences, and on the two short sides by residential dead-end streets. About two-thirds of the way through, you enter a dense forest, a veritable grove of trees. This city park has no facilities other than a few hand-hewn benches, providing a Spartan atmosphere for navel contemplation or tail chasing, your preference. The sand and gravel pit on the south side is a mild distraction; otherwise, there is nothing going on here. Cooper wants his buddies to know that Cherry Park has some serious squirrel action.

Take Exit 19 from I-205, going east on S.E. Division Street. Turn left on 112th Avenue, left on Market Street, and left on 106th Avenue to wind your way into the dead-end at the park.

28 Woodstock Park

🐾🐾 🐕 (See Greater Portland map on page 109)

There are a bunch of neighborhood dogs who take advantage of the off-leash area at Woodstock Park on the west side of the park along 47th Avenue, south of Steele. It's slightly hilly and has neat green grass and big deciduous trees. In response to a problem complying with waste pickup laws, there are giant, blue plastic trash cans cabled to each of the trees bordering the OLA as a major hint. There is no fence around the area and you need to stay well clear of busy Steele Street. Playgrounds, a wading pool, and the restrooms are near the dog play area.

From Highway 99E, go east on U.S. Highway 26, S.E. Powell Boulevard. Turn right on S.E. 52nd Avenue, right on S.E. Steele Street, and left on S.E. 47th Avenue. Street parking is available along 47th. OLA hours are complicated and vary by the season; call 503/823-3647 or go to www.portlandonline.com/parks and select "Dogs" under the "Recreation" tab.

29 Sellwood Riverfront Park and Oaks Bottom Trail

🐾🐾 🐕 (See Greater Portland map on page 109)

The off-leash area at Sellwood carves out a healthy center section of the nine-acre city park in the center of the intersection of S.E. Spokane and Oaks Parkway. You'll need excellent voice control of your dog, as there is no fencing nor natural features to separate the OLA from other park uses.

Many parts of Sellwood are worth exploring on leash. The riverfront part of the park is easy to reach by means of a ramp, and it extends around the bend all the way to Portland's historic Oaks Amusement Park, operating since 1904. The views of the city and Sellwood Bridge are great.

Sellwood also connects to the Oaks Bottom Trail, a 1.5-mile, soft-surface hike through a wildlife refuge packed with more than 140 species of birds, mammals, reptiles, and amphibians. You're most likely to see great blue herons, beavers, and muskrats in addition to the usual geese and ducks. It's a level and shady walk with late summer blackberries free for the picking.

From I-5, take exit 297 south on S.W. Terwilliger Boulevard for 0.9 mile, turn left onto S.W. Taylors Ferry Road for one mile, and right on S.W. Macadam Avenue 0.5 mile to the Sellwood Bridge. Cross the bridge and immediately turn left on S.E. 7th Avenue to S.E. Oaks Parkway. OLA hours vary by the season; call 503/823-3647 or go to www.portlandonline.com/parks and select "Dogs" under the "Recreation" tab.

30 Brentwood Dog Park

🐾 🐕 (See Greater Portland map on page 109)

Although trees and grass have been planted, the fenced off-leash area at Brentwood City Park is a muddy patch of rectangular earth carved out of an existing park. It sits in a depression, gathering runoff from the sprinklers on the sports fields. After 15 minutes with her beloved soccer ball ("The ball, the ball, PUULEEEZ the ball!"), Isis came away with enough earth caked in her fur to bake four-and-twenty blackbirds into a mud pie. She suggests you give in to it and get covered head-to-toe. As any dog will tell you, that whole cleanliness-is-next-to-godliness thing is overrated. Bring your own bags, water, and a stack of towels.

From I-205, take Exit 17 west toward S.E. Woodstock, turn left at the next intersection on S.E. 92nd Avenue, then right on S.E. Duke Street, and left on S.E. 62nd. The OLA is on the southeast corner of 62nd Avenue and S.E. Rural Street. Street parking is on 62nd, south of S.E. Cooper Street. Open 5 A.M.-midnight. S.E. 60th Ave. and Duke St.

PLACES TO EAT

Berlin Inn: Dogs, that's *hunds* in German, have their very own Patio Pooch Menu for dining in the *biergarten* at this upscale Bavarian restaurant. Canine connoisseurs can select from items such as Lollipups, a peanut butter biscuit on a rawhide stick; a Bag-O-Bones sampler of treats; or Mutt Mix, two turkey hot dogs sliced and tossed with biscuits. Humans are treated to filling gourmet fare, fine wines, sponge cake tortes, and, of course, German beer. 3131 S.E. 12th; 503/236-6761; www.berlininn.com.

Cooper's Coffee: Our Cooper could barely maintain his composure when he discovered this fine establishment with lots of room for outdoor eating, named for another honorable furry four-legger whose portrait hangs on the wall. Fill out your sandwich order card with a grease pencil and hand it to the kind people behind the counter, or pick from a light menu of lasagna, quiches, and salads. Stop by after a visit to nearby Mount Tabor, and stay for evening acoustic music sets. 6049 S.E. Stark St.; 503/805-2835.

Dingo's Fresh Mexican Grill: Dingo's has dozens of picnic tables, a full bar, sit-down service, and inventive Mexican food, all on a hip street within a few blocks of Mount Tabor Park. The restaurant is popular for tequila samplers and breakfast, although perhaps not together. 4612 S.E. Hawthorne Blvd.; 503/233-3996; www.dingosonline.com.

The Lucky Lab Brew Pub: Some people would have a tough time choosing between beer or their dog as their truest best friend. Fortunately, they can have both, and decent grub, at this pub that's famous in canine social circles. Outside is a big, covered patio with dozens of picnic tables; inside, the walls are lined with photos of the many Labs and other breeds who have paid a visit. Add a little extra to your beer money to buy a Lucky Lab T-shirt or hat. 915 S.E. Hawthorne Blvd.; 503/236-3555; www.luckylab.com.

Two more locations celebrate life's good things: the Lucky Labrador Beer Hall at 1945 N.W. Quimby (503/517-4352) and Lucky Labrador Public House at 7675 S.W. Capitol Highway (503/244-2537).

PLACES TO STAY

Jupiter Hotel: Props go to the Jupiter for being the most mod, looking straight out of the 1960s after a 2004 update. In the Bohemian Hollywood District, the rooms fit right in, with unique murals, chalkboard art doors, and shag throw rugs. Don't let the kitsch fool you; modern amenities include Wi-Fi, HDTVs, iPod docks, and bamboo floors. This is not the place to stay for peace and quiet. It's a party town, especially weekends, with the largest independent music venue on the grounds (called Doug Fir) and wee-hour cocktails under the Dream Tent. The dog gift basket is unbelievable. Yours to keep are collapsible bowl and water bottle dispensers, a coupon book for pet-friendly businesses, bags, a box of designer treats, a map of local parks, and so on. Rates range $90–150. The pet fee is $30 a night, up to $90 per stay. 800 E. Burnside; 503/230-9200 or 877/800-0004; www.jupiterhotel.com.

est Portland

.west Portland is green with money as well as trees. The real estate taxes in this area climb in direct proportion to the elevation, all the way to the city's highest point at Council Crest.

PARKS, BEACHES, AND RECREATION AREAS

31 Marquam Nature Trail and Council Crest Park

🐾🐾🐾🐾 (See Greater Portland map on page 108)

On a very clear day at the 1,043-foot summit of Council Crest, you can see the city and the Mounts of Hood, Adams, Jefferson, St. Helens, and even Rainier. And, if you time it right, your dog can enjoy the off-leash area on the southeast hillside, although it's steep and has no fence or dog amenities.

The tip of Council Crest is panoramic in every direction, but the point of including this park in the book, according to Cooper, is to access the Marquam Nature Trail. It's a great city escape through a primal fern-filled canyon forest. On this steep, lung-capacity-challenging hike, there are so many things outdoor dogs love: trees, wildflowers, squirrels, and plump banana slugs, whose slime creates a favored hair gel for Isis. For stretches of the trail's 1.5-mile length, you'll feel lost in the woods, until you see the West Hill mansions tucked in the green space. On the trail, use the leash, pick up the poop, and don't pick the purple trilliums.

To corkscrew up the hill to Council Crest, take S.W. Broadway Drive south through downtown, stay in the far right to avoid the Barbur Boulevard/99W interchange, and follow Broadway another 1.3 miles. Turn left on S.W. Greenway Avenue, go another 0.7 mile, and take the right fork onto S.W. Council Crest Drive. Council Crest's OLA hours are 5–11 A.M. and 6–10 P.M. April–October, extended from 4 P.M. the rest of the year. The top of the hill within the boundaries of the circular drive is added to the OLA during these extended winter hours (bring the glow-in-the-dark toys). S.W. Council Crest Dr.

32 Willamette Park

🐾🐾🐕 (See Greater Portland map on page 109)

Willamette has a choice waterfront location, south of the city. The unfenced off-leash area is a good-sized landing strip, half open and half shaded. The grass is thick and green, a nice playground for those with paws. Soccer fields occupy the south end of the park, so the best time to enjoy this spot is midday weekdays, when there are no games. The only other users are boaters headed straight for the water; you can watch them unload and take off down the river while you play. If your loved one smells too much like a dirty dog after a day of play, the Wiggles and Wags Dog Wash is across the street (6141 S.W. Macadam; 503/977-1775).

From I-5, take Exit 299A and go south on S.W. Macadam Avenue and turn right on S.W. Nebraska Street. The OLA is on the north end of the park, to your left past the pay booth at the entrance. This park has a rare parking lot, which costs $3 per day Memorial Day–Labor Day and on weekends March–Memorial Day. Open 5 A.M.–10 P.M.

33 Gabriel Park

🐾🐾🐾🐾🐕 (See Greater Portland map on page 109)

The grass is soft and green on the rolling hills of Gabriel Park, no mean feat, even in the fully fenced off-leash area. We're talking some serious trees here, and the benches and chairs are comfy. It's definitely one of Portland's fanciest OLAs. The only drawback is that there are separate summer and winter areas to allow the turf to recover in the off-season. The summer area is bordered by the tennis courts, which had Isis doing the Wimbledon head wobble watching the balls go to and fro.

The two-acre winter site, dubbed "Little Gabriel," is unfenced, with fewer amenities, and it's a bit hard to find. Walk south of the summer area, down wooden steps and across a bridge to the paved path. When you come into a clearing, you are there, bordered by a baseball diamond and the community garden. The rest of the park's 90 acres provide amiable on-leash walks.

From I-5, take Exit 297 and continue straight onto S.W. Bertha Boulevard. Turn left on S.W. Vermont Street, pass the park, and turn left on S.W. 45th Avenue. There's a parking lot that's often full. To better your chances, continue south on 45th, turn left on S.W. Multnomah Boulevard, left on S.W. 40th

left on S.W. Canby Street to park by the winter area and sneak in
ʲ. Open 5 A.M.–midnight. S.W. 45th Ave. and Vermont St.

PLACES TO EAT

Fat City Café: The owners of this country café have four dogs, and they wish
they could provide outdoor seating, but the sidewalk's too narrow and the
codes are too strict in Historic Multnomah Village. They'll provide a water
bowl and treats for your pet while he waits for you to order to go and take your
homemade, good lovin' cookin' to Gabriel Dog Park around the corner. 7820
S.W. Capitol Hwy.; 503/245-5457.

PLACES TO STAY

Hospitality Inn: Both the motel rooms and the complimentary continental
breakfast spread are cheery and large at the inn. Dogs up to 40 pounds are
allowed. Rates range $80–100, plus a $10 pet fee. 10155 S.W. Capitol Hwy.;
503/244-6684; www.hospitalityinnportland.com.

Hillsboro

As an affluent suburb of Portland, Hillsboro brought considerable resources
to bear in opening a beautiful dog park in 2007. During inclement weather,
local dogs can be found at **Schroeder's Den,** an indoor dog park at a day-
care and training facility (2110 N.W. Aloclek Dr., Suite 620; 503/614-9899;
www.schroedersden.com).

PARKS, BEACHES, AND RECREATION AREAS

34 Hondo Dog Park

🐾🐾🐾🐾🐕 (See Greater Portland map on page 108)

Your water bowl runneth over, and not just from the water gushing out of the
doggy drinking fountains in two of the three five-foot-high, black-vinyl-coated,
chain-link-fenced, off-leash areas of this purpose-built dog park. It's the first ever
OLA for this suburb, honorably named for the city's only, and we hope ever, K-9
dog officer to lose his life in the line of duty, commemorated by a plaque on-site.

Hondo is 3.75 acres in toto for Toto, separated into the main mixed-use dog
area, a small/timid dog area, and a giant sandbox intended as a winter area
to allow the grass to get some breathing time. Each space has fire-engine-
red benches and garbage cans, bag dispensers, defunct and decorated fire
hydrants, healthy grass, gravel walkways, and young trees that will grow up
to provide decent shade. Everything is still shiny and new, so come and get it
while it lasts. Humans get sloppy seconds in the form of a lowly portable potty.
The water fountains are turned off in the winter.

Take Highway 26 west 11.5 miles from the intersection of Highway 405 to

the Cornelius Pass Road South exit, Exit 62A. Take a left onto Cornelius Pa
Road, a right on N.W. Evergreen parkway, and a right on N.W. 229th Avenue.
The park will be on your left. Open dawn–dusk most days; opens at noon on
Mondays and Thursdays to allow for maintenance. 4499 N.W. 229th Ave.;
www.hillsborodogs.com.

PLACES TO EAT

Iron Mutt Coffee Company: Combining a love of coffee and canines, Iron
Mutt provides a fenced-in side patio with gravel and wood-chip areas where
lovable mutts can roam free while their owners IM using free Wi-Fi, eat panini
and ice cream, and drink milkshakes and bubble tea and coffee. Inside, there
are dog books on every surface and floor-to-ceiling shelves packed with treats,
toys, and dog-themed gifts. A portion of proceeds goes back to non-profit animal organizations. 530 S.W. 205th; 503/645-9746; www.ironmuttcoffee.com.

PLACES TO STAY

In this area, chain hotels listed in the *Resources* section offer the best choices
for dogs and their owners.

Beaverton

Beaverton is Oregon's fifth-largest city. Seven miles southeast of Portland, it
is the heart of the state's "Silicon Forest," an economic artery pumping capital
into a healthy business environment. Silicon or no, this forest is worthy of a
side trip from Portland just for its dog park.

PARKS, BEACHES, AND RECREATION AREAS

35 Hazeldale Dog Park

🐾🐾🐾🐾 🐕 (See Greater Portland map on page 109)

This full-time off-leash complex devoted to the art of being a dog deserves all
four paws, one for each of its four separate, fully fenced areas. There are two
dog runs for the big boys and two for the little fellas. They're used in pairs, one
set each for the summer and winter, allowing the opposites to repair themselves for half the year.

Each area is long and thin. There's some openness, but most of the space
is covered with short, stocky pine trees for games of hide and seek. They are
beautifully equipped. The fences are high and secure and there are double
gates to create leash-transition zones. There are picnic tables, bags tucked in
the fence, and water brought in bowls and buckets from elsewhere in the park.
Perhaps best of all, the people and dogs are exceptionally friendly and take
great pride in maintaining the OLA in tip-top shape.

From U.S Highway 26, exit to State Route 217, then exit on State Route 10

⌐OG-EAR YOUR CALENDAR

Beaverton has a beautiful dog park, and the city wants to keep it that way. Every August it holds a **Dog Day Afternoon** fundraiser at the Hazeldale Dog Park. There are vendor booths, a raffle, blessing of the animals, and contests and demos for lure coursing, agility, and flyball. Be a vendor, donate raffle items, or come and participate to raise rent and maintenance money for a great regional dog park. Email hazeldaledogpark@yahoo.com for more information.

westbound and follow it past Beaverton until you see signs for Aloha. Turn right on S.W. 192nd Avenue, then turn left on the third street, Prospect Street. There's plenty of parking. Everyone is vigilant about keeping their dogs on leash until inside the gates. Managed by Tualatin Hills Parks and Recreation, 503/645-6433.

PLACES TO EAT

Mingo's West: From the parking area, it's hard to see what everyone is getting so excited about. Pass through the archway, however, and everything becomes clear as you step onto a half-moon garden patio called The Round, with multiple canine-friendly culinary options. One look at the plump tomatoes and roasted garlic cloves at Mingo's had us salivating, an Italian grapefruit margarita drew us in, and gnocchi *alla Romana* sealed the deal. The bar menu, served 2–5 P.M., makes for the happiest of happy hours. 12600 S.W. Crescent; 503/646-6464; www.mingowest.com.

PLACES TO STAY

In this area, chain hotels listed in the *Resources* section offer the best choices for dogs and their owners.

Tigard

It's TI-gard, as in Tiger, and according to statistics on the city's Parks and Recreation website, approximately zero tigers and 9,200 canines call this Portland suburb home. Woof.

PARKS, BEACHES, AND RECREATION AREAS

36 Summerlake Dog Park

🐾🐾🐾🐕 (See Greater Portland map on page 109)

Suburban dogs idle away their days at Summerlake, a mid-sized field of a couple of acres, one of a few excellent off-leash areas created and maintained by the Tigard Dog Park Committee. Summerlake's off-leash area is crowded and friendly, with a large covered shelter that makes for a nice people hangout while the dogs go about their business. It's got all the goods, including garbage cans, pooper-scoopers and bags, running water, a secured fence with double-gated entry, and just enough tree cover for a bit of shade and a couple of suicidal squirrels.

From State Route 217 southbound, take Exit 4B (Exit 4 northbound), and go west on Scholls Ferry Road for a mile. Take a left onto 130th Avenue and go 0.4 mile, straight through a couple of stop signs, until the road becomes S.W. Winter Lake Drive. The OLA and the parking lot will be on your left, past the sports courts and the restrooms. Open dawn–dusk. 503/639-4171; www.tigard-or.gov/community/parks.

37 Potso Dog Park

🐾🐾🐾🐾 (See Greater Portland map on page 109)

Potso pups long for summer evenings and winter weekends, when this great part-time dog park is open to them for unleashed play. Potso is open 4:30 P.M.-dusk Monday–Friday May–Oct., and dawn–dusk on weekends and holidays all year. Cooper and Isis had a ball chasing balls in the open field's healthy green grass. They wanted to take a moment to thank the Bichon Frise who inspired this playground, as well as Coe Manufacturing for allowing a dog park to be built on their spare property.

Potso comes well equipped with poop bags, garbage cans, and sheltered picnic tables. It is completely fenced, with a double gate, and, as an extra bonus, has a separate off-leash area for smaller dogs (yip, yip, yippee!).

From State Route 217 southbound, take Exit 7, make a right onto 72nd Avenue, follow the cloverleaf and immediately turn left on S.W. Hunziker. Turn left on Wall Street in front of the Coe Manufacturing building. Park only in designated spots with giant paw prints painted on them. 7930 S.W. Hunziker; 503/639-4171.

PLACES TO EAT

Max's Fanno Creek Brew Pub: Nachos, fries, and mozzarella sticks are meant to be shared by human and dog alike, says Coop, and the proof is in the pub, or, rather, outside of it at multiple picnic tables packed with happy eaters from both species. Add a schooner of summer blonde or a pint of IPA and some caramel fudge pecan cake and discover what it means to be blissed out. 12562 S.W. Main St.; 503/624-9400; www.maxsfannocreek.com.

PLACES TO STAY

In this area, chain hotels listed in the *Resources* section offer the best choices for dogs and their owners.

Lake Oswego

As you approach this well-to-do bedroom community, you'll see forested landscapes and expansive views of the Willamette River, along with formal landscapes and expansive homes. The few blocks of downtown have a dense concentration of trendy shops, galleries, and a sculpture garden on A Avenue along the Millennium Plaza Park.

PARKS, BEACHES, AND RECREATION AREAS

38 Tryon Creek
🐾🐾🐾 (See Greater Portland map on page 109)

There are eight miles of hiking tails in this 645-acre State Natural Area, plus three miles reserved for equestrians, and another three-mile paved path along the east edge. Pick any trail in the ravine and you'll enjoy plenty of shade among the cedar, fir, and big leaf maples, while your dog appreciates the mixed bouquet of the forest and occasional horse puck. If there's anyone in your group who thinks the last one in the creek is a rotten egg, the fastest route to the water is along the Middle Creek Trail from the nature center to High Bridge, returning on the Old Man Trail to make a quick one-mile loop. Many lunchtime and after-work joggers take to Tryon's hills; the park is strict about enforcing leash laws on the tight and narrow trails. The 0.4-mile Trillium Trail is fully accessible. There are drinking fountains and restrooms at the nature center, at the main entrance.

From I-5, take Exit 297 and stay in the right lane to cloverleaf around south onto S.W. Terwilliger Boulevard. The park entrance is 2.5 miles down on your right. Open 7 A.M.–dusk. 503/636-9886.

39 George Rogers Park
🐾🐾 (See Greater Portland map on page 109)

Life is pretty relaxed on the swimming beach at this city park. Many of the park's 26 acres are taken up by baseball diamonds, tennis courts, a children's play area, and the formal, landscaped Memorial Garden. Pass all of that up and head down the hill to the sandy banks of the Willamette River to mingle with the geese at a natural open-space area.

George Rogers is the site of Oregon's first iron smelter in the 1890s. You can view the preserved historic chimney behind a fence on the grounds.

From I-5, take Exit 299A and travel south on State Route 43, S.W. Macadam Avenue, into Lake Oswego. The road becomes N. State Street through downtown; a few blocks later, watch closely for Ladd Street. Turn left, past the athletic fields, and then right at the Main Parking Lot sign. Open 6 A.M.–10 P.M. 611 State St.; 503/797-1850.

40 Luscher Farm Dog Park

🐾🐾🐾🐾🐕 (See Greater Portland map on page 109)

There's no getting up at the crack of dawn to milk the cows and feed the hens here. Well, there is, on the portion of land still maintained as a working farm, but the only chores you're likely to face are throwing a slimy ball a hundred times for your happy-go-lucky farm animal and picking up the fertilizer he leaves in the field.

Dogs will find any excuse to escape to the countryside if it means coming to this pair of popular off-leash parks in Hazelia Field. Gorgeous, and new in 2008, are two securely fenced and gated OLAs with generous field grass and woodchip trails around the inside perimeters. The timid-dog section is completely separate from the larger area, about a hundred yards away, so there's no barking at the fence.

There are clusters of trees in each OLA, with covered seating areas for humans to sit and shoot the breeze. It can be hectic, but you can get 40 dogs inside the fence and still have room to run. Each OLA has separate entrance and exit areas, to help with crowd control. A paved pathway winds around the farm if you want a leashed stroll to take the edge off. Biodegradable cleanup bags and water are provided. Decent restrooms and a playground are next to the larger field.

From I-205, take Exit 3 north on S.W. Stafford Road for two miles. Take a right on Overlook Drive into the park. A gravel parking lot is on the right. If you continue north on Stafford, it becomes McVay Avenue into downtown Lake Oswego. Open 6 A.M.–10 P.M.

PLACES TO EAT

Port City Pasta Co.: Get your turkey sandwich to go, take it one block south to George Rogers Park, and relish every bite of the focaccia bread that *Gourmet* magazine called "the Best in the West." Your dog would rather have bits of the turkey filling anyway. 333 S. State St.; 503/699-2927.

Zeppo: The salads are so gorgeous at this fine Italian eatery, you may never make it to the thin-crust pizzas, al dente pastas, or low-carb dinners. Your pup may join you on the piazza, a sunny brick plaza. 345 First Street; 503/675-2726; www.zepporestaurant.com.

PLACES TO STAY

Crowne Plaza: This swank property, favored by business executives, got full room renovations in 2008. They like to place pets in rooms on the second floor, saving other floors for those who may have allergies. Rates range $125–155; the pet fee is $20. 14811 Kruse Oaks Dr.; 503/624-8400; www.crowneplaza.com/lakeoswegoor.

More Accommodations: Please look under *Chain Hotels* in the *Resources* section for additional places to stay in this area.

West Linn

With a median household income approaching the six figure range, this affluent suburban city survived fires and floods in the early years to emerge as a
comfortable place to live and play. With a descriptive nickname, "The City of
Hills, Trees, and Rivers," West Linn has no established commercial downtown, which doesn't hurt a dog's feelings at all. **The Dog Club** in West Linn
is posh and well equipped for a day of play, a wash or groom, or to pick up
quality chow, toys, and accessories (18675 Willamette Dr.; 503/635-3523;
www.dogclub4u.com).

PARKS, BEACHES, AND RECREATION AREAS

41 Mary S. Young

🐾🐾🐾 🦮 (See Greater Portland map on page 109)

If your dog is stir-crazy but you don't have time for a drive to the country, take
her to the trails and the pet exercise area at this state recreation site. The off-
leash area is a couple of acres, protected by a ring of trees on three sides. It's
wide open and unfenced, yet remote enough to feel reasonably secure. There's
some shade at picnic tables huddled in one corner, restrooms, and a water
pump for dog drinking and bathing. Bring your own pickup bags.

The trail system is a bit vague in the forested section of the park. The city
narrows it down to somewhere between five and eight miles of trails through
the fir, maple, and alder. The paths you can easily find begin across the parking

DIVERSIONS

Fleece feels good on fur in these damper climes, and there's no
better fleece dog sweater collection than the one at **Sellwood Dog
Supply** (8334 S.E. 17th Ave.; 503/239-1517; www.sellwooddogsup-
ply.com) in none other than the historic Sellwood neighborhood. The
owners used to run Pacific City Beach Dog Supply on the Oregon
Coast, but even that got too cold for their taste. Hence, perhaps, the
sweaters.

A dog is not well and truly spoiled until she's paid a visit to
Bone-Jour GourMutt Bakery (5656 Hood Street, Suite 107, Central
Village; 503/557-2328; www.bonejourdogbakery.com) in West Linn
for some of the most amazing treats ever created for those who are
crated. The variety of savory and sweet biscuits laid out before her
will look almost too pretty to eat. The store itself is decked out in soda
fountain colors. Pearls before swine or divine for canine? She'll let
you know, in between bites.

lot from the dog run, leading down to the southwest bank of the Willamette River.

From I-205, take Exit 8 north on Willamette Drive (State Route 43). Turn left toward Lake Oswego and go two miles. To find the OLA, drive past the athletic fields to the end of the circular parking loop. Open 7 A.M.–dusk. Mary S. Young is owned by Oregon State Parks and managed by West Linn Parks and Recreation, 503/557-4700.

PLACES TO STAY

Best Western Rivershore Hotel: Not only does this lovely hotel take dogs, but they've had a chimpanzee stay once. The only four-legged creatures they turn away are those with hooves. While your livestock may have to lodge elsewhere, your dog is welcome to join you for a $5 fee per night, soaking up Willamette River views from the balcony. Although technically in Oregon City, it is just across the river, and the highway, from West Linn. Rooms regularly go for $95–230 a night. 1900 Clackamette Dr.; 503/655-7141.

Milwaukie

Between Portland and historical Oregon City, this City of Dogwoods is a taste of small-town charm, close to the city.

PARKS, BEACHES, AND RECREATION AREAS

42 North Clackamas Park

🐾 🐕 (See Greater Portland map on page 109)

This fenced off-leash area is a prized privilege for Milwaukie dogs, even though it's smallish, a bit under two acres. Word of mouth says it can get really crowded on weekends, and Cooper thought the supervision was too minimal and play allowed here was too rough for his taste. There's even a local gang of Akitas who act tough in the after-work hours, so we're told. We're also told that a separate small-dog area is in the works for late 2008, but nothing has materialized yet.

It's a wood-chip area, a bit dusty in summer and certainly muddy the rest of the year. Through the double-gated entry, you'll find picnic tables and a muddy water pump. Bring pick up bags.

From Highway 99E, take State Route 224, the Milwaukie Expressway. Turn south on S.E. Rusk Road, and when this arterial road curves around to the left, continue straight to enter the park. To find the OLA, turn right at the Area A&B sign, pass the Milwaukie Center, and park behind the peaked-roof picnic shelter. Walk a few hundred feet west to the fenced area on your right. 5440 S.E. Kellogg Creek Dr.; 503/794-8002.

PLACES TO EAT

Bob's Red Mill Whole Grain Store: From the Milwaukie Expressway, you can't miss Bob's big red barn. This specialty mill grinds whole-grain, organic flours for sale at health food grocery stores around the country. There is a deli, whole-grain store, and visitors center on-site. Kids can watch the water wheel turn and sample Bob's breads and cookies. If the patio is iffy for pets, get your hearty sandwiches to go. 5000 S.E. International Way; 503/607-6455; www.bobsredmill.com.

Gresham

While these parks are still technically within Portland city limits, they are far enough east to use the heavy retail suburb of Gresham as a home base.

PARKS, BEACHES, AND RECREATION AREAS

43 Powell Butte Nature Park

🐾🐾🐾 (See Greater Portland map on page 109)

Pick a clear day when the mountains will be out and rain is not expected within 24 hours to head to the top of this 570-acre park, an extinct volcano with a nine-mile trail system for hikers, cyclists, and equestrians. In addition to the indigenous forest, trees include old apple, pear, and walnut orchards from the 1900s farm of Henry Anderegg. Powell Butte is exceedingly popular with mountain bikers, and you'll have to tolerate them buzzing by you at the beginning of the trail until you can break off onto a walkers-only path. There's a gravel parking lot with restrooms, a drinking fountain, and a trail map at the start. At the top is a rolling meadow where Anderegg's cattle used to graze within sight of Mount Hood and the tips of a few other peaks. Underneath it all is a 500-million-gallon reservoir, part of the Bull Run system, the primary water source for the Portland metro area.

From I-205, go east on S.E. Division Street for 3.5 miles. Take a right on S.E. 162nd Avenue and continue 0.7 mile to the park entrance. Open 7 A.M.–6 P.M. or later as the sun stays out. To protect the ecosystem from hillside erosion, the butte closes when measurable rain falls; call 503/823-1616 to get recorded status information before you go. www.friendsofpowellbutte.org.

44 Lynchwood Park

🐾🐾 🐕 (See Greater Portland map on page 109)

The Wonder Wieners will be the first to admit that this park is obscure. Its remote location and lack of other specific use are the very things that make it an ideal off-leash area. A grove of dense tree canopy forms a semicircle around the flat field, protecting it from the only adjacent road, which isn't very busy

anyway. The other three sides of the rectangle are enclosed by residential and school fences. You'll feel like the free fun zone on the east side of the park is your own secret discovery. Benches under the trees are the only amenities. You should go potty before you leave the house and bring anything you'll need, including bags, water, and your pooch's favorite UFO.

From I-205, go east on S.E. Division Street for four miles, take a right on S.E. 174th Avenue, and a right on S.E. Haig Street. Park along Haig where it dead-ends. OLA hours vary by the season; call 503/823-3647 or go to www .portlandonline.com/parks, and select "Dogs" under the "Recreation" tab.

PLACES TO EAT

Subs on Sandy: This tiny corner shop in the strip mall makes enough fat, messy sandwiches to order a different one every day of the month and teriyaki on weekends. An outdoor picnic table looked weary. 13912 N.E. Sandy Blvd.; 503/252-7827.

PLACES TO STAY

In this area, chain hotels listed in the *Resources* section offer the best choices for dogs and their owners.

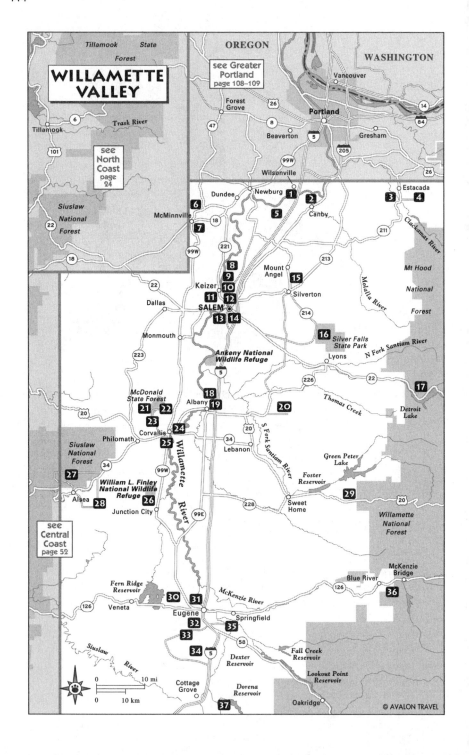

CHAPTER 5

Willamette Valley

From 1843 to 1869, a half million pioneers hitched up their wagons and traveled the 2,000-mile Oregon Trail from Missouri to reach the promised land of the Willamette Valley. As you travel through, you can see why they came, and reap the fruits of their labors. Tucked between the Cascade and Coastal mountains, the abundant valley sits on the same latitude as France's Burgundy wine region and is perfect for growing grapes. The climate is also ideal for hazelnuts, also called filberts, producing 99 percent of the nation's entire supply. Tree farms and nurseries line the rolling hillsides, with thousands of identical conifers in soldierly order. The valley's abundance includes a cornucopia of off-leash areas as well, within state parks and in the region's three major college towns of Eugene, Salem, and Corvallis.

PICK OF THE LITTER—WILLAMETTE VALLEY

BEST PARKS
Eagle Fern, Estacada (page 150)
Willamette Mission, Salem (page 156)

BEST DOG PARKS
Dog Runs at Keizer Rapids Park, Salem-Keizer (page 156)
Alton Baker Dog Park, Eugene (page 171)

BEST HIKE
Ridgeline Trail System, Eugene (page 173)

BEST EVENT
Silverton Pet Parade, Silverton (page 160)

BEST PLACES TO EAT
Bistro Maison, McMinnville (page 155)
Fleur de Lis, Cottage Grove (page 177)

BEST PLACES TO STAY
Wayfarer Resort, Blue River (page 176)
Village Green Resort, Cottage Grove (page 177)

Water is the source of life in the valley, and its rivers and reservoirs are the primary source of recreation. To cross the multiple tributaries of these major rivers, Oregon pioneers built bridges with buildings over them to protect the wooden trusses from accelerated decay in rainy weather. The state has preserved the largest number of historical covered bridges west of the Mississippi, most of them in the Willamette Valley, each county featuring a different design. Covered bridge tour maps from city visitors centers provide a perfect excuse to explore scenic roads.

The top two tourist attractions in Oregon are in the Willamette—the Champoeg and Milo McIver Pet Exercise Areas. No, actually they are Spirit Mountain Casino (www.spirit-mountain.com) and the upscale outlets at Woodburn Company Stores (www.woodburncompanystores.com), but dogs may beg to differ.

NATIONAL FORESTS AND RECREATION AREAS

Willamette National Forest
🐾🐾🐾🐾

This playground has more than 80 developed campgrounds and 1,700 miles of hiking trails. The forest service's interactive trip planning map, online at www.fs.fed.us/r6/Willamette, is a great way to find recreational opportunities far beyond what we have room to mention in this book. For the McKenzie River Recreation Area, along State Route 126, stop into the ranger station in McKenzie Bridge (57600 Hwy. 126.; 541/822-3381).

Wilsonville

This fast-growing city hosts corporate biggies like Xerox and Hollywood Entertainment. At the same time, it has a Tree City USA designation to keep it green.

PARKS, BEACHES, AND RECREATION AREAS

1 Memorial Bark Park
🐾🐾🐾🐕 (See Willamette Valley map on page 144)

This popular off-leash area is where local dogs come to blow off steam after a hard day's nap waiting for their humans to come home from work. The city says the 1.5-acre park has been left in its natural state except for the occasional mowing, but the Dachshund Duo found it to be in much better shape than many parks they've seen. Gopher holes are the main hazard, also providing something to stick a nose in for a snout full of rodent spoor. There's no long list of rules, merely the statement that only good dogs are allowed.

A chicken-wire fence surrounds the field with a perimeter path, tables in either corner, and gates on both ends. There are a few shade trees along one side and bag dispensers, which were all empty. Bring your own bags and water.

From I-5, take Exit 283 and go east on Wilsonville Road for 0.3 mile, turn right on Memorial Drive and almost immediately turn left. The OLA is around the corner to your left past the sports fields, down a short path from a gravel parking area. Open dawn–dusk.

PLACES TO EAT

Country Grains Bread Co.: It's only a couple of blocks from Memorial Bark Park, but you may want to eat at this deli's picnic tables to avoid mass

begging. In addition to sandwiches and low-carb choices, there's chili to go by the quart. Open Monday–Friday. 8553 S.W. Main St., in the Village at Main Street; 503/682-5857.

PLACES TO STAY

In this area, chain hotels listed in the *Resources* section offer the best choices for dogs and their owners.

Canby

Canby sits in the state's garden spot for tree nurseries, flax, and floral, the latter most visible in the summer at the Swan Island Dahlia Farm, the nation's largest dahlia grower. Other local landmarks include the Canby Depot Museum, one of the oldest remaining railroad stations in Oregon, and the Canby Ferry across the Willamette to Wilsonville.

PARKS, BEACHES, AND RECREATION AREAS

2 Molalla River

🐾🐾🐕 (See Willamette Valley map on page 144)

Since the last edition came out, the state park moved the pet exercise area to a four-acre sloped field. The park has land, lots of land, under starry skies above, with no fence to keep you in. If your dog is tempted to take off, he can go for miles on adjacent farmland before you can catch up with him. Also, it seems to the Dachsie Twins that the usability of the OLA depends on how ambitious the driver of the riding lawnmower is that week, carving a playground out of five-foot-high field grass. It's not very soft on the paws, and any animal with more hair than a Chinese crested is likely to come away with half the native groundcover stuck to his fur.

So, the Dachsie Twins give the off-leash area at this state park only one paw, with an extra paw thrown in for the riverfront trails. Starting west of the boat ramp, opt for a 0.75-mile hike along the Willamette River to where it joins with the Molalla then loops back around through the woods for a total of about 1.5 miles. There's a garbage can and bag dispensers, and running water nearby at a restroom drinking fountain.

A quarter mile downstream from the park is the Canby Ferry across the Willamette; pedestrians and bicycles cross for no charge, cars, with dogs allowed in them, are $1.25 each way. For information call 503/650-3030.

From Highway 99E northeast of Canby, turn right on N.E. Territorial Road, turn north on Holly Street, and travel 2.2 miles. The park entrance comes up suddenly on the left after a bend in the road. Open 7 A.M.–9 P.M.

Estacada

Estacada is the gateway city to the Clackamas River Recreation Area of the Mount Hood National Forest. Ask at the ranger station (595 N.W. Industrial Way; 503/630-6861) for a long list of scenic hikes and river boat ramps. Despite early years of logging and dam development to supply nearby Portland with hydroelectric power, the area remains beautiful for hiking, fishing, camping, and hounding around.

PARKS, BEACHES, AND RECREATION AREAS

🖪 Milo McIver State Park

🐾🐾🐾🐾🐕 (See Willamette Valley map on page 144)

Sometime in the 1970s, according to a local historian, this state park hosted its first and only government-sponsored concert event, called Vortex. Supposedly, the goal was to keep all the hippie activists happy and busy, away from Portland while President Nixon was in town. Local farmers were reputedly paid to drop off bags of food and smokable plants for the 35,000 people.

While the flower power days of the 1970s may be over, at least your dog can enjoy a carefree existence at Milo McIver's off-leash pet exercise area. Even though the area is not fenced, the rest of the park's designated areas are miles away in this 951-acre sprawling park on the Clackamas River. There's a garbage can, a bag dispenser, and a huge, wide-open field of tender, green grass—real grass, not dirt or wood chips. You can enjoy the shade of one gigantic tree and an amazing view of Mount Hood while developing a case of tennis elbow from tossing.

It's easy to spend an entire vacation at this pet-friendly park and not get bored. There are miles of Milo along the riverbanks, hiking trails with long beaches and convenient splash points. Rafting down the river from Milo McIver to Barton Park is another popular pastime, plus there are equestrian trails, a campground, a fish hatchery, and several picnic areas.

From Estacada, travel southwest on State Route 211 for a mile, turn right on Hayden Road, and right on Springwater Road for another mile. The off-leash area is to the right along the main park road. Open 7 A.M.–sunset. Parking is $3. 503/630-7150.

◳ Eagle Fern

😺 😺 😺 😺 (See Willamette Valley map on page 144)

The county's largest and most doggone divine park is tucked deep in the woods in one of the few remaining old-growth timber stands in the valley. There is an excellent kiosk of information presented by the forest service to give you an idea of the treescape around you. Each of many individual picnic areas along Eagle Creek has convenient water and garbage cans nearby. Across a bouncy suspension bridge are short and sweet hikes, from 0.5 mile to 1.25 miles each, through towering Western red cedars, Douglas firs, hemlocks, and maples. The water is inviting for fishing and dog paddling. It is a relaxed and relaxing atmosphere for people with pets.

From State Route 224, four miles north of Estacada, follow the sign to Eagle Fern Park/Dover District, turning on Wildcat Mountain Road and traveling two miles to bear right onto Eagle Fern Road and another 2.3 miles to the park. Open 6 A.M.–9 P.M. May–September, until 6 P.M. in the winter. A $3 parking fee is charged weekends and holidays Memorial Day–Labor Day. 503/794-8002; www.clackamas.us/parks.

PLACES TO EAT

Colton Café: It's the perfect little country café, a cheery yellow building with curtains in the windows and a picnic table on a side lawn shaded by a huge maple tree. The gravel parking lot is five times the size of the building, hinting at the restaurant's popularity for b'fast and lunch. 12 miles from Estacada; 21038 S. Hwy. 211; 503/824-5111.

PLACES TO STAY

Clackamas Inn: This friendly highway stop in Clackamas (Exit #12 off I-205) is the closest motel to Estacada. Management caters to seniors and pet owners, and non-smoking rooms are available. Rates range $70–100, plus a $10 pet fee. 16010 S.E. 82nd Dr.; 800/874-6560; www.clackamasinn.com.

Milo McIver Campground: The 44 electric sites at Milo are friendly for RVs or tents, for $13–17. There are also nine primitive tent sites available for a measly $6–9 per night. 800/452-5687; www.reserveamerica.com.

Newberg

This city was the boyhood home of Herbert Hoover, the 31st president of the United States. It's a popular stop along the "Wine Highway," State Route 99W, 25 miles southwest of Portland.

PARKS, BEACHES, AND RECREATION AREAS

5 Champoeg State Park

🐾🐾🐾🐾 🦮 (See Willamette Valley map on page 144)

After her first visit to the pet exercise area at this state heritage area, your dog's tail will start wagging if you even think the word Champoeg (sham-POO-ee). The park's designated off-leash area is a five-acre field that seems much larger, in the middle of 615 acres of white oak forests, fields, and wetlands along the Willamette River. The pet area is not secured, but it is far enough removed from everything else to present no problems for well-managed dogs. The park sits on the site of the ghost town of Champoeg, where Oregon's first provisional government was established. The town was destroyed in an 1861 flood and abandoned after more floods in 1890.

There are other activities to enjoy with a leashed pooch. The Riverside Picnic Area is nearby, and if you walk on the trails west of the Pioneer Mother's Cabin, there are a few informal areas along the river to catch the drift. There is a four-mile paved trail from the park to the Butteville General Store, where you can rent bicycles for the day. A large campground, visitors center, historic buildings, hiking trails, and disc golf course occupy other areas of the large park.

We say phooey to the convoluted signs to Champoeg. Instead, take the Charbonneau exit (282B) from I-5, go west on winding Butteville Road for five miles, then bear right onto Champoeg Road for another three miles. To find the OLA, turn down the hill to the left toward the Riverside Area and Pioneer Mother's Cabin and go 0.7 mile to parking along a gravel lane at the far end of the field. Parking is $3. 503/678-1251.

PLACES TO EAT

Butteville General Store: First opened in 1863, Oregon's oldest continually operating store carries on the tradition of being the social center of a rural community. It's a deli, an art gallery, a historical museum of local photographs, a venue for local musicians, and a bicycle rental shop for treks to

DETOUR

Take your dog to a drive-in movie, before this endangered species becomes extinct. The **99W Drive In Theatre** in Newberg runs double features of first-run titles on summer weekends, with real-butter popcorn and original, restored 1950s trailers before the show and between features. Cash only; 503/538-2738; www.99w.com.

The drive-in's pet policy is priceless:

Question: Can I bring my dog/cat/ferret/elephant?

Answer: Yes, as long as the animal is harmless to the customers and our operation. Management reserves the right to refuse any animal (including human) admission. Elephants and other larger animals will be charged a single-occupant car admission due to the fact they would take up a car space by themselves. You will be solely responsible for damage caused by your animal to the drive-in, yourself, other drive-in patrons or property. You must keep your animal secured to your vehicle/parking space. NOTE TO ELEPHANTS AND GIRAFFES: Our ticket window height clearance is 8 feet.

nearby Champoeg. Plan your vacation to coincide with pizza or gourmet burger nights. Pets are warmly welcomed on the front porch or in garden seating. Open seasonally, May–September. 10767 Butte St.; 503/678-1605; www .champoeg.com.

PLACES TO STAY

Avellan Inn: This exquisite bed-and-breakfast is a haven of country peacefulness. Once you've lain down on the downy featherbeds and sat in a swinging chair on your private enclosed deck, you may never want to leave. Neither will your dog feel any desire to part from the hazelnut orchards and fields of the 12-acre property, where he's free to roam off-leash. Sally's Room is $125 per night, Emily's Room is $155 with a suite area and a private entrance for pet people. Children are also welcome. 16900 N.E. Hwy 240; 503/537-9161; www.avellaninn.com.

Champoeg Campground: There are 79 RV sites for $16–20, and six walk-in tent sites for $12–16 at this state park in a remote setting on the plains by the Willamette River. 800/452-5687; www.reserveamerica.com.

More Accommodations: Please look under *Chain Hotels* in the *Resources* section for additional places to stay in this area.

McMinnville

Historic downtown McMinnville, along 3rd Street, is an enjoyable place to stroll, shop, and eat. It's the hub for wine country tours of the valley, catering to travelers with its quaint bed-and-breakfast inns and a pretty city park.

PARKS, BEACHES, AND RECREATION AREAS

6 Joe Dancer Park

🐾🐾🐾 (See Willamette Valley map on page 144)

J.D. is a huge, sparkling city park, opened in 2008, with an excellent soft-surface perimeter trail, massive fields of tender manicured grass, and, someday, an official off-leash area at adjacent Kiwanis Marine Park. Isis was impressed by the landscaping, with giant stones lining all the newly paved roads and parking areas. While much of the park is reserved for ball fields, a skate park, and playgrounds where dogs are not allowed (officially, dogs must stay off the groomed lawn areas), at least check out the perimeter trail loosely following the South Yamhill River and lose a tennis ball or two in the back fields. There's plenty of space for every dog to have his day.

From 99W into downtown McMinnville, take 3rd Street east, which becomes Three Mile Lane. Turn left on Brooks Street into the park. The first pullout holds only a couple of cars; there are better spaces in the next lot and you can find join the trail a ways behind the skate park.

7 McMinnville City Park

🐾🐾 (See Willamette Valley map on page 144)

Conveniently located at the end of the downtown historic district, this city park has two levels. Dogs are not allowed in the upper park, with a gigantic wooden play castle for the kids, sandwiched between the library and city pool. The lower level is more informal and dog-friendly, with a short walking path and picnic tables along woodsy Cozine Creek.

DETOURS

Oregon is deservedly gaining fame from wineries in the Willamette, several of which you can visit with your dog. The golden retriever, blue heeler and Pomeranian who live at **Elk Cove Winery** (503/985-7760, elkcove.com) will sit with you under a giant oak tree overlooking the La Bohème vineyard and brag to your dogs how they made it into the *Wine Dogs USA* picture book. Dog treats are available, but other begging is discouraged.

In what was once a decaying industrial area of McMinnville, Oregon, an old turkey processing plant, a grass seed company, and a steam-generated power plant have been converted to produce something that tends to get better with age. Owners of these upstarts call themselves either the "Pinot Quarter" or the "Wine Ghetto." At one of these wineries, Douglas Drawbond of **Anthony Dell** (503/910-8874; anthonydell.com) has produced 50 cases of 2005 Pinot Noir under the label Homeward Bound, and all sales benefit the local no-kill animal shelter of the same name. Enjoy a nice Oregon pinot noir, and help save the lives of shelter animals.

Dogs are also welcome in the picnic areas of **Duck Pond Cellars** (23145 Hwy. 99 W; 800/437-3213; duckpondcellars.com), and **Sokol Blosser** (5000 Sokol Blosser Ln.; 800/582-6668; sokolblosser .com), if they can get along with the winery dogs.

As you enter town from the north, State Route 99W becomes Adams Street southbound. The park is located at the intersection of 3rd and Adams Streets. If you are entering from the south, 99W merges onto Baker Street northbound. Turn left on Third Street and drive one block to Adams.

PLACES TO EAT

Bistro Maison: Deborah Chatelard, owner of this dog-friendly restaurant in McMinnville, called to invite us onto her beautiful patio to hang out with her boxer and indulge in a menu that won a Best of Fine Dining award from City-Search in 2006. It is a French menu, and as such, the *pomme frites* with saffron aioli are de rigueur. Reservations highly recommended. 729 N.E. Third St.; 503/474-1888; www.bistromaison.com.

Harvest Fresh Grocery and Deli: Hearty soups, fresh salads, and sandwiches of substance including tempeh, tarragon chicken, and turkey meatloaf are only the beginning at the deli side of this health food grocery store a couple of blocks from the city park. The fresh vegetable and fruit juice blends are refreshing, sipped at a sidewalk table. 251 E. 3rd St.; 503/472-5740.

PLACES TO STAY

Baker Street Inn: "Just be honest about your dogs," asks owner Cheryl Hockaday, and they will be welcome to stay in Le Petite Chateau, a two-bedroom, 700-square-foot cottage, fully renovated in 1994 and updated in 2004. They may choose to hang out with you on the back porch, and may stay in the chain-link-fenced dog run while you're away if they're comfortable in their own skin. Rates range $150–160; the pet fee is $20 total per stay. 129 SE Baker St.; 503/472-5575; www.bakerstreetinn.com.

More Accommodations: Please look under *Chain Hotels* in the *Resources* section for additional places to stay in this area.

Salem-Keizer

In 1864, the capital of Oregon was moved from Oregon City, near Portland, to its present location in Salem. Perhaps they realized how convenient this centrally located city is to all that the valley has to offer in Marion and Polk counties.

The gardens around the Salem suburb of Keizer are well known as the center of the world's iris industry. May and June are the months to see this tall flower in bloom.

PARKS, BEACHES, AND RECREATION AREAS

8 Willamette Mission

🐾🐾🐾🐾🐕 (See Willamette Valley map on page 144)

This 1,600-acre state park is a time capsule and a hands-on agricultural lesson, with an off-leash dog park thrown in for good measure. The history is visible against the sky in the form of ghost structures, metal sculptures that trace the outlines of the original Methodist mission, established in 1834 by Reverend Jason Lee. You can hike up to 12 miles through vineyards, fields of hops, mission roses, and habitat restoration projects, and, in the fall, you can gather hazelnuts in the picnic orchards. (Don't pick them off the trees; they're not ripe until they fall.)

As for the real reason you came here, to find the pet exercise area, turn left at the entrance booth and go a mile toward the picnic facilities, to the parking lot for the nation's largest black cottonwood tree. To your left is an unfenced off-leash area, another orchard with many trees to inspect. There's a garbage can and a bag dispenser. The OLA is close to group picnic areas, providing an opportunity to practice tough love to keep your German shepherd from snagging a bratwurst off someone's grill.

From I-5, take Exit 263 and drive two miles west on Brooklane Road. After a right turn on Wheatland Road, it's another 2.5 miles through hazelnut orchards and hops fields to the park entrance. Parking is $3. Open 7 A.M.-sunset. 503/393-1172.

9 Spong's Landing

🐾🐾 (See Willamette Valley map on page 144)

You'd never suspect that such a great countryside watering hole can be found five minutes from the commercialism of the main drag in Keizer. There is some serious running around going on, on the fields of Spong's Landing. It's also an excellent hidden river spot with bark dust trails down to a little beach on a wide bend in the Willamette River.

From River Road, turn west on Lockhaven Drive for 0.9 mile, right on Windsor Island Road for 0.7 mile, and left on Naples for 0.6 mile. Opens at sunrise; closes a half hour after sunset.

10 Dog Runs at Keizer Rapids Park

🐾🐾🐾🐾🐕 (See Willamette Valley map on page 144)

The city has grand plans for this park—building a boat ramp to connect it to regional river trail systems, creating a non-motorized transportation corridor, expanding it from 85 to 119 acres, you name it—but they did the most important thing first: They created an excellent dog park.

As canine celebrities, Cooper and Isis were granted access a couple of days early (they snuck in), as the field was being mowed before the grand opening on June 8, 2008. It's about time they leveled the playing field, literally, for Keizer canines, with kudos to Keizer Veterinary Clinic for financial support.

Bordered by rows of hazelnut orchards are two double-gated, fenced, wide-open areas blanketed with heavy-duty grass that might actually last a while under the punishment of happy paws. We guarantee that the field in the big-dog area is longer than the Salem-Keizer Volcanoes pitcher can chuck a ball. Cooper laughed to discover that the fence surrounding the small-dog area is shorter than the one for the big boys. There are cans and bags and we'll look for the city to add water and human perks such as shelter and real bathrooms in place of the portable potty as the park matures.

Take a moment to look in an information box for trail maps down to the river and peek at the park's grand master plan on the bulletin board. Enjoy the trails on leash, and watch out for poison oak.

Take Exit 260 from I-5 going west on Lockhaven Drive, and take the first left at the light after the railroad tracks onto Chemawa Road. Stay on Chemawa for 2.8 miles, until it ends at the park. You'll see the dog runs on your left; take the long drive past the fence to reach the gravel parking area. Open sunrise–sunset. 1900 Chemawa Rd. N.

11 Orchard Heights Park

😾 😾 🐾 (See Willamette Valley map on page 144)

Cooper and Isis pulled up, saw a small, unfenced, and roughly mowed field marked as a dog exercise area, and thought, "Ho hum, pretty ordinary." Then they crossed a bridge behind the tennis courts and their eyes went wide as a brief woodchip trail opened up to a hillside with the largest oak tree they'd ever seen, one of a hundred oak, alder, and cottonwood trees in this city park. The field is overgrown with waist-high grass, so all but very leggy and adventurous dogs typically stick to the gravel trail, leading back to a stream with several easy water entrance points. Parking, playgrounds, restrooms, mutt mitt dispensers, and garbage cans are all in close proximity.

From downtown Salem, go west over the bridge for State Route 22 West, staying in the right-most lane to peel off onto State Route 221 North. Go north toward West Salem and Dayton, and take a left on Orchard Heights Road. The park will be on your right at the corner of Parkway Drive and Orchard Heights Road. Open 5 A.M.–midnight. 1165 Orchard Heights Rd. N.W.

12 Salem Riverfront Park

😾 😾 🐾 (See Willamette Valley map on page 144)

We'll admit to the dogs up front that this park plaza is included primarily for your people. The main attraction is the Riverfront Carousel, with $1.25 rides on its colorfully restored horses. Wet-nosed ones won't mind the stroll along the Willamette River down to the *Willamette Queen* sternwheeler paddle-boat and the Eco Globe, a former acid tank for the Georgia Pacific paper mill transformed into a work of art using 86,000 mosaic tiles. The luxurious grass of the elevated amphitheater steps is tailor-made for picnic blankets.

From I-5, take Exit 256 and go west on Market Street through town and turn left on Front Street. Parking is immediately south, under the highway overpass.

13 Minto Brown Island Park

🐾🐾🐾🐕 (See Willamette Valley map on page 144)

Today, the former farmsteads of Isaac "Whiskey" Brown and John Minto have been combined into a 900-acre park with a 20-acre off-leash area. Through cooperative use agreements, some of the land continues to be farmed, while 12 miles of paved and soft-surface trails wind through the remaining wildlife areas. If there's a dog in your life who needs some space, this is an ideal place to bring him. The dog run at Minto Brown is just that, a long field, not fenced or secured, separated from the park road by a row of trees and large boulders. There's not much traffic to worry about in the middle of an island surrounded by low-usage orchards, gravel pits, timber, dense underbrush, and grassy meadows. Trash cans are provided; bring your own bags and water. A nearby trail, the A-Loop, is a good 1.5-miler.

Regular volunteer park patrols have significantly diminished the park's reputation as an unsafe place in the 1990s. It's still best to stick to the daylight hours in this remote area.

From I-5, take Exit 253 west on Mission Street. Turn left on Commercial Street and, shortly thereafter, turn right on Owens Road. Then you'll bear left onto River Road, and right onto Minto Island Road. The park entrance is a mile from the turn onto Owens Road. The dog run is between parking areas #2 and #3, 0.6 mile into the park. 503/588-6336.

14 Bush's Pasture Park

🐾🐾🐾 (See Willamette Valley map on page 144)

You can go for a long walk on the gentle bark-dust Outer Loop Trail of 95-acre Bush's Pasture. As the joggers pass you, you'll pass wide fields, mature oak trees and apple orchards, and a playground designed specifically for handicapped users. You'll skirt Willamette University's stadium and historic Deepwood Estate and Bush House Museums. You can detour through a 2,000-bloom rose garden and along Pringle Creek. Also at this city park is a track dedicated to Soap Box Derby racing; Salem is one of the few cities in the nation to have one. For a serious dose of lighthearted fun, check the schedule at www.salemsbd .org and catch a race. There's more here, but you get the idea. Salem dogs are lucky to have such a diverse urban park, and the Dachsie Twins thank them for sharing.

From I-5, take Exit 253 west on Mission Street, less than a half mile to the park on your left. Turn into the first parking lot for trail access. To find the

Municipal Rose Garden, continue on Mission and turn left on High Street. Open 5 A.M.–midnight.

PLACES TO EAT

Arbor Café: In the heart of the Capitol Mall area, this deli and bakery serves a half dozen daily specials in addition to a long list of delicious sandwiches and salads. Your eyes might glaze over as you gaze at the glazed tarts in the pastry case. There's plentiful courtyard seating. 380 High St.; 503/588-2353.

Gerry Frank's Konditorei: You can't miss the big sign that reads Extravagant Cakes Etc. on your way to Minto Brown park. The "etc." stands for traditional soups, salads, and sandwiches, but Isis couldn't take her eyes off the rotating pastry case of those aforementioned extravagant cakes. 310 Kearney S.E.; 503/585-7070.

La Margarita Express: This Mexican restaurant with colorful umbrella tables may very well be your elected government representative's favorite lunch haunt. It'll win your vote with vegetarian specialties and a light menu. 515 Chemeketa St.; 503/371-7960.

PLACES TO STAY

In this area, chain hotels listed in the *Resources* section offer the best choices for dogs and their owners.

Silverton

On your way to Silver Falls State Park, enjoy Silverton's excellent galleries, boutiques, and antique stores along its historic main thoroughfare, Water Street.

PARKS, BEACHES, AND RECREATION AREAS

15 The Oregon Garden

😊😊😊 🐾 (See Willamette Valley map on page 144)

Isis was surprised to learn that the internationally renowned Oregon Garden opened only in 2001. It seems much more established and sophisticated than the years would indicate, located on 80 acres on the site of a former Arabian horse ranch in historic Silverton. Pets who won't pee on the flowers and people who pick up after their pets are welcome to walk together through 20 specialty gardens and around Oregon's only house designed by Frank Lloyd Wright.

Among the themed gardens is a pet-friendly educational garden designed to demonstrate how to keep pets from harm in the yard and from causing harm in the flower beds. There's information on edible plants and a take-home brochure listing toxic plants. Water bowls and a canine cooling station help those without sweat glands keep their cool.

DOG-EAR YOUR CALENDAR

The **Silverton Pet Parade,** on the third Saturday in May, is the longest running pet parade this side of the Mississippi. It was started by the American Legion as a way to get kids out for some fun after the Great Depression and has blossomed into a way to promote an animal-friendly community. The parade is free to enter and free to watch. The lineup starts at Coolidge McClaine Park and wanders through downtown Silverton. 503/873-5615; silvertonchamber.org.

For the famished, Wagger's Barkery dog treats are sold in the gift shop. Admission is $10 for adults, $8 for children. 879 W. Main St.; 503/874-8100 or 877/674-2733; www.oregongarden.org.

16 Silver Falls

🐾🐾🐾 🦴 🐕 (See Willamette Valley map on page 144)

There's no doubt that dogs will enjoy a hike on any stretch of the 18 miles of trails open to pets in the 8,700 acres of Oregon's largest state park. Yet, for their humans, it's a bit of a cruel tease, because pets are not allowed on the park's most famous trek, the seven-mile Canyon Trail loop, a.k.a. the Trail of Ten Falls. It is simply too crowded and too precipitous to allow dogs. As a condolence, there is an unfenced off-leash pet exercise area in the South Falls day-use area.

Despite the restrictions, you shouldn't pass up this park. You can see South Falls, the most popular, and two other falls from viewpoints accessible by car or along the 2.7-mile Rim Trail, where dogs are allowed. If possible, bring some

friends and tag-team it, a couple of you hanging with the dogs while the others take to the trail. The waterworks are truly spectacular, and you can walk behind four of the falls for the full sound-and-spray experience.

From downtown Silverton, the drive out State Route 214 to the park passes through beautiful farm country, rolling hills of tree farms and grass seed fields. After the park, the road loops down to intersect with State Route 22 in Salem. Park hours vary widely with the seasons; call 503/873-8681. Parking is $3.

PLACES TO EAT

Gingerbread House: Sure, it looks like a typical drive-through order window with burgers and fries, until you try the warm gingerbread with vanilla ice cream sprinkled with nutmeg. A blue X taped in the window is the secret code for the days when there's fresh banana bread. There are lounge chairs with side tables lined up out front. 21935 Gingerbread St.; 503/859-2247.

Silver Creek Coffee House: Just when you thought you couldn't stand to hear Coop go on about another coffee shop, in this case he feels justified, as Silver Creek serves full gourmet fare from a regularly changing seasonal menu. Additionally, this particular establishment does double duty for Howard Hinsdale Cellars wine tasting. So, please forgive the dog if he does go on. 111 Water St.; 503/874-9600.

PLACES TO STAY

Oregon Garden Resort: Moonstone properties built 17 cottages on a tiered hilltop meadow adjacent to the Oregon Garden, so that every room is a room with a view from private, landscaped patios. Six of the rooms in one building

DIVERSION

Lassie and Rin Tin Tin ain't got nothing on **Silverton Bobbie.** In one of the greatest true dog stories ever told, Bobbie was a Scotch collie who got separated from his family on a vacation to Indiana in 1923. Distraught, the family stayed in the area for a month trying to locate the dog, but left despondent and unable to do so. Six months later, Bobbie appeared on their doorstep, worse for wear but spirited, after covering nearly 3,000 miles on foot to find his way home. The story made national news, and over the next year, the family received letters with stories from people who remembered seeing and helping Bobbie on his journey. Stop in the visitors center to ask about his statue, doghouse and mural, located in town. There are more statues of him in the **Oregon Garden,** and several fiction and non-fiction books about this wonder dog in their gift shop. Visit silvertonbobbie .com for more.

will allow two pets per room. Opened in September 2008 with the latest in amenities, the rooms are luxuriously appointed and range $90–200, depending on the season; $15 pet fee. The garden theme is accented with occasional tables made from birdbaths and headboards that are modeled after garden gates. 895 W. Main St.; 800/966-6490; www.moonstonehotels.com.

Silver Falls Campground: There are 47 electrical sites open year-round for $16–20 and 46 tent sites open May–October for $12–16. 800/452-5687; www.reserveamerica.com.

Detroit Lake

It's torturous for the Dachsie Twins to limit what's in this guide, especially here in the North Santiam Canyon recreation area. There are dozens of picnic parks and campgrounds along the North Santiam and Little North Santiam Rivers. You could work your way into the Opal Creek Wilderness (www.opalcreek.org), or fish at the bend in the river in North Santiam State Park. Whatever you choose, as you travel State Route 22 southeast from Salem, it's along the river and through the woods you go to hound heaven.

PARKS, BEACHES, AND RECREATION AREAS

17 Mongold Picnic Area at Detroit Lake

😺 😺 (See Willamette Valley map on page 144)

In and of itself, Detroit Lake is primarily designed for water recreation, with two beautiful boat ramps and a paved swim beach where dogs are not allowed. The Mongold day-use area has picnic tables all along the lake with great views, and a few tables tucked in the woods.

It's better to use this area to hike around and up above the lake. Pick up maps for the Tumble Creek Trail #3380, Dome Rock Trail #3381, and Stahlman Point Trail #3449 at the ranger station in Mill City on the way to the lake. Now you're talking.

The lake is four miles east of the town of Detroit on Highway 22. Detroit Lake has the only camping for miles. $3 day-use permit required. 503/854-3366.

PLACES TO EAT

KC's Espresso and Deli: The folks at Fodor's love KC's and the dogs do too, relaxing on the lawn by makeshift picnic tables. You can't miss the bright purple fence and you won't want to miss the old-fashioned milkshakes and made-to-order meatloaf sandwiches. You might meet the town mayor, coming in for his morning jolt. 210 Forest Ave.; 503/854-3145.

PLACES TO STAY

All Seasons Motel: Other than camping, this is it. The rooms are serviceable at prices of $50—70 per night. There's no charge for dogs yet, but they are toying with the idea of adding a flat $5 per visit cleaning fee. There are picnic tables and a propane grill out front for guests. 130 Breitenbush Rd.; 503/854-3421; www.allseasonsmotel.net.

Albany

Despite a difficult economy, residents of this historic town are working to restore the Victorian homes and the high concentration of covered bridges surrounding the city, reminders of a vital role this central town played in the trade and commerce of the early valley. Call 541/928-0911 for your copy of *Seems Like Old Times*, the self-guided tour brochure that will take you time traveling, walking or driving through the town's historic districts, including the Monteith House Museum, said to be the most authentic restoration project in Oregon.

PARKS, BEACHES, AND RECREATION AREAS

18 Simpson Park Trail

😾😾😾 (See Willamette Valley map on page 144)

The Wonder Wieners were glad they went out of their way to visit this trail, reminiscent of a Sunday stroll down a quiet country lane. Neither the faint whiff from the wastewater treatment plant in the beginning nor the low hum of the highway in the distance or the occasional train whistle could deter them from their appointed rounds. The path is wide, level, easy, soft, and shaded, 1.3 miles each way, in between murky First Lake and the Willamette River. You'll end up in a field, with one very narrow, overgrown path heading to the river.

There are no amenities other than what nature intended, so humans go pee somewhere else first, bring bags and water, and pack everything in and out. From a parking circle, the trail curves around to the right, past the metal gate.

Take Exit 234 from I-5 and swoop into town on South State Route 99E, Pacific Boulevard. Exit onto Lyons Street, one-way into town. Turn north on 2nd Avenue, travel a mile, and turn left on Geary Street. Take a right on Front Avenue, which curves around to become Waverly Drive. Cross a one-lane bridge over Cox Creek to gravel parking on your left. Open 6 A.M.–10 P.M.

19 Takena Landing–Eagle Trail

😾😾 (See Willamette Valley map on page 144)

The picnic area and restrooms of this city park are under a highway overpass, but you lose the traffic noise after about a quarter mile on the Eagle Trail, named by default as the ongoing project of the local Eagle Scout troop. This 1.7-mile one-way walk parallels the Willamette River on the opposite shore from the city. The scouts are doing a good job maintaining the hard pack and

trimming back the blackberry bushes just enough to give you peek-a-boo water views. As for getting into the water, where there's a will, there are pathways. Your companionable river walk should be shady, serene, and private.

The park is a mile from State Route 99E. Turn west on Lyons, which crosses the bridge over the river and curves around to West U.S. Highway 20, and turn left onto North Albany Road. Open 6 A.M.–10 P.M. 541/917-7777; www.cityofalbany.net/parks.

20 Larwood Wayside

🐾🐾🐾 (See Willamette Valley map on page 144)

On a Linn County covered-bridge tour, pause at this countryside gathering place to soak up the timeless fun of a dog-day afternoon. The park looks much as it must have 70 years ago, when the Larwood Covered Bridge was wet with whitewash in 1939. Farm kids hang off the sides of the bridge, wave at passing cars, then jump into the water. Others float by on inner tubes past the ruins of the water wheel power plant on the riverbank. For sustenance, there's a U-Pick blueberry field two miles down the road and fishing. Once featured in *Ripley's Believe It or Not,* this is the only place in the United States where a river (Roaring River) flows into a creek (Crabtree Creek), instead of the other way around.

From State Route 226 east of Albany, Larwood is 6.7 miles down Fish Hatchery Road.

PLACES TO EAT

Loafers and Szabos: Primed to earn your vote for the hangout of the summer, this hybrid restaurant is a bread bakery and bistro by day, switching over to serve surf and turf (heavy on the turf) by night. They share the same historic building, the same boomerang-shaped patio with palm trees, and the same parking lot. The deli salads and dessert bars look especially good by day; see the specials board in the evening for chicken fried steak, a pound of shrimp, and halibut fish and chips with key lime pie and mile-high mud pie to top it all off. 222 S.W. Washington St.; 541/926-8183.

PLACES TO STAY

Peggy's Alaskan Cabbage Patch B&B: As retired Alaskans, Peggy and her husband, son, and two dogs are enjoying the not-so-cold weather and the company of lodgers in their two upstairs rooms: one lodge-themed, called Bear; and one frilly, called Wildflower. You can have either room for $75 with a shared hall bath, or for $125 to keep the bath to yourself. A six-foot fenced dog run is available in the unfenced yard, if you feel comfortable leaving your pet for a while. It's a no-frills, unfussy place to stay. No pet fees or restrictions. 194 S. Second St., in Lebanon, southwest of Albany; 541/258-1774; www.cabbage-patch-b-and-b.com.

More Accommodations: Please look under *Chain Hotels* in the *Resources* section for additional places to stay in this area.

Corvallis

Corvallis is the home of Oregon State University and their mascot the Beavers. It's fairly difficult to live in Oregon without being a rabid fan of the Beavers or of their rival from Eugene, the University of Oregon Ducks.

All city parks are open 6:30 A.M.–10 P.M. The Dachsie Twins applaud Corvallis for having six off-leash areas, although most of them can only be described as having rough ground cover, and they leave a bit to be desired in terms of creature comforts like shade, water, seating, and human facilities. On the other side of the coin, dogs are prohibited in Chintimini, Central, Franklin, Lilly, and Washington city parks. For heavier-duty hiking than the Wieners can manage, on primitive trails in the foothills, contact the OSU Research Forest Department regarding hiking trails in Dunn and McDonald State Forests. 541/737-4452.

One thing the dogs love about college towns is that there's a great variety of restaurants to serve a hungry student body. The highest concentration of prime outdoor eating is along 1st Street downtown, across from Riverfront Commemorative Park, and a block over on 2nd Street. For legit dog food and other goodies, visit **Animal Crackers** pet supply (949 N.W. Kings Blvd.; 541/753-4559; www.animalcrackerspetsupply.com).

PARKS, BEACHES, AND RECREATION AREAS

21 Martin Luther King Jr. Park

🐾🐾🐾 (See Willamette Valley map on page 144)

MLK Jr. Park was Walnut Park until a name change in 2005. At first, the designated off-leash area at MLK/Walnut is as clear as mud. From the parking lot, head due south about three-quarters of the way through a field. On the right, you'll see a painted brown wooden bridge and a Public Urban Stream Corridor sign. Cross the bridge and follow the gravel path, and you'll break out into a clearing with a post marking the dog area. It is effectively secured by the surrounding woods and a stream, with the added bonus of a landscaped private garden on the southern, fenced border. Once you've run the gauntlet to find it, you are rewarded with big meadows of wildflowers and field grass to play in, at least part of which has been mowed to dachshund height. There are no amenities other than a lonely shaded bench. A gravel path bisects the area, leading you back to the north end by the parking lot.

From 99W, turn west on Walnut Boulevard. The park is on the right as the road swings to the south, immediately as it becomes 53rd Street.

22 Chip Ross Park

🐾🐾🐾 (See Willamette Valley map on page 144)

This city park is composed of 125 acres of savannah, oak, and upland prairie in the foothills north of town. A 1.5-mile loop takes you through, and your sidekick will be thrilled to discover that he's allowed off leash on the trail. It's a bit of climbing to reach the summit, where you can connect to the Dan Trail in the McDonald Forest if, for example, your vizsla hasn't yet exhausted his supply of boundless energy. Cooper opted to rest and absorb the vistas of Coast and Cascade Mountains from summit benches before returning to a couple of picnic tables at the trailhead for a bite of bologna and cheese. You may pass horses and their riders along the hot, sunny trail. There are portable potties; bring your own drinking water.

From 3rd or 4th Streets, the main north–south thoroughfares through town, go west on Harrison Avenue to 10th Street. Follow 10th northeast through town until it turns north and becomes Highland Drive, and continue until the road starts to climb. Turn left on Lester Avenue, which dead-ends at the park. Closed November 1–April 15 for snow conditions.

23 Woodland Meadows

🐾 (See Willamette Valley map on page 144)

Rough and tumble pups only need apply at this city park. The off-leash area is essentially the back 40 of the farm, behind the historic Corl House. The field grass is like hay, and it's rarely, if ever, mowed. Any dog with hair longer than a Chinese crested is likely to come away with half the park's native groundcover stuck to his fur. The hilly area is not secured in any way, and is marked only by signposts. Things like shade, or a bench, or water have probably escaped the tight budgets of city planners. Avoid the side of the hill along Circle Avenue, a busy arterial street, and bring a wide-brimmed hat for self-made shade. The park on the west side of Circle Avenue only is off-leash, past the perimeter around the historic house.

From 99W, turn west on Circle Boulevard to the park. Turn north on Witham Hill Drive and right at the Corl House sign to the gravel parking lot.

24 Riverfront Commemorative Park

🐾 🐾 ◄💧 (See Willamette Valley map on page 144)

The banks of the Willamette River have served as the focus for commerce in Corvallis since the 1860s. Flour mills, grain warehouses, sawmills, rail lines, and even the city jail occupied the lots along the 11 city blocks of what is now the downtown core. In order to create a place for people to gather, the city had to remove 110,000 pounds of concrete rubble, asphalt, scrap metal, car bodies, and other debris as part of the riverfront restoration project.

The results speak for themselves. Even the garbage cans double as flower planters along this pretty city parkway. You and your mutt mate can stroll the promenade, day or night, to take in the gardens, artwork, and views of the river. Across the street are excellent restaurants, many with outdoor seating where your dog is allowed. Riverfront Park connects to Pioneer Park and Avery Park on the south. Dogs must be leashed, especially enthusiastic water dogs, to keep them from jumping into the spray fountain and scaring the toddlers.

The park is along 1st Street, from Washington to Van Buren. There's a large, free parking lot and restrooms south of the intersection of 2nd Street and B Avenue, and cheap metered parking along the walk.

25 Willamette Park

🐾 🐾 🐾 🐾 🐕 (See Willamette Valley map on page 144)

Coop 'n' Isis had encountered so many wonderful off-leash areas in the valley that they had become critical and jaded by the time they reached Corvallis—until they came here. At this big park close to downtown, the city has found a way for "civilized man" and "beast" to co-exist. It is complicated, so check the map at the north entrance information kiosk if you're unsure. Willamette is three parks in one. Dogs are always allowed off leash on Willamette Park trails, to the east along the river and in the Kendal Nature Park, the latter including informal trails to the west of the sports fields. Dogs are allowed off leash on the open Crystal Lake Sports Fields November–March. Dogs are not allowed off leash in the campground or south of Goodnight Avenue in the playground. Basically, stick to the trails until the whole park goes to the dogs in the winter. Behind the kiosk, only a short run from the parking lot, is a wide dirt ramp straight down into the wonderful Willamette River.

The off-leash areas and, more importantly, the map are easiest to reach from the north entrance to the park. From 99W, which is 4th Street downtown, turn left on Crystal Lake Drive, the opposite direction from Avery Avenue on the west. Curve around past the Evanite Glass Fiber factory and left into the park on Fisher Lane. 541/766-6918.

26 Bellfountain Park

 (See Willamette Valley map on page 144)

A visit to Benton County's oldest park is worth a side trip from the highway for the unique and memorable experience of visiting the world's longest picnic table, a single slab of wood milled by the Hull Oaks Lumber Co. to 85 feet long and half a foot thick. With a peaked shelter covering the whole length, it even resembles an upside-down feed trough. The gleam in your dog's eye is him imagining the world's largest pot luck where all the humans have mysteriously disappeared, leaving him no choice but to save the food from spoiling.

From State Route 99W south of Corvallis, turn west on Dawson Road and travel 4.3 miles to the park entrance. To reserve the table for yourself, call 541/766-6871.

PLACES TO EAT

American Dream Pizza: Make your own pizza dreams come true with a huge list of meat and veggie combos served by the slice at a couple of picnic tables or to go. 214 S.W. 2nd St.; 541/753-7373. For delivery of whole pies to most of Corvallis, call the campus branch of the Dream at 541/757-1713.

Fox and Firkin: What we didn't know was that a firkin is a type of wooden keg. What we do know is that a menu of pub grub, including shepherd and vegetable pot pies, tastes best when washed down with one of the 46 beers on tap or 32 single malt scotches. The Fox has more seating outside than in, along the riverfront. 202 S.W. 1st St.; 541/753-8533.

New Morning Bakery: This shop is so much more than a bakery. It delivers the one-two punch, first with a glass case full of beautiful salads, then with even more beautiful desserts. 219 S.W. 2nd St.; 541/754-0181; www.newmorningbakery.com.

Sunnyside Up: Breakfast is the dogs' favorite meal of the day, especially when it is served all day at this café. The Sunnyside concentrates on organic, wholesome food served in very large portions, which shouldn't be a problem when you have a four-legged food-disposal device sitting at your feet. Outdoor seating and wireless Internet. 116 N.W. 3rd St.; 541/758-3353.

PLACES TO STAY

Hanson Country Inn: People flock to this former poultry farm for its rural setting, still within city limits. Charlie the dog and his feline friends, of the city's oldest and classiest bed-and-breakfast, are often out front to greet arrivals. Smaller or particularly well-mannered pets may be allowed in the posh, restored 1928 main house. The only slightly more rustic detached cottage is suitable for more rambunctious Rovers. There are extensive fields to roam if your dog is careful not to disturb the neighbors' sheep and chickens. Rates range $95–145. 795 S.W. Hanson St.; 541/752-2919; www.hcinn.com.

More Accommodations: Please look under *Chain Hotels* in the *Resources* section for additional places to stay in this area.

Alsea

Named for a native tribe that lived at the north of the river, Alsea is a gorgeous, second-growth wooded area that has recovered beautifully from early logging and settlement. Fishing, especially for steelhead, is the most popular pastime in local parks along the Alsea River.

PARKS, BEACHES, AND RECREATION AREAS

27 Siuslaw National Forest–Mary's Peak

🐾 🐾 🐾 🞀 (See Willamette Valley map on page 144)

Even if you don't hike any of the 12 miles of trails on this peak, you owe it to yourself and your dog to visit Observation Point at the top of the 4,097-foot mountain, the highest in the coastal range. If you want to hoof it, come in at the north end, off U.S. Highway 20, to the Woods Creek Trailhead. From there, it is a heat-up-your-haunches 5.8-mile climb to the top on the North Ridge Trail. If you'd rather stick your heads out the window and drive 9.5 miles to the top, enter from the south, off State Route 34, to Mary's Peak Road. From the parking lot, it's a short, easy 0.5-mile walk to the tip top. Once there, you'll be so inspired by the 360-degree vistas you may want to circle the peak on the Meadowledge Trail, an easy 1.6-mile loop near the summit. Come for sunsets over the ocean; and, should you decide to stay overnight, there are two primitive, first-come, first-served campgrounds on the peak for $10 a night.

The signs are clear at the north entrance on Forest Road 2005, Woods Creek Road, and on the south from Forest Road 30, Mary's Peak Road. Mary's Peak Road is closed at milepost 5.5 December–April; foot traffic is welcome in the snow. Parking is $5. 541/563-3211.

28 Alsea Falls

🐾 🐾 🐾 (See Willamette Valley map on page 144)

The coastal forest at the Alsea Falls Recreation Site is thick enough to grow in an arch over the road. As you hike along the South Fork of the Alsea River, 0.5 mile in one direction to the campground or a mile the opposite way to Green

Peak Falls, you can see the remains of old growth, last logged in 1945. Life persists, reclaiming the forest in thick carpets of springy moss, giant ferns, red vine maple, and sapling Douglas firs. The sun filters through the trees in dapple patterns, lending an air of enchantment.

The falls are a short series of segments tumbling over a wide ledge. How close you can get to the falls depends on mountain runoff. Picnic areas are hidden within their own private groves. On a hot day, Alsea offers cool relief in the river and a popular picnic spot. Camping at the falls is on a first-come, first-served basis, for $10 a night.

From the town of Alsea on State Route 34, turn south on State Route 201 for one mile and left on the Back Country Byway for nine miles, two of which are on a nicely graded gravel road.

Sweet Home

This small town of about 9,000 (not including dogs) is built on a vast, prehistoric petrified forest. While it may seem pointless to pee on petrified trees, it does make rock hounds happy to hunt for agates, jasper, and crystals.

Again, Cooper and Isis were forced to leave out many recreational opportunities, but you don't have to. The Sweet Home Ranger District (4431 Hwy. 20; 541/367-5168) publishes an excellent free guide to the hikes following the Santiam Wagon Trail along U.S. Highway 20 southeast from Albany, paralleling the South Fork of the Santiam River. A self-guided nature walk on Iron Mountain comes highly recommended, as does taking to the Tombstone Prairie nature trail, or just lounging around Foster Lake.

PARKS, BEACHES, AND RECREATION AREAS

29 Cascadia

🐾🐾🐾 (See Willamette Valley map on page 144)

This state park captures much of what makes the Pacific Northwest such a great outdoor destination. There's a quiet 25-tent campground in the woods behind the South Santiam River. The east picnic area has a wide, sunny field. The west picnic area is shaded under big trees. The paved Soda Springs Trail follows the springs, which divides the park east to west, and then down to the river. A 1.5-mile out-and-back trail runs along the creek to Soda Creek Falls. It's an easy magical mystery tour through a dense forest of ferns, moss, and old growth, a quintessential Northwest forest.

Cascadia is off U.S. Highway 20, 8.5 miles east of Green Peter Dam. The first-come, first-served campground, $14 per night, and east picnic area are open May–September. The west picnic area and the trails are open year-round. 541/367-6021.

Eugene-Springfield

Eugene is the birthplace of Nike (now headquartered in Beaverton), with a long-running tradition of long-distance runners that dates back to the 1970s, when Steve Prefontaine broke every record in the world for races of 2,000 meters and above. Needless to say, there's no shortage of places for your dog to get her exercise in the hometown of the University of Oregon Ducks. When it's time for a little time apart, pack Fido off to **Dogs at Play** for the day (590 Wilson St.; 541/344-3647). City parks are open 6 A.M.–11 P.M. unless posted otherwise.

In downtown Springfield, step into the alley on 5th Street between Main and A Streets to give your pet a moment to commune with the 11-foot by 16-foot mural titled *Bob the Dog Visits the Old Growth*.

PARKS, BEACHES, AND RECREATION AREAS

30 Candlelight Park OLA

😊 😊 🐾 (See Willamette Valley map on page 144)

Should you find yourself in the residential 'burbs of Bethel-Danebo west of downtown Eugene, there's a good-sized dog park out here, at the corner of Royal and Throne (we're not kidding!). An unofficial off-leash area since about 1991, now it's official with fence posts and mesh, gates, water pumps, and plastic pools for paw washing. There are two divided areas, the East and West Meadows, with a wood-chip trail around the inner perimeter. The West Meadow is reserved for small or timid dogs on Wednesdays and Sundays, and one of the areas may occasionally be closed in winter to allow turf to take a breather.

The leash-up area is nice and large, and an Eagle Scout built boxes around the dog parks to encourage people to recycle their home plastic bags. Not only does it save the city money, it's the environmentally responsible thing to do. Outside of the dog park are play fields, a playground, restroom, and picnic benches.

Take 6th Street west through town and stay on it until it becomes Highway 99 North. Turn left on Royal Avenue and go one block past Candlelight. Street parking is available along Throne. Royal Ave. and Throne Dr.

31 Alton Baker Dog Park

😊 😊 😊 😊 🐾 (See Willamette Valley map on page 144)

It is not easy to get to Alton Baker. Once there, you could try your dog's suggestion of never leaving, and, thus, never having to worry about trying to find your way back. This wonderful off-leash area has everything a dog park should. Its big, grassy fields are fenced with double gates for leash maneuvers.

DIVERSIONS

Eugene's historic 5th Street Public Market is famous for high-end designer shopping, and **Lexi Dog Boutique** is no exception. It's geared toward glamour and accessorizing (248 E. 5th Ave.; 541/343-5394; lexidog.com). Don't miss Yappy Hour on the patio, a mixer for both species featuring the valley's fine wines for the two-leggers. For a larger selection of everyday stuff in Eugene, The Healthy Pet is the place (2777 Friendly St.; 541/343-3411; www.thehealthypet.net).

It has covered picnic tables, shady benches, and hefty trees. There's water galore in the form of drinking fountains, water pumps, and wading pools to dunk in. Garbage receptacles and bags are plentiful. Outside the gates, you can connect to miles of Ruth Bascom's Riverbank Trail, paved multi-use pathways that follow the Willamette and Steve Prefontaine's four-mile soft jogging trails. As you can imagine, its popularity sometimes makes it a crazy place. The only time it's not good to visit is prior to and after a sporting event; get a list of game dates for the stadium at www.goducks.com to avoid rowdy sports fans.

If you're already in downtown Eugene, it's much easier to get to the park. Take 5th Street downtown heading east, follow the signs for I-105/206/Coburg Road, cross the bridge, and peel off to the right at the sign for Autzen Stadium/MLK Boulevard and right on Leo Harris Boulevard. Park at the Alton Baker Park Eastern Natural Area lot. Cross the wooden bridge to the dog area. Whew. 541/682-4800.

32 Amazon Dog Park
🐾🐾🐾 🦴 (See Willamette Valley map on page 144)

"Our dog has such a high ball drive, I don't know what we'd do without a dog park," said the owner of a 16-month-old black Lab Cooper met at Amazon's off-leash park. Although the smallest of the OLAs, this off-leash area is perfect for a game of toss. The wide field is level and open, fenced, and gated. In between rounds, there is a water station and plastic wading pools for cooling off. Our friend warned us that the park can get a little rough. People come to cluster around the single covered picnic table and chew the fat, and sometimes they don't pay enough attention to what their dogs are doing. If you're worried about the pack mentality getting out of hand, it wouldn't hurt to go up and introduce yourselves first and ask people to watch their charges around your timid or small dog.

From 6th and 7th Streets, the main east–west thoroughfares downtown, turn south on Pearl Street and stay in the right lane until the road merges onto Amazon Parkway. Continue in the right lane until 29th Street, then turn left into the parking lot behind the bus terminal. It's a total of two miles from the center of downtown.

33 Wayne Morse Ranch Dog Park

🐾🐾🐾🐕 (See Willamette Valley map on page 144)

This off-leash area is the place to perfect the precision of your throw to avoid tossing your dog's favorite ball or toy into the fenced-off, protected drainage areas in the middle of the park. There are three large, fenced meadows and lots of grass at Morse Ranch, with several gated entry points and natural bridges to cross in between. The ground in all three pastures is uneven and hilly; bigger trees to the west, and more open to the east, along Lincoln Street. Your Aussie can pretend he's patrolling the farm and then reward himself with a quick swim in the wading pools. There are historic buildings outside the OLA, several of which house Willamette Wildlife Rescue.

From 7th Street, eastbound downtown, turn south on Willamette Street and go 2.2 miles, then take a hard right up the hill on Crest Drive and go another 0.4 mile to the parking lot at the intersection of Crest and Arden, past the fenced-off areas. The east pasture is open shorter hours, 8 A.M.–8 P.M., to be kind to nearby neighbors. 595 Crest Dr.

34 Ridgeline Trail System

🐾🐾🐾🐾 (See Willamette Valley map on page 144)

We got the lowdown from a park maintenance supervisor in Eugene that this is where he takes his lab pal Zac for a jaunt out of town to a more relaxed environment. While our short-legged companions barely scratched the surface of these trails, they liked what they saw. Totaling about 14 miles from Spencer Butte to Mount Baldy, there are well-marked, regularly maintained treks from easy to challenging and everything in between. The hills are alive with the sound of barking.

To start at the Spencer Butte Park trailhead, turn south onto Willamette Street from downtown and go five miles, watching carefully to stay on

Willamette as it twists and turns. Plenty of parking and a couple of portable potties are available.

𝟑𝟓 Howard Buford Recreation Area–Mount Pisgah

🐾 🐾 🐾 🐕 (See Willamette Valley map on page 144)

You can see the mound of Mount Pisgah as you drive into HBRA, named for the Biblical summit from which Moses sighted the Promised Land. We say "Hallelujah!," for dogs are allowed to hike off leash on five of the 2,363-acre county park's seven trails. Only on Trails #1 and #2 are pups required to wear an eight-foot or shorter tether. Hikes are 0.7 to 3.9 miles in length, and some to the 1,531-foot summit are tougher than others that circle the base. Cooper can't promise your pet a religious experience, but he finds off-leash hiking to be nothing short of a revelation. One caution: Some trails are hiker only and some are designated for horses and hikers. Maps are available at visitors centers in town or at the bulletin board by the arboretum entrance. Hiking on the hill can be hot and dry. Bring plenty of water and poop bags.

From I-5, take Exit 189 to the east and go a block north on the frontage road. Turn right on Franklin Road for 0.4 miles, and left on Seavey Loop Road for 1.8 miles. Parking is $2 May–September; free in the off-season. www .bufordpark.org.

PLACES TO EAT

Hideaway Bakery: If local Jeannine and her miniature schnauzer hadn't shared their favorite spot with us, we never would have found it, living up to its name, hidden behind Mazzi's Italian Restaurant. The Mazzi's make amazing, rustic, baked goods in an earthen oven fired by recycled wood from a sawmill. Hideaway's trellis-covered patio is huge and warmed with heat lamps on cold days. People often have dogs with them, coming to and from Morse Ranch or Amazon Park to enjoy a pot of tea and piping hot panini. 3377 E. Amazon; 541/868-1982; www.mazzis.com/bakery.php.

Steelhead Brewing Co.: When the brewpub garage door is rolled up, it reveals a sidewalk sports bar, complete with TVs, homebrews on tap, and plenty of room for dogs to sit at their owners' elbows. The only thing missing is your lumpy couch. 199 E 5th Ave.; 541/686-2739; www.steelheadbrewery.com.

P.S.: The Lucky Noodle across the street is also a delicious choice.

Sweet Life Patisserie: It is indeed sweet to see row upon row of gleaming, gorgeous pastries in this bakery's case, with many good choices for people with food allergies, such as gluten-free, dairy-free, and vegan options. Sidewalk tables are open early and stay open late. They make cakes, tortes, and tarts, and yes, there really is a dessert called the Nipple of Venus. 755 Monroe; 541/683-5676; www.sweetlifedesserts.com.

PLACES TO STAY

Blue Rooster Inn: This is the place to stay if you want to visit the wineries in the valley. This 1865 historic farmhouse, 20 minutes from Eugene, is nestled on 68 acres where your dog is free to roam with Nancy's three dogs. It is absolutely postcard perfect. Turn-of-the-last-century antiques furnish a large lower room and parlor. The Garden Room upstairs may also be available. Call and discuss your dogs with her for details. Rates are $90 downstairs, $80 upstairs. 82782 Territorial Rd.; 541/684-3923; www.blueroosterbnb.com.

Campbell House: You have to really want to stay at this bed-and-breakfast, with its steep dog fee of $50 per pet per night, plus tariffs (that's British for rates) of $130 per night for the Frazer Room and $245–350 for the Celeste Cottage, the two rooms where pets are allowed. If you can swing it, you'll be a temporary resident at the most elegant address in town, a four-diamond property a few blocks from the desirable 5th Street Public Market. 252 Pearl St.; 541/343-1119 or 800/264-2519; www.campbellhouse.com.

Valley River Inn: This rambling, corporate motel is so pet-friendly, they like to say that The Pampered Pooch Pet Package is only $180, $200 for river view rooms, and owners stay free! Also just for pooch is a yappetizer menu of locally made gourmet treats in the gift shop. The motel's mall location seems a bit odd, but the back faces the banks of the river, with bike and jogging paths. Pets are allowed in ground-level rooms only. 1000 Valley River Way; 541/743-1000; www.valleyriverinn.com.

More Accommodations: Please look under *Chain Hotels* in the *Resources* section for additional places to stay in this area.

Blue River and McKenzie Bridge

From Eugene, State Route 126 leads you to the McKenzie River Recreation Area, 60 miles of swimming, boating, and fishing pleasure. The **McKenzie River National Recreation Trail** runs 27 miles along the whitewater tumbling down from the Cascades. From 11 well-marked parking areas, you can access 600-year-old stands of trees, waterfalls and turquoise pools, log bridge crossings, and hardened lava flows. The first trailhead is 1.5 miles east of McKenzie Bridge. Sahalie and Koosah Falls and Tamolich Pool are two highly recommended hikes. Directions and maps are available at the ranger station (57600 S.R. 126; 541/822-3381).

PARKS, BEACHES, AND RECREATION AREAS

36 Delta Old Growth Trail

🐾🐾 (See Willamette Valley map on page 144)

This half-mile stroll through old-growth forest is a synopsis of the unique features of a Pacific Northwest temperate rainforest. Soft, pine-needle-carpeted trails and three wooden bridges take you past giant hemlock, fir, and cedar trees draped in moss. Your footsteps are hushed by the surrounding undergrowth of lichen and thick ferns. This trail is at the northern end of the Aufderheide Scenic Byway, a 19-mile drive through the Willamette Forest skirting the edge of the Three Sisters Wilderness.

From State Route 126 east of Blue River, turn on Forest Road 19 and, shortly thereafter, turn right into the Delta Campground. The trail is at the very end of the campground, 1.3 miles from the turnoff. Parking is $5.

PLACES TO EAT

Harbick's Country Store: If you forgot anything for your road trip along the river, Harbick's has it, including deli food and groceries for you and pet provisions for you-know-who. They also loan out narrated CDs or cassettes of the journey along the Aufderheide Scenic Byway; there's no charge if you return the borrowed disc or tape. 91808 Mill Creek Rd.; 541/822-3575.

PLACES TO STAY

McKenzie River Inn: Dogs may run free in the orchard and along 500 feet of riverfront at this bed-and-breakfast, as long as they are on leash in and around the buildings and other guests. The cabins are best for dog owners, with separate entrances and river-view decks, ranging $115–165 per night with steep winter discounts and no pet fees. 49164 McKenzie Hwy.; 541/822-6260; www.mckenzieriverinn.com.

Wayfarer Resort: Across a covered bridge and into the woods are 12 dog-friendly cabins, much too luxurious to be called cabins, on a 10-acre property surrounded by the McKenzie River and Martin Creek. Rates range $80–105 for studios for two, $290 for a house that sleeps six; there is a three-night minimum Memorial Day–Labor Day, and a $10 dog fee. Ironically, the only unit dogs are not allowed in is The Dogwood unit. There's a stocked pond where the kids can fish, tennis and basketball courts, and easy river access. Quiet dogs may be left unattended if crated. 46725 Goodpasture Rd; 541/896-3613; www.wayfarerresort.com.

Cottage Grove

This township is proud of its claim to fame as the location where Buster Keaton starred in the film *The General* in 1926. Today, it is known more as the starting point for a covered bridge scenic tour featuring five of Oregon's oldest covered bridges.

PARKS, BEACHES, AND RECREATION AREAS

🐾 Row River Trail

🐾🐾🐾 (See Willamette Valley map on page 144)

The river got its name from a row over cows, a dispute between two pioneer men over cattle-grazing rights in the 1850s. You can take it fast or slow on the paved 15.6-mile trail, originally the line of the Oregon Southern & Eastern railway nicknamed "The Old Slow and Easy." There are nine trailheads to reach trail segments from Cottage Grove to the mining and lumber towns of Dorena and Culp Creek. The most scenic part of the trail begins at Mosby Creek, three miles outside of town, passing the shores of Dorena Reservoir.

A trail map from the Cottage Grove visitors center shows restroom and water stops, trailheads, camping parks, and historic covered bridge sites along the trail. To reach the Mosby Creek Trailhead, take Exit 174 from I-5 and turn east at the bottom of the exit ramp onto Row River Road. Drive three miles and turn left onto Layng Road. Open dawn–dusk.

PLACES TO EAT

Fleur de Lis: An amazing painting of Notre Dame graces one wall, and outside, you'll be sitting alongside a trompe l'oeil park painted on boards covering up an empty lot between two buildings. The croissants and cakes in the pastry case are just as artistic at this bistro and bakery. Cooper couldn't decide between the chicken curry and pasta salads, so he ordered both. Meanwhile, Isis got up on her hind legs for the Princess Cake, a pink dome of marzipan covering raspberry jam, white sponge cake, and whipped cream. 616 Main St.; 541/767-0700; www.fleurdeliscafe.net.

PLACES TO STAY

Village Green Resort: "Pets stay free!" reads the ad at this older motel on 14 acres of theme gardens and walking paths. Moonstone Properties is slowly upgrading the rooms, so some look more dated than others. An entire building is reserved for dog and their people, and includes singles, doubles, smoking, and nonsmoking rooms. The staff are super dog friendly, handing out treats and love at check-in. Rates range $80–120; there's no pet fee, except a $50 penalty if you don't declare your dog at registration. 725 Row River Rd.; 541/942-2491; www.villagegreenresortandgardens.com.

More Accommodations: Please look under *Chain Hotels* in the *Resources* section for additional places to stay in this area.

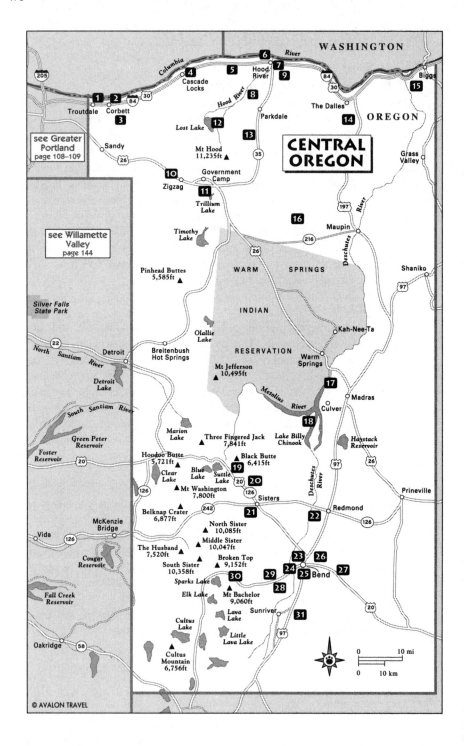

WASHINGTON

CENTRAL OREGON

OREGON

see Greater
Portland
page 108–109

see Willamette
Valley
page 144

© AVALON TRAVEL

CHAPTER 6

Central Oregon

From the high desert of the Oregon Outback in the south to Mount Hood and the Columbia River Gorge bordering Washington, Central Oregon is expansive and majestic, full of the kind of splendor that makes nature photographers drool like dogs. While traveling in this dry and sunny region, you'll often encounter more wildlife than people. Watch for deer on the road, elk in the mountains, and squirrels and chipmunks everywhere. Cooper has developed a deep, abiding love affair with the golden-mantled ground squirrel, small and striped like a chipmunk, numbering in the billions in Central Oregon's mountains and high plains.

The top boundary of the region is the Columbia River, the fourth largest river in the United States, with a water volume twice the Nile in Egypt. Before multiple dams and development, it is believed to have had the largest salmon runs in the world, between 6 and 10 million per year.

PICK OF THE LITTER—CENTRAL OREGON

BEST PARK
Mount Hood National Forest–Lost Lake Resort,
Mount Hood (page 190)

BEST DOG PARK
Big Sky Dog Park, Bend (page 203)

BEST EVENT
Fourth of July Pet Parade, Bend (page 204)

BEST PLACES TO EAT
Elliot Glacier Public House, Mount Hood (page 191)
Petite Provence, The Dalles (page 194)
Terrebonne Depot, Redmond (page 201)

BEST PLACES TO STAY
Columbia Gorge Hotel, Hood River (page 188)
The Dalles Inn, The Dalles (page 194)
Five Pine Lodge, Sisters (page 199)
Champagne Chalet at Cricketwood Country B&B,
Bend (page 207)

NATIONAL FORESTS AND RECREATION AREAS

Columbia River Gorge National Scenic Area
😺😺

Columbia River residents brag that their gorge is gorgeous, and they're not suffering from delusions of grandeur. In the 292,500-acre protected area, you can walk under waterfalls, wade through wildflowers, and retrace the route of Oregon Trail settlers in two states. You can windsurf until your lips turn blue and ski until you're blue in the face, on the same day. Nearly every hike is a bun-buster. You are, after all, hiking up out of a gorge that's 80 miles long and up to 4,000 feet deep. On the downside, access to much of the area's recreation requires four-wheel driving on rough dirt roads following vague directions. Weather conditions vary dramatically, often in the same day, and you and your pooch need to be safely equipped for the rigors of backcountry travel. Hood River Ranger Station; 541/352-6002; www.fs.fed.us/r6/columbia.

Deschutes National Forest
😺😺😺😺

The Deschutes invites 8 million people annually to come out and play in its 1.6 million acres (that's twice the size of the state of Rhode Island). Its diverse regions include the Crooked River National Grassland, Newberry National Volcanic Monument, eight wilderness areas, and the Pacific Northwest's largest ski area at Mount Bachelor. Its recreation opportunities could fill a library, much less a book. Where does a dog begin? In addition to our suggestions in this chapter, try the links under "Recreational Activities" at www.fs.fed.us/r6/centraloregon, or call the Bend–Fort Rock Ranger Station, 541/383-4000. On many trails, dogs are allowed off leash October–April.

Mount Hood National Forest
😺😺😺

At the summit of 11,235-foot Mount Hood, the largest mountain in Oregon, is the grave of Ranger, a dog who was said to have climbed the volcano 500 times in his life from 1925 to 1938 with his owners and friends. Only 20 miles from Portland, this national forest is an easy recreation area for you to reach, following in Ranger's footsteps to create your own feats of athleticism on more than 1,200 miles of trails. Powder hounds can schuss and skijor on Mount Hood's five ski areas. www.fs.fed.us/r6/mthood. Mount Hood Chamber of Commerce: 503/622-3017; www.mthood.info.

Cascade Lakes Recreation Area
😺😺😺😺

From Bend, Century Drive leads to State Route 46, also called the Cascade Lakes National Scenic Byway. The nonprofit organization Scenic America has named it one of the Top 10 most important byways in the country, with extravagant views of mountain peaks, and access to alpine lakes, campgrounds, hiking, and skiing at **Mount Bachelor.** In the summer, dogs are allowed to ride the scenic chairlift and hike to the summit, led by a Forest Service Guide (541/382-7888; www.mtbachelor.com). For the drive, there's a cool downloadable Print-n-Go Map at www.byways.org (click "Explore Byways" and scroll down to "Oregon").

Troutdale

This period town welcomed travelers in their new-fangled Model Ts when the Columbia River Highway opened in 1915. Travelers rested up in auto courts, predecessors to today's motels, before their adventures on the King of Roads. Merchants in Troutdale sold tyres (tires), fuel, and parts, now replaced by antiques, gifts, and clothing boutiques. Isis barked at the dog on the *Hitchin' a Ride* bronze sculpture at the corner of Dora Avenue on Main Street.

NATURE HIKES AND URBAN WALKS

On the Historic Columbia River Highway, between Exit 22 and Exit 35 from I-84, you can drive or walk to 10 **Columbia Gorge waterfalls.** Half of them require fancy footwork to see; the rest are visible from highway stops.

Upper and Lower Latourell: It's a short walk from the parking lot viewpoint to the base of 249-foot Lower Latourell Falls. A 2.3-mile circuit takes you to 100-foot Upper Latourell, where you can walk behind the falling water and through the peaceful picnic area of Guy W. Talbot Park. On Highway 30, 3.4 miles west of Exit 28 from I-84.

Shepperds Dell: Two tiers of falls can be viewed from the bridge crossing. The upper tier is a straight plunge of 35 feet, the lower is a horsetail formation, falling 60 feet. From I-84, take Exit 28 and drive 2 miles west on Highway 30.

Bridal Veil: There's a mile hike down steep switchbacks and stairs to the base of Bridal Veil, which plunges twice—first 100 feet, then another 60 feet. The basalt formation Pillar of Hercules can be seen from a separate wheelchair-accessible path around the cliff above Bridal Veil. The falls is in a state park that includes a picnic area and restrooms. Near milepost 28 on Highway 30, accessed from I-84 at Exit 28.

Wahkeena: These 242-foot fantail falls are described by the Yakima tribe's word meaning "most beautiful." They can be seen from a picnic area, or you can walk 0.2 mile to a bridge viewpoint, close enough to feel the spray. Wahkeena is 0.5 mile west of Multnomah Falls on Highway 30.

Multnomah: The highest and most famous of the falls, Multnomah cascades 620 feet in two sections from the top of Larch Mountain to the Columbia River. Two million people crowd the 0.2-mile trail to the bridge viewpoint each year. Fewer hardy souls climb the 1.2 miles from the visitors center to the top of the falls, and those of you with haunches of steel may want to tackle the six-mile trail to the top of Larch Mountain or trek the equally long loop to Wahkeena Falls and back. Multnomah has a lodge, restaurant, gift shop, and snack bar. Exit 31 from I-84; 503/695-2372.

Horsetail and Ponytail: This 176-foot swisher can be seen from a turnout on Highway 30, 2.5 miles east of Multnomah Falls. Viewing the smaller Ponytail Falls requires a short, steep hike.

Oneonta and Triple Falls: Starting at Horsetail Falls Trailhead (#438), it's a mile uphill to Oneonta Falls, with the added treat of a footbridge over Oneonta Gorge on the way. From there, it's a 1.7-mile climb on Trail #424 through wild canyon scenery to the log bridge viewpoint of Triple Falls, with parallel chutes ranging from 100 to 135 feet. Round-trip is 5.4 miles.

Dogs are prohibited at nearby Glenn Otto, Oxbow Regional, Blue Lake Regional, and Dabney State parks.

PARKS, BEACHES, AND RECREATION AREAS

🔢 Lewis and Clark State Recreation Site

🐾🐾🐾🐕 (See Central Oregon map on page 178)

About a third of the grounds at this state recreation site is designated as a pet exercise area. While there are no fences to separate the space, signs clearly mark where your dog may be off leash. It's hemmed in on three sides by bushes, an inviting place to spend a leisurely afternoon on the grass under the shade trees by Sandy River. There are restrooms, picnic tables, and interpretive signs for the Lewis and Clark Trail.

Across the street from the park is the easiest access to the Sandy River. You'll see cars parked in the dirt and in the roadside pullout before the Troutdale bridge. Portlanders bring their dogs here to walk along the river and go for a swim.

From I-84, take Exit 18 and turn left at the bottom of the cloverleaf exit ramp. You'll see the recreation area to your left around the bend under the railroad trestle. Closes at 9 P.M.

PLACES TO EAT

Jack's Snack 'n' Tackle: Drive or step up to the window at this tackle shed that's been semi-converted to a sandwich place. Fresh-squeezed lemonade, power smoothies, and zero-carb drinks taste so good when slurped at a picnic table around the corner from Lewis and Clark's off-leash area. 1208 E. Historic Columbia River Hwy.; 503/665-2257; www.jackssnackandtackle.com.

Troutdale General Store: This double-duty shop has good taste, both in the food they serve on a covered sidewalk patio and in the gifts and goodies they carry inside. The apple and bacon breakfast casserole is a great choice, and the smoked salmon chowder comes highly recommended for lunch. 289 E. Historic Columbia River Hwy.; 503/492-7912.

PLACES TO STAY

In this area, chain hotels listed in the *Resources* section offer the best choices for dogs and their owners.

Corbett

For the best gorge views, the curviest section of the Historic Columbia Gorge Highway, and the highest concentration of waterfalls in the United States, take Exit 22 from I-84 and follow the signs to Corbett. Your first stop should be the Portland Women's Forum, and then you'll rise to Crown Point and the Vista House.

PARKS, BEACHES, AND RECREATION AREAS

2 Rooster Rock Pet Exercise Area

😻 😻 😻 🐾 (See Central Oregon map on page 178)

Dogs are allowed off leash in this state park, as are unclothed people; Rooster Rock is one of Oregon's two public clothing-optional beaches. There are some restrictions: Dogs are not allowed on the nude beaches to the far east of the park, and nude sunbathers are not allowed in the dog area to the far west of the park. The dogs definitely got the better end of the deal.

The off-leash area is a lengthy, hefty field, partially shaded by old-growth trees, yet open enough to break into a run after a ball. The only oddity is that the state is waiting for funds to replace the decayed wooden tops and benches of the picnic tables, leaving the concrete bases as mini-monoliths for your dog to sniff and lift a leg on.

From I-84, Exit 25 is an exclusive road into the park. Parking is $3. Park closes at 10 P.M.

3 Larch Mountain

😻 😻 🐾 (See Central Oregon map on page 178)

On a clear day at the Sherrard Viewpoint picnic area, at an elevation of 4,055 feet, you can see Mount Rainier, Mount St. Helens, Mount Adams, Mount Hood, Mount Jefferson, and the Columbia River Gorge. It's as if you're in an airplane with a much bigger window. From the parking area, it's only a 0.25-mile climb to the picnic spot.

For a true test of endurance, you can hike 6.6 miles straight up Larch Mountain from Multnomah Falls to this glorious spot. Bring plenty of water and protein bars. This is summer and fall recreation only; the road is snowed in half the year.

From I-84, Take Exit 22 and follow the signs to Highway 30. Go east from Corbett to Larch Mountain Road, turn right and follow the main road 14 miles to the viewpoint sign.

Cascade Locks

If you get as excited by technical marvels as you do by wonders of nature, let the dogs take a backseat and drive through the grounds of the Bonneville Locks and Dam and watch the fish play chutes and ladders.

Native American oral history tells of a natural bridge across the Columbia created by a landslide, but evidence of the crossing was lost by the time Lewis and Clark arrived, and the explorers had to portage over a difficult section of rapids. The more recent Bridge of the Gods is a steel toll bridge, costing $1 to drive over to Stevenson, Washington.

PARKS, BEACHES, AND RECREATION AREAS

◢ Marine Park

😺😺 (See Central Oregon map on page 178)

This scenic city park is the site of frequent weddings and also the port for Sternwheeler paddleboat cruises along the gorge. There's a rose garden, pristine lawns, and a seawall walk along a fishing canal. The coolest part of this park is the trek over to Thunder Island, a man-made berm once part of an elaborate and expensive boat locks system that was never fully successful. A historical museum and interpretive signs tell the saga of humans' attempts to control the forces of nature, from the Lewis and Clark expedition to the crossing of Oregon Trail pioneers and the debacle of building and tearing down the locks.

From WaNaPa Street in Cascade Locks, turn north on N.W. Portage Road, down the hill and under a tunnel with a 12-foot clearance to enter the park. Open a half hour before sunrise to 10 P.M.

PLACES TO EAT

Johnny's Ice Cream and Deli: All hail the spud, one of the most popular lunch items on the menu, next to burritos, soup, and other simple, homemade, tummy-filling food. Johnny's is not fancy, so don't worry about your dog putting his paws up on the secondhand dining room sidewalk furniture. 424 WaNaPa St.; 541/374-0080.

PLACES TO STAY

Bridge of the Gods Motel: A surprising number of amenities are packed into the rooms at this laid-back mom-and-pop motel in the locks. Cheerful hanging flower baskets provide a signature welcome. Inside, you'll find jetted tubs, HDTV, Wi-Fi, and kitchenettes in tidy rooms. Smaller rooms upstairs are $70 and larger rooms with kitchenettes downstairs are $90 a night; $10 pet fee. 630 WaNaPa St.; 541/374-8628.

More Accommodations: Please look under *Chain Hotels* in the *Resources* section for additional places to stay in this area.

Hood River

Vibrant and outdoorsy, this city is a magnet for young and energetic sailboarders and kiteboarders pumped to ride the crests of the Columbia River. To hang out and watch the boarders, ask for directions to The Hook or The Spit. Between town and the mountains is an agricultural valley you can tour with a

DIVERSIONS

When you go away, the very least you can do is take your four-legged kids to **Cascade Pet Camp** to stay. They can bed down in the bunkhouse or in private cabins, some with patios and, um, even TVs tuned to Animal Planet. Daytime includes a heavy schedule of play, cuddles, treats and snacks, and naps, and can include special services such as training, grooming, and therapeutic massage. The facility must be seen to be believed. It is gorgeous and state–of–the art. Your little darling will want for nothing, other than you, of course. Day camp is $24 weekdays, $32 weekends. Overnights are $30–50, depending on accommodations. Check online for the whole list of optional services and goodies. 3085 Lower Mill Dr., Hood River; 541/354-2267; www.cascadepetcamp.com.

Fruit Loop brochure from the visitors center (405 Portway Ave.; 541/386-2000; www.hoodriver.org). While most places prefer that you leave pets in the car, your dogs can relax in the picnic area at Hood River Vineyards while you enjoy wine-tasting (4693 Westwood Dr.; 541/386-3772; www.hoodriver vineyards.us).

The **Gorge Dog** (412 Oak Ave.; 541/387-3996; www.gorgedog.com) is in town for accessories for your best friend. They can recommend great hiking in the area, and you can check their website for local pet-friendly services. **Hannah's Great Dog Store** (2940 West Cascade Ave.; 541/386-8844, www .hannahs4dogs.com) is another great stop, just west of downtown.

PARKS, BEACHES, AND RECREATION AREAS

🔟 Starvation Creek

🐾🐾 (See Central Oregon map on page 178)

It's easy to miss this tiny spot as you whiz by on I-84, especially since it can be accessed only via the eastbound lanes. If you seek it out, what you'll find is an enchanting forest glade, with three lovely picnic areas beside a stream underneath a cascading waterfall. This magical pixie-sized park gets its dramatic name from a band of holiday train passengers who were trapped here for three weeks in a snowstorm. Nearby residents rallied to their aid, snowshoeing in supplies. Everyone emerged safely, if a bit thinner.

You can work on trimming your figure on the park's spur trails that head straight up the gorge walls a mile on the Starvation Ridge Trail to Warren Falls and six miles to Mount Defiance. For an easier, accessible stroll, follow the restored mile of the Historic Columbia River Highway State Trail eastbound to Viento State Park. At least walk to the gently cascading waterfall.

Exit 54 from I-84 is available eastbound only, 10 miles west of Hood River.; westbound, take Exit 51 and return three miles on the eastbound side.

6 Port Marina Park–Port of Hood River

🐾🐾 (See Central Oregon map on page 178)

The port's a busy place, with boat builders, surfboard rentals, docks, and the Hood River County Historical Museum. All the activity makes for good people-watching: novice sailboarders trying to take off from a nearby sand spit, toddlers with water wings splashing in the shallow cove, a Chihuahua swimming on leash as her owner wades alongside. The picnic tables are in front of the surfboard shop, and a huge lawn by the museum is popular with the Frisbee crowd.

From I-84, take Exit 64 and turn north toward the river. Before you cross the Hood River Bridge, turn left into the marina and follow the signs to the left. Closes at 10 P.M.

7 Wilson Park

🐾🐾 (See Central Oregon map on page 178)

"There are always dogs at Wilson," said Jessie at the visitors center. There's a little bit of shade and a little bit of sun on an Irish-green lawn, with primary-colored playground equipment and just enough room to throw a ball around. The park is out of the way on a quiet residential street with a fence along one side.

From Oak Street, turn south on 13th Street and left on May Street to 2nd Street.

8 Tucker Park

🐾🐾🐾 (See Central Oregon map on page 178)

Tucker is tucked into a bend in Hood River, offering camping with showers and flush toilets, which is pretty swank for a county park. When views of the river simply won't suffice, there's a quickie river trail across the picnic meadow from the parking lot. Water dogs will find several swimming holes while picking their way along the sandy and rocky trail. Tent sites are $13 a night.

From Oak Street, turn south on 13th Street, which will merge into Tucker Road. The park is 5.5 miles from the Oak Street turnoff.

9 Mark O. Hatfield–Mosier Twin Tunnels Trail

🐾🐾🐾 (See Central Oregon map on page 178)

Before this old section of the Historic Columbia River Highway was restored and paved, trail users were 80 percent off-leash dogs and 20 percent mountain bikes. Now, it's 80 percent bicycles and 20 percent dogs *on* leash. Either way, you get 100 percent of the best views in the gorge. Dog activists in town are trying to secure a couple of off-leash hours per day; so far, no luck. We say, if you can't beat 'em, join 'em. Rent a bike at Mount View Cycles in Hood River (205 Oak St.; 541/386-2453) and pedal the 10-mile round-trip with your dog jogging alongside. You'll pass through two radically different climate zones, from lush forest to arid desert, two rock tunnels with windows on the gorge, and an engineering marvel designed to keep rocks from falling and crushing trail users.

The two trailheads are named for Senator Mark O. Hatfield, who was active in promoting highway restoration and park projects. From I-84, take Exit 69 and turn left on Rock Creek Road to the East Trailhead. In Hood River, take Exit 64 and turn right at the Historic Columbia River Highway State Trail sign for the West Trailhead. Plentiful parking is $3 per day, and there are restrooms and water at both ends. This trail is excellent for wheelchair users.

PLACES TO EAT

Double Mountain Brewery and Taproom: You can never have too many brewpubs, insists Cooper, although it seems Hood River is pushing the limit. The dogs' choice appears to be the sidewalk outside the brew room here, where garage doors are rolled up to reveal seating, a stereo blaring, and content humans drinking and eating from a short menu of pizza, brats, and the like. Dinner only; lunch on weekends. 8 Fourth St.; 541/387-0042; www.double mountainbrewery.com.

Mike's Ice Cream: Mike's Adirondack chairs, picnic tables, and glass-topped café tables rest on a corner lawn that is probably the busiest patch of turf in town. You and your malamute have it made in the shade, slurping down ice cream, shakes, malts, and floats. 504 Oak St.; 541/386-6260.

South Bank Kitchen: Passionate foodies will be in gourmet deli heaven at South Bank. Salads have dreamy combinations such as spinach and pears, pralines and chicken, and Asian noodle and cabbage. Sandwiches are dressed in spreads; for example, curried chicken with golden raisins or cranberry turkey and hazelnut cream cheese. Wraps, cookies, and pastries, plus daily soup specials and shelves of delicacies, help you pack the picnic basket. Pass the Grey Poupon. 404 Oak St.; 541/386-9876; www.southbankkitchen.com.

PLACES TO STAY

Columbia Gorge Hotel: This 1921 grande dame is the Hope Diamond of hotels, voted the most romantic in Oregon year after year, and the site of more than 100 weddings annually. For $35 per stay, dogs receive treats stored in a Waterford crystal jar, blankets, and a dog dish to keep. An original Otis Elevator, with an operator, whisks you to your timeless, antique-filled room with a Mount Hood or Columbia River view. The price of your room, ranging $200–250, includes a five-course farm-style breakfast and afternoon

champagne and caviar. The grounds are a park in themselves, with 208-foot Wah Gwin Gwin Falls and lavish formal gardens. Go on, your dog deserves it! 4000 Westcliff Dr.; 541/386-5566; www.columbiagorgehotel.com.

Hood River Hotel: The best rooms in this historic hotel are reserved for dogs, three ground-floor suites that have been graciously restored into vintage masterpieces with antique reproductions, wood floors, and four-poster beds. Suite rates are $90–170; the pet fee is $15. 102 Oak St.; 541/386-1900; www.hoodriverhotel.com.

Hood River Vacation Rentals: The great thing about renting a house is that you can find one with a fenced yard if you'd like to sneak away for a movie or to shop without your terrier in tow. This property listing service has eight dog-friendly homes from two to four bedrooms, in a variety of price ranges, available nightly or weekly. Dog fees are $8 per night or $50 per week. 541/387-3113; www.hrvacations.com.

Pheasant Valley Bed and Breakfast: Dogs who can be sociable with resident dogs, cats, and namesake pheasants can stay with you in The Cottage, a stylish two-bedroom apartment in the pear orchard of this winery, farm, and inn. The private deck can be securely fenced to give your dog a comfy place to hang out. Nightly rate is $135, and there's no pet fee as long as they don't have to clean up after your dog; the five-day minimum in the summer rents for $500. 3890 Acree Dr.; 541/387-3040; www.pheasantvalleywinery.com.

More Accommodations: Please look under *Chain Hotels* in the *Resources* section for additional places to stay in this area.

Mount Hood

In the Mount Hood Territory, you can start a hike to Mexico on the Pacific Northwest Trail or watch the birds migrate there on the Pacific Flyway. You can water ski in the morning on the Columbia River and snowboard in the afternoon on the largest night ski area in the nation. Dogs are not allowed to stay at the historic Timberline Lodge, but if you *had* to leave your loved ones at home and needed a fix, stop by and pet the lodge's Saint Bernards Bruno and Heidi. Each village has its own name—ZigZag, Rhododendron, Welches, Government Camp, Brightwood, Parkdale—but ask even Portland natives where Welches is, and they'll scratch their heads. It's all Mount Hood to them.

PARKS, BEACHES, AND RECREATION AREAS

🔟 Wildwood Recreation Site

🐾🐾🐾 (See Central Oregon map on page 178)

There is something for every ability and interest at this family-oriented interpretive nature site. The biggest draw for the kids is the underwater fish-viewing window on the 0.75-mile Cascade Streamwatch Trail. Adults may enjoy the Wetland Boardwalk Trail more, suspended over the ponds and marshes. Both trails are wheelchair accessible, and picnicking spots are nearby. If you and your dog are looking for a better workout, the Boulder Ridge trail climbs 4.5 miles one-way up steep and narrow switchbacks into the Mount Hood wilderness. Open 8 A.M.–sunset May–September. Parking is $3. 503/622-3696.

🔢 Trillium Lake

🐾🐾🐾 (See Central Oregon map on page 178)

Mount Hood towers in all its glory above the crystal-clear lake, easily one of the best views of the mountain in the region. Only two miles off State Route 35, this mountain gem has an easy mile loop around the lake, alternating between hard pack, pavement, and boardwalks. There are dog-paddling opportunities galore. Drive past the Day Use/Boat Ramp sign to another parking lot by the dam to reach the lake loop trailhead.

The lake entrance is 0.25 mile west of the junction of State Route 35 and U.S. Highway 26. Parking is $3. Winter use of the Trillium Sno-Park for snowmobiling and cross-country skiing requires a separate permit November 15–April 30.

🔢 Mount Hood National Forest–Lost Lake Resort

🐾🐾🐾🐾 (See Central Oregon map on page 178)

This destination deep in the woods of Mount Hood National Forest is full of perks for all, from spectacular views of the lake and Mount Hood to pockets of old-growth cedars and firs and plenty of places to take a swim. The hike around the alpine lake is an easy 3.2 miles on soft dirt track and alternating boardwalks, starting from the viewpoint parking lot. There's a general store, paddleboat rentals, cabins, and camping at the lake as well. It's peaceful; motorboats are strictly prohibited and cell phones stop working about a quarter mile before the park. The picnic area closes at 9 P.M. Maps are available at the general store for a half dozen additional hikes in the area. September is a stunning time to visit after the crowds have thinned.

From Oak Street in Hood River, turn south on 13th Street, which merges onto Tucker Road. Follow Tucker as it becomes State Route 281 into Dee. From there, the only way to avoid getting lost on the 28-mile journey to Lost Lake is to carefully follow the signs as the road twists and turns to your destination. Parking is $6 per day; the Northwest Forest Pass does not apply. Closed October–May.

13 Mount Hood National Forest–Tamanawas Falls Loop

🐾🐾🐾🐾 (See Central Oregon map on page 178)

Dog owners at both the Gorge Dog boutique and the visitors center recommended this moderate trail through a cool forest glade along Cold Spring Creek to the falls viewpoint. It's four miles round-trip, with only a few huff-and-puff sections. First, you cross a springy suspension bridge over the East Fork of the Hood River, then turn right after the bridge. Stay to the left at the remainder of the trail junctions to stay on the Tamanawas Trail #650A. The hike is typically doable April–November. It's a beautiful hike, one that's easy to get to, and it provides several places where your dog can go for a quick swim in the creek.

From I-84, take Exit 64 and go south on State Route 35 for 25.3 miles to a gravel parking area on the right side of the road. The trailhead entrance is 0.2 mile north of the Sherwood Campground.

PLACES TO EAT

Elliot Glacier Public House: It's dog central on the lawn out back by the patio seating of this brewpub, where your pal can hang with the local ruff-raff. The food tastes great and it's cheap; Monday night is $1 taco night! Don't miss the porter brownies. 4945 Baseline Rd., Parkdale; 541/352-1022.

Soup Spoon: Gourmet soups and daily specials are served in a pretty garden setting behind the Heart of the Mountain gift shop. Shop, slurp, and go home happy. Well-behaved dogs are welcome. 67898 E. Hwy. 26, Welches; 503/622-0303.

PLACES TO STAY

Lost Lake Resort: Lost Lake has private tent sites available for $15 per night, $20 if you want a lake view on F loop. All campsites are on a first-come, first-served basis. Showers are coin operated. If you'd rather stay warm and dry, dogs are allowed in the seven cabins, $60–120 per night; $10 pet fee. They are various sizes, sleeping 2–10 people, and guests must provide their own cooking utensils and bedding. There's a two-night minimum on weekends and holidays. Lost Lake; 541/386-6366; www.lostlakeresort.org.

Old Parkdale Inn: Mary puts out a whole spread for dogs, including bowls, bags, blankies, treats, and a letter of behavioral expectations. The gorgeous Monet Suite has a kitchen, and breakfast can be served in your room, so you don't have to worry about leaving your pal unattended. Dogs are allowed free on the acre property, but please stay out of the pond and away from the resident cats. The room is $135–145 per night; the pet fee is $25 per stay. 4932 Baseline Rd., Parkdale; 541/352-5551; www.hoodriverlodging.com.

Resort at the Mountain: The Scottish were the first to play golf, so it's appropriate that this resort on the grounds of the first golf resort in Oregon (a nine-hole hayfield in 1928) has a Scottish theme. Thankfully, the tartan isn't overdone, nor is the snob factor. The older Croft Rooms allow two pets for a $25 fee per stay; rates are $90–100. In 2004, the resort opened a few fancier rooms to pets, ranging $100–185. 68010 E. Fairway Ave., Welches; 503/622-3101; www.theresort.com.

More Accommodations: Please look under *Chain Hotels* in the *Resources* section for additional places to stay in this area.

The Dalles

We're pretty sure this is the only city in the United States that officially has the word "the" as part of its name. The French translation of the town's unusual moniker means "river rapids flowing swiftly through a narrow channel over flat, basaltic rocks." The rapids have disappeared, drowned in the rising waters of The Dalles Dam, locks, and irrigations systems. The dam visitors center is open 10 A.M.–5 P.M. Wednesday–Sunday April–October. 541/296-1181.

Cars can pick up another segment of the Historic Columbia River Highway from The Dalles to the east in Mosier. It's another stunner, with a terrific viewpoint at the Rowena Crest Overlook. From this apex, you'll descend again in loops that Agent 007 would love to take on in his Aston Martin.

PARKS, BEACHES, AND RECREATION AREAS

14 Sorosis Park

🐾🐾🐾 (See Central Oregon map on page 178)

Never mind that it sounds like that disease of the liver, drinking in the intoxicating sights and smells in this city park can only be good for you. The buzz starts right in front of the park at the Kelly Viewpoint, with a panoramic vista that includes the Columbia River and Gorge and the city of The Dalles below. It continues at the park entrance with a fragrant and beautiful rose garden, in the center of which is a towering water fountain, given to the city in 1911 by Maximillian Vogt. Kids will get giddy just looking at the Treetop Play Park, one of those gigantic playground castles that'll keep them occupied for days.

Finally, it's the soft grass and the trees—immensely tall and fat pines thickly grouped together—that make dogs dizzy with delight. We're not sure how they managed it, but it looks like the city cleared 15 acres of forest floor and laid a carpet of sod, without touching a single tree.

From the city center on 3rd Street westbound or 2nd Street eastbound, turn south on Union Street, right on 9th Street, and left on Trevitt. Continue on Trevitt past 17th Street, where it becomes W. Scenic Drive, winding up several spirals into the foothills before you'll see the park on your right and the viewpoint on your left. Open 6 A.M.–dusk.

Atiyeh Deschutes River Trail

🐾🐾 (See Central Oregon map on page 178)

Oregon's thirty-second Governor, Victor Atiyeh, was a smart man who led an effort to combine public and private funds to protect the lower 18 miles along the Deschutes River as public land in 1987. Now everyone can responsibly enjoy their piece of the 8,320 acres along both sides of the river without bugging anyone else.

Horses have their 22-mile round trip, bicycles have a 32-mile loop on the abandoned railroad grade, and hikers have several 2–4 mile loops of their own. The two-mile Lower Atiyeh Trail wins the dogs over for having the most shade and places to jump in the water in a valley where 100–110 degree summer heat is common. The trails begin at the back of a field, past the picnic grounds and campground, where the Deschutes meets the Columbia River. Watch for rattlesnakes and check for ticks after hiking.

The trimmed and watered greens of the day-use area are a delicious place to relax before, after, or instead of a hike, scoping the river from under the

NATURE HIKES AND URBAN WALKS

At the start of the **Lewis and Clark Riverfront Trail** in The Dalles, there are authentic covered wagons to fuel your imagination as you travel what was a treacherous final section of the Oregon Trail for thousands of pioneers. Your journey along the Columbia River should be a much easier one, up to five miles one-way on a smooth asphalt path, and you won't have to lug provisions other than plenty of drinking water. The starting point is the Columbia Gorge Discovery Center, and the trail ends at the boat basin downtown, near Riverfront Park. It's also a great way to observe the present, watching the commercial freighters and tugs navigate the river.

From I-84, take Exit 82 and go west on U.S. Highway 30 to Discovery Drive. 541/296-8600.

protection of the white alder tree canopy. The dogs envied the anglers floating in armchair inner tubes, launching at Heritage Landing across the river. Serious hikers can pick up a spur of the original Oregon Trail; couch canines can read the excellent interpretive markers about the Trail's history.

Deschutes State Park is 17 miles east of The Dalles on State Route 206. Heading eastbound on I-84, take Exit 97; westbound, take Exit 104 at Biggs Junction; and follow the signs. 89600 Biggs-Rufus Hwy.; 541/739-2322.

PLACES TO EAT

Big Jim's Drive In: Big Jim's has held its own against the golden arches for 40-plus years, promising hamburgers, chili, and chowder made with love, and ice cream made 50 ways to sundae. As tastes have leaned toward the leaner side, they've added chicken, fish, shrimp, and salads to the menu. Dogs can take their rightful place at the drive-through or on patio seating. 2938 E. 2nd St.; 541/298-5051.

Holstein's Coffee Co.: Who knew this many specialty drinks could come from a bean and an udder? If the Holy Cow, with three shots of espresso with ground chocolate and steamed milk, doesn't take you to a higher plane, nothing will. While chewing your cud, check your email on wireless Internet. Moo if you like outdoor seating! 811 E. 3rd St.; 541/298-2326.

Petite Provence: Soak up the sunny flavors of Southern France while basking in the glow reflected off the distinctive bumblebee-inspired facade of this full restaurant. The victuals are certainly inspired, as are the intricate pastries and breads. 408 E. 2nd St.; 541/506-0037.

PLACES TO STAY

Cousins Country Inn: On the outside, this motel invokes the relaxed comfort of a country home with a big red barn replica housing the lobby and restaurant. Inside, it's fairly standard. They have no official restrictions, but said, "Please don't bring herds." Rates are $65–110; pet fee is $10. 2114 W. 6th St.; 541/298-5161; www.cousinscountryinn.com.

The Dalles Inn: Isis was psyched to find out that the #1-rated property in town welcomes dogs in the back building. After staying here, this is what she knows: The rooms are lovely and the staff will take good care of you. Other items worthy of mention are that your room or suite will be close to historic downtown for great strolls, breakfast includes D.I.Y. Belgian waffles, and the outdoor pool opens Memorial Day. The pet package includes bowls, towels, treats, and scoop bags for use at a small pet exercise area. Rates start at $90; $10 pet fee. There are no pet restrictions. 112 W. 2nd St.; 541/296-9107; www.thedallesinn.com.

More Accommodations: Please look under *Chain Hotels* in the *Resources* section for additional places to stay in this area.

Maupin

The main draw in Maupin is the Deschutes River Recreation Area for life-vest-wearing, rubber-raft-carrying crowds intent on fording the river's low-level rapids and fishing its swells. None of the local companies allow Rover to raft with you. For that, try Ferron's Fun Trips on the Rogue in the *Southern Oregon* chapter. For rafting, fishing, horseback riding, camping, and hiking along the banks of the Deschutes, check out the Bureau of Land Management's information center at 7 N. Hwy. 97; 541/395-2778.

PARKS, BEACHES, AND RECREATION AREAS

16 White River Falls

🐾🐾 (See Central Oregon map on page 178)

The river lives up to its name in the hottest months as melting glacial water deposits silt and sand into the water. This turbulent waterfall is the site of a former hydroelectric plant, built in 1901 to power the gristmill of the Wasco Warehouse Milling Company, grinding the grain from local farmers into flour. In the picnic area above the falls, each tree guards its own picnic table, providing precious shade. Your dog's reward for waiting patiently while you look at the falls lies across a wooden bridge and down a rough, short trail to a swimming hole below, near the stone remains of the mill. For a quick peak at the one-mile round-trip down into the canyon, see the hiking guide at www.nwhiker.com. As they obviously note, rattlesnakes in the area don't make good playmates for your dog, so leashes are vital.

From U.S. Highway 197 in Maupin, travel 10 miles north and turn east on White River Road for 3.8 miles to the State Park.

PLACES TO EAT

Imperial River Company: This business is a triple treat of white-water rafting rental company, excellent restaurant, and great lodge. Dogs are not allowed in the picnic area of Maupin City Park, so walk on over to the picnic tables on the lawn or the backyard patio tables, where you and your dog will be warmly welcomed and well fed with steaks, burritos, chicken, pastas, and other big-appetite pleasers. 304 Bakeoven Rd.; 541/395-2404; www.deschutesriver.com.

PLACES TO STAY

Imperial River Company: Dogs are allowed in rooms #3, #4, #11, and #12 on the ground floor of this nonsmoking lodge. Also pet friendly, the Bunkhouse for $110 per night and the Imperial Suite with kitchen, TV, fireplace, and private deck for $150 are modern with a Western flair, as big as the open prairie. The pet fee is $10. 304 Bakeoven Rd.; 541/395-2404; www.deschutesriver.com.

Madras-Culver

A drive along U.S. Highway 197 through the golden wheat fields of this arid desert region is a cure for feeling overcrowded. It looks like the plains extend to the Cascades without interruption, and until you're right on the brink of it, you can't see the immense Crooked River Canyon extending from Madras to Culver. For better canyon views, less traffic, and quicker park access, drive the **Cove Palisades Tour Route.** Maps are available in Madras (366 5th St.; 541/475-2350).

PARKS, BEACHES, AND RECREATION AREAS

17 Round Butte Overlook
🐾🐾 (See Central Oregon map on page 178)

Thanks to the Portland General Electric Company, park visitors can look into the workings of the dam and the hydroelectric power it produces to learn much about the history of the Warm Springs Indians, including Billy Chinook and Chief Simtustus. Next to the free educational center, there's probably more exquisite shade on the spruced-up grass than in the rest of the valley combined.

From Madras, turn west on Belmont Lane and south on Mount View Drive, following the signs to the park. Open 10 A.M.–8 P.M. Thursday–Monday.

18 Cove Palisades
🐾🐾🐾🐕 (See Central Oregon map on page 178)

It took a darn big dam to create this watery playground in the Crooked River Canyon. The majority of people come to this state park for the water sports on Lake Billy Chinook, named for the tribesman and scout to Captain John C. Fremont on his explorations of the Oregon Country in 1843. Water sport rentals of all kinds are available at the marina.

This rambling 5,200-acre park has two campgrounds and its own pet exercise area. The off-leash area is a fenced and gated acre of rarely mowed field, simple and desirable for a leisurely stroll and sniff. There's no immediate parking; park at the Upper or Lower Deschutes day-use areas and walk a short ways on a trail to the dog area.

After you drive your way down into the canyon, you can hike your way back out on the Tam-a-Lau Trail. It's a difficult, steep, hot hike topped off with seven stunning mountain peaks, one for each mile of the seven-mile loop. There are thousands of harmless whiptail lizards living in the area, an added bonus and distraction for dogs.

From U.S. Highway 97, turn west onto State Route 361, the Culver Highway, and follow signs six miles to the park. Parking is $3. 7300 Jordan Rd.; 541/546-3412.

PLACES TO EAT

Beetle Bailey Burgers: The restaurant selection isn't huge in Culver. This burger shed on the way to Cove Palisades is about it, which is probably why the half dozen picnic tables out front are always packed. 403 W. 1st, Culver; 541/546-8749.

PLACES TO STAY

Hoffy's Motel: Hoffy's rooms are neat, comfortable, and inexpensive at $50–60, plus $12 per pet per stay. 600 N. Hwy. 26; 541/475-4633.

    Cove Palisades Campground: Cooper highly recommends sites #B18–#B22 in the Deschutes River Campground, five miles into the park. They are pleasantly shady, and, most importantly, they line up against the fence of the off-leash area. There are a total of 92 tent sites and 82 hookups in Crooked River and the Deschutes Campgrounds, both in the park. $13–21; 800/452-5687; www.reserveamerica.com.

Sisters

The Three Sisters—Faith, Hope, and Charity—are mountains, tremendous and snow-capped year-round. In the valley below, the town has cultivated the Western frontier look, where you might expect the sheriff to stroll around with his six-shooters and shiny star. It is the gateway to the Metolius River Recreation Area and the Three Sisters Wilderness.

In the winter, downhillers come to **HooDoo Ski Area** (541/822-3799; www.hoodoo.com) and cross-country skiers and snowmobiles share the trails at Corbit and Ray Bensen SnoParks. You'll see evidence of a massive 2007 fire as you drive and hike through this area.

Dogs are required to be on leash July 1–September 30 in the following areas of the surrounding Deschutes National Forest: Moraine Lake, Green Lakes, Todd Lake, and Broken Top with its associated trails. Otherwise, voice control is acceptable. For trail details, call the Sisters Ranger District at 541/549-7700.

PARKS, BEACHES, AND RECREATION AREAS

19 Deschutes National Forest–Black Butte Trail

🐾🐾🐾 (See Central Oregon map on page 178)

Occasionally, Cooper and Isis like to include more challenging trails for their longer-legged friends, and this calf-burning climb takes you 1,585 feet up to the top of a 6,436-foot cinder cone. The reward for climbing to this high point is the 360-degree vista of the Metolius Valley, the Three Sisters, and all of the nearby Cascade Peaks from the historic fire lookout.

Take U.S. Highway 20 four miles west of Sisters and turn right on Green Ridge Road (Road 11). The sign says Indian Ford Road/Green Ridge Road/Indian Ford Campground. Follow the signs 3.8 miles to Forest Road 1110, turn left and travel 4.2 miles to Forest Road 700, turn right and continue 1.1 miles to the trailhead. All this driving means there's less climbing, but not much. Bring lots of refreshing water.

20 Metolius River Recreation Area

🐾🐾🐾 (See Central Oregon map on page 178)

Eons ago, the green ridge volcanic fault cracked open, releasing the Metolius River to the surface from its glacially fed source high in the Cascade Mountains. The temperature and flow rate are cold and constant, producing a crystal clear waterway to play in and around. From the Head of the Metolius Observation Point, you and your trail hound can walk for miles through ponderosa pine and Douglas fir in the 4,600-acre corridor, jumping in and out of the river at will. Brrrrr. The level trail is easy for all ability levels.

From U.S. Highway 20, take the Camp Sherman Road (Road 14) and follow the Campground signs. To pick up the trail, park in the observation point lot, go back out across the road and a few yards down, across from the Riverside Campground. Additional trailheads start at the Wizard Falls Fish Hatchery and the Canyon Creek Campground off Forest Service Road 1420. Metolius Recreation Area maps are available at visitors centers in the area. Metolius Recreation Association: 541/595-6711; www.metoliusriver.com.

21 Village Green

 (See Central Oregon map on page 178)

In the village of Sisters, population 2,000, this block of picnicking green is a welcome respite from the heat. It has restrooms, picnic tables, and… a good sprinkler system, as Coop 'n' Isis unexpectedly found out early one morning.

The park is on Elm Street, two blocks south of State Route 20/126, which is Cascade Avenue through town.

PLACES TO EAT

Martolli's: Order hot subs, calzones, and authentic, hand-tossed pizza by the slice, or create your own pie to wolf down at the restaurant's outdoor tables, for takeout, or to take and bake yourself. 220 W. Cascade St.; 541/549-8356.

Ski Inn: Rumor has it that breakfasts at this classic greasy spoon are bountiful and wonderful. As for lunch, the tiny inside of this hut was crammed when we stopped for fat burgers and fries, which made us especially thankful for the much larger lawn, outdoor order window, and bright blue metal picnic tables covered with Pepsi umbrellas. 310 E. Cascade; 541/549-3491.

PLACES TO STAY

Cold Springs Resort: All of the privately owned rental cabins allow pets for $8 per pet per night. Each modern, fancy cabin sleeps six people. You can fight over who gets the loft, the separate bedroom, or the queen-size sofa bed in the living room. The river is right outside your doorstep, burbling by your private deck, and you can pick up the Metolius River Trail to follow it. Winter rates are $120 for two people, up to $155 for six. Summer rates range $165–195. 25615 Cold Springs Resort Ln., Camp Sherman; 541/595-6271; www.cold springs-resort.com.

Five Pine Lodge: The Harrington and The Hitchcock, a.k.a. classic cottages #20 and #21, are as grandiose as they sound, with pillow-top king-size beds, two-person Japanese soaking tubs (the water comes from the ceiling!), wet bars, 52-inch flat-panel TVs, gas fireplaces, and authentic Amish Craftsman furniture. It doesn't get any better than this, folks. For Fido, hiking trails are out your patio door, past your Adirondack chairs. For you, there's a pool, an athletic club, and Shibui Spa. As an added bonus, you and your pal are also welcome on the patio at the brew pub. The rates are amazing for what you're enjoying, at $150–210, plus a $20 pet fee, limit two pups. 1021 Desperado Trail; 541/549-5900; www.fivepinelodge.com.

Lodge at Suttle Lake: Of the resort's pet-friendly options, Isis votes for the Falls Cabin ($200–300), originated in 1929 and renovated in 2008. It's closest to the water along Lake Creek and has the best front deck. Cooper's choice is the authentic 1959 Ranger Guard Station ($215–250), with its summer camp character and backyard seclusion. The other six are rustic camping cabins ($100–130), what our folks used to call Mattress Camps, without kitchens or bathrooms, fun to reserve in groups if everyone is down with trudging to the bathhouse.

You'll have easy access to trails all the way around the lake from Cinder Beach, and the day-use area is open 7 A.M.–9 P.M.; you can use it even if you're not staying at the resort. The pet fee for up to two dogs is a hefty $40 a night; it includes a package with mats, bowls, and treats. 13300 Highway 20; 541/595-2628; www.thelodgeatsuttlelake.com.

More Accommodations: Please look under *Chain Hotels* in the *Resources* section for additional places to stay in this area.

Redmond

While it may not be as glamorous Bend or as scenic as Sisters, Redmond is a central location to use as home base for exploring the region. It's also the site of Central Oregon's only commercial airport. On your way through, stock up on chow at **The Feed Barn** (2215 Hwy. 97; 541/923-3333; www.feedbarn.net).

Although energetic people are crawling all over the walls at nearby Smith Rock State Park, an internationally famous, technical rock-climbing Mecca, we chose not to include it because it's not a dog-friendly destination. Shade is hard to come by; the rim of the main developed hike is called Misery Ridge for a reason. The local ranger's biggest pet peeve is an off-leash dog and he'll slap you with a $104 fine if your terrier is caught off his tether.

PARKS, BEACHES, AND RECREATION AREAS

22 Dry Canyon
🐾🐾🐾 (See Central Oregon map on page 178)

The Dry Canyon cuts through the middle of the city, providing a three-mile paved path that you'll share with cyclists and inline skaters out for exercise or their morning commute. Dogs may prefer the narrow dirt track that parallels the main trail to the west. This single track will give your dog a more interactive experience with the gully's natural environs. It's not marked, but you'll easily see it leading from the south end of the trailhead parking lot. There are no restrooms or water in the gulch. However, right about mid-point in the trail is a road that leads up to West Canyon Rim Park. Relax, water, and refresh yourselves at this green space before descending again from the rim.

From U.S. Highway 97 north of Redmond, turn west on Pershall Way and travel a mile to the trailhead entrance sign on your left by the City of Redmond Water Pollution Control.

PLACES TO EAT

Terrebonne Depot: One sip of the basil-infused orange martini sent us over the moon. One bite of the seared ahi tacos with mango cabbage left us clamoring for more. Suffice it to say that even if they didn't put water bowls on the wide and sunny deck for the pooches, we'd be back for this bistro's new American menu and long cocktail list. The curb appeal of the beautifully restored, 100-year-old railroad station adds to the ambiance. 400 N.W. Smith Rock Way; 541/548-5030; www.terrebonnedepot.com.

Bend

Bend is gorgeous, a high-desert playground stacked against the Cascade Mountains. Locals who moved here years ago to get away to a quiet mountain town are bemoaning the fact that Bend has become "the Aspen of Oregon." Nothing this good stays undiscovered for long, and Bend draws as many mountain bikers, hikers, and anglers in the summer as nearby Mount Bachelor calls boarders and skiers to the slopes in winter. Bendites are a highly fit, outdoorsy bunch who have dogs in tow where e'r they go. Official city stats say 49 percent of households have 1.2 dogs. Downtown, along four blocks of Wall and Bond streets, is packed with hip shopping and delicious outdoor dining.

Dogs are allowed in all city parks as long as they are on a leash and you pick up after them. To assist you in this task, Bend Parks and Recreation has installed Dog E Rest Stops, bag dispenser stations with a witticism borrowed from Smokey the Bear: "Only *you* can prevent dog piles." Pick up an Urban Trails Map at the visitors center (917 N.W. Harriman, 541/382-8048, www .visitbend.com).

PARKS, BEACHES, AND RECREATION AREAS

23 Sawyer Park

🐾🐾 (See Central Oregon map on page 178)

Robert W. Sawyer River Park, which was a state park and is now part of the City of Bend, is a sampler platter of regional recreation. It has interesting rock formations, picnic benches under ponderosa pines, a bridge over the Deschutes

DIVERSIONS

There are a couple of great options for dog shopping in Bend. For high-end glamour and fanciful dog treats, toys, and accessories, **Downtown Doggie** is the place, near the Old Mill district. 55 N.W. Wall St.; 541/389-5138; www.downtown-doggie.com.

For a huge selection of all things pet, there are two locations of **Bend Pet Express.** The Eastside store has self-serve dog wash stations and the Down Dog Bakery for homemade-with-love treats. Eastside: 420 N.E. Windy Knolls; 541/385-5298. Westside: 133 S.W. Century Dr.; 541/389-4620; www.bendpetexpress.com.

Bend is the headquarters for RuffWear, a national retailer of serious outdoor gear for active pets on-the-go. Your best bet is to shop online at www.ruffwear.com. Also manufactured here are safety dog collars and leashes at Tazlab (www.tazlab.com) and ultra-impressive dog-powered scooters and trikes and skateboards (www.dogpoweredscooter.com). Get your dog to pull you; he needs more exercise than you do!

river, and an outstretched circle of turf over the hill with a Dog E Rest Stop bag dispenser. A piece of the Deschutes River Trail follows the water, past squirrels and wildlife popping in and out of ground holes. You can get your fill and be wanting more a few hours later.

From U.S. Highway 97/20 North, turn left on O. B. Riley Road and left into the park.

24 Shevlin Park

🐾🐾🐾 (See Central Oregon map on page 178)

This hillside of shady pines became a city park in 1920, the same year as Drake Park below. Its six miles of looped paths are a popular spot for trail runners and joggers. Mountain bikers take their cycles for a spin on parallel, separate tracks. Tumalo Creek rambles through the park, with bridges to cross here and there. Shevlin is on the outskirts of town, but not for long. As high-profile housing developments pop up around it, its sampling of the Oregon Outback topography will be appreciated even more by canines who prefer parks to pavement.

Turn west on Business 20 from U.S. Highway 97. Stay in the right lane to remain on Newport, which leads to Shevlin Park Road. The park is 4.8 miles from the turnoff onto Business 20. 18920 Shevlin Park Rd.

25 Drake Park

🐾🐾🐾 (See Central Oregon map on page 178)

Isis thinks this gorgeous park, named for Bend founder Alexander M. Drake, should be renamed Mrs. May Arnold Park, for it was she and early women of Bend who were responsible for its establishment in 1920. They gathered 1,500 signatures in a fledgling town of 5,400 to convince the city council to purchase the land.

No mere asphalt will do for strolling the greens centered around Mirror Pond—the walking paths are of intricate flagstone. Over an arched wooden footbridge in the middle of the 13-acre park is Harmon Park, with a playground for kids and placards telling the early history of the pond's famous Swan Pageant. The pageant is no more, but the swans and geese remain, as does their prodigious poop.

Dog E Rest Stops are found on the Harmon end of the footbridge and the west end of the park, which is where the dogs tend to hang out, a bit farther away from downtown.

Follow the signs from U.S. Highway 97 to downtown and turn west on Franklin Avenue from Wall Street. If you can't find street parking, there is a public lot on the east side of the park. It's free for the first two hours, $1 per hour thereafter.

26 Pilot Butte

🐾🐾🐾 (See Central Oregon map on page 178)

About 19,000 years ago, a cinder cone erupted, leaving this peak in the middle of the flats. Civilization has overtaken the butte, and now it's an oddly located State Scenic Viewpoint in the middle of a busy suburban area on auto row. There are two ways to hike to the top of Bend's natural answer to the Stairmaster: alongside the road on a one-mile trail, or up the shorter but steeper 0.8-mile nature trail. You'll see all of the city and the mountains beyond. It's a fine place to catch the high country's colorful sunsets.

For dogs who would rather stick their heads out the window on a drive to the top, the summit access road is 0.75 mile east of the trailhead entrance.

From U.S. Highway 97, turn east on Greenwood Avenue and follow it to Summit Drive and the Trailhead Parking signs.

27 Big Sky Dog Park

🐾🐾🐾🐾 🐕 (See Central Oregon map on page 178)

Bend's first and largest off-leash park is a four-acre, fenced playground on the east side of town. It's a rough-and-tumble, natural park among the juniper trees and sagebrush behind the youth sports complex. Short trails from a

DOG-EAR YOUR CALENDAR

If your pup is feeling patriotic, she can prance in the annual **Fourth of July Pet Parade** in Bend. The organized chaos starts at Drake Park at 9 A.M. and winds through downtown on Bond and Wall Streets. It's huge. Estimated attendance in recent years counts more than 6,000 walkers and another 6,000 onlookers participating in a tradition that dates back to the 1930s.

Although dogs are the primary species, there have been lizards, rats, goldfish, cows, donkeys, llamas, and more on parade with kids walking, pulling wagons, and riding bicycles and tricycles. Everyone is welcome to come in costume, and kids can join in with a stuffed animal if there are no live, tame animals in the family. All participants get a collector's button and Popsicle at the finish line. There's no registration, no fees, and no solicitation. It's a free-for-all in every sense. 541/389-7275.

Dogs are also welcome to hold down their corners of the picnic blanket at **Free Summer Sunday Concerts** in the Old Mill District (www.theoldmill.com). Gates open at 1 P.M., concerts start at 2:30 P.M.; B.Y.O. lunch or get your delicacies at food court vendors. See www.bendconcerts.com for the full list of sweet, soothing music.

couple of double-gated entry points lead down to a centralized open space with a picnic table and a water spigot.

The area can be dry and dusty, prickly and brambly, and overrun by chipmunks. In short, the Dachsie Twins loved it. You're likely to come away coated in fine red dust in the summer and rich mud after a rain.

Turn east on Olney from 3rd Street/Business 97. Continue onto Penn, which becomes Neff Road. Follow Neff until you see the park, 3.5 miles from the turnoff at 3rd. Pass the BMX track and the fields to the end of the parking lot marked with large rocks and a Dog E Rest Stop bag dispenser. 21690 Neff Rd.; 541/389-7275; www.bendparksandrec.org.

28 Farewell Bend Park
🐾🐾🐾 (See Central Oregon map on page 178)

Bend used to be called Farewell Bend until a lazy postmaster decided plain ole Bend was enough. Easily four out of five cars are unloading dogs at the city's namesake park, but you may be puzzled at the lack of people on the wide, groomed lawns. It's because most of them are saying farewell to the city and heading around the bend. They're taking to the Deschutes River Trails, crossing the bridges and hiking upriver starting at this easy-access point in the Old Mill District. Some are even launching self-propelled watercraft and floating the water from put-ins along the shores. Either way, we suspect this is how the lazy postmaster chose to spend his summer afternoons.

From downtown, take Wall Street southbound. Go straight through the light at Arizona, then take the roundabout to the left onto Industrial Way. Stay on Industrial Way as it curves to the right to become Bond Street. Follow Bond all the way around the Mill District, and take the roundabout to the right onto Reed Market Road.

You can only access the four-hour parking lanes along the park from Reed Market Road westbound.

29 Upper Deschutes River Trails
🐾🐾🐾🐾 🐢 (See Central Oregon map on page 178)

You can walk a little or a lot on this easy, family-friendly trail system closely following the banks of the tumbling Deschutes. There are seven trailheads, two picnic areas, and three waterfalls (Dillon, Lava Island, and Benham), along a 10-mile stretch from Bend south to Sunriver. Hiker, biker, and horse trails are separated to give you room to spread out. Dogs have to be on leash May–September, darn it, because the trails are so popular; otherwise, voice control is acceptable. The drier and hotter the weather, the more you'll come away with a fine sheen of red dust on your skin or fur from the dusty paths.

Patrick, CEO of RuffWear, takes his dogs Otis and Gordo to the Meadow

Camp Picnic Area, six miles west of U.S. Highway 97 on Century Drive (follow the signs toward Mount Bachelor). Immediately before the Widgi Creek Golf Course, turn left on the gravel road with the little brown park sign. Local Justin and his dog Shadow recommend going another mile, past the Seventh Mountain Resort, and turning up Forest Road 41 for the other trailheads. Parking is $5 at all marked trailheads: Lava Island, Aspen Falls, Big Eddy, Dillon Falls, and the Slough.

30 Tumalo Falls

 (See Central Oregon map on page 178)

The amount of work it takes to see these beautiful falls depends on the time of year and the snow pack. When melted, the gates to the 2.5-mile dirt road are opened, and you may drive along Tumalo Creek all the way to the impressive waterfall. In winter, the road becomes part of the fun for the very fit, either on snowshoes or cross-country skis.

Out this way, in the Deschutes National Forest, there's a whole mess of trails for hikers and cyclists, some of them many miles, leading from both the trailhead and the falls. Your journey will be somewhat shaded by pines, junipers, and alder trees and there are opportunities to slip into the water for a quick swim or to fish for rainbow trout, but watch those currents.

For the falls and the trails, take Exit 137 from U.S. Highway 97, and go straight south on Wall Street. Take a right on Franklin Avenue, which becomes Riverside Boulevard almost right away. At the stop sign, take a right on Tumalo Avenue and go straight through the roundabout onto Galveston Avenue. On your 10-mile journey out to the trailhead, it will become Skyliners Road, then Tumalo Falls Road. Parking is $5.

PLACES TO EAT

Bendistillery Martini Bar and Sampling Room: Sidewalk seating at the martini bar in the alley overlooking Drake Park is the nightspot in Bend, with a dizzying list of specialty martinis and everything from chichi appetizers of brie and fruit to comfort food interpretations. Patrons 21 and over only, please; that's about three in dog years. 850 N.W. Brooks St.; 541/388-6868; www.bendistillery.com.

Cascade Lakes Brewing Company Lodge: The dudes who came up with the clothing line featuring stick people enjoying the good life had to have been inspired by a heated brewpub patio such as this one, on the way to and fro all the recreational wonder of the Cascade Lakes. Drink some beer, grab a burger. Guzzle some brew, devour a taco. Sip a cold one, shred a brat. You get the idea. 1441 S.W. Chandler Ave.; 541/388-4998; www.cascadelakes.com.

Kebaba: A small restaurant that serves modern Middle Eastern food, Kebaba is all about choice. Choose your meat and veggies on a skewer or in a pita; select beer or wine from a daily list; pick between flagstone patio seating or a handy drive-up and drive-off option. Whatever you decide, don't miss the great "fries" made out of sliced and spiced flatbread. 1004 Newport Ave.; 541/318-6224; www.kebaba.com.

Merenda Wine Bar: Please your palate with more than 60 wines by the glass, and hors d'oeuvres and small plates with interesting combinations like fennel, grapefruit, and avocado salad or asparagus and prosciutto pizza. It's sidewalk dining at its finest. 900 N.W. Wall St.; 541/330-2304.

Mother's Juice Café: Mother wants to make sure you eat your apple a day, provided with every sandwich. But the health-conscious flock to Mother's mainly for the list of more than 30 fruit juice and smoothie blends, made from whole, fresh fruit. An impressive list of metabolic accessory nutrients, stuff like spirulina, psyllium, echinacea, and ginseng, can be added for that extra performance punch. 1255 N.W. Galveston St.; 541/318-0989.

Soba Asian Bistro: Everything is made to order and served in a bowl, be it a rice dish, a noodle dish, or a salad. Recipes are from all regions of Asia; there's sure to be something your shar-pei will love. You'll love the shaded sidewalk tables and cold Asian beer or ginger-peach iced tea on a hot day. 945 N.W. Bond St.; 541/318-1535; www.eatsoba.com.

Strictly Organic Coffee Co.: The cement patio is huge at this fair-trade coffee cooperative, but even it pales in comparison to the size of the breakfast burritos and lunch wraps. It feels good to sit in the sun and eat good food and drink strong brew with a clear conscience. 6 S.W. Bond; 541/330-6061; www.strictlyorganic.com.

Victorian Café: There's usually a dog or two hanging out on the lawn beside glass-topped patio tables where people enjoy a comfy-casual menu of breakfast scramblers with thick hobo potatoes and hot sandwiches and fresh salads for lunch. So popular, it can be hard to eke out a spot. 1404 N.W. Galveston St.; 541/382-6411.

The Village Baker: You'll be thrilled you took the time to hunt down this little storefront, even if you have to wait in line for superb sandwiches and baked goods. 1470 S.W. Knoll Ave.; 541/318-1054.

PLACES TO STAY

Absolutely Bend Vacation Homes: For a variety of pet-friendly rental properties, for longer stays on long summer days, the Cascade, Honeysuckle Lane, Bear's Den, and Kingston are pet friendly. There's no pet fee as long as there's no damage and no hair all over the place. 541/280-1813; www.abvhs.com.

Champagne Chalet at Cricketwood Country B&B: Heated Italian tile floors, two-person hydrotherapy tub, see-through gas fireplace, these the humans in your party can appreciate while the pups experience what a guest once called "Disneyland for dogs." Your pal can cavort in the five-acres of native grasses and wildflowers on a fenced, rural property down a dirt road with very little traffic. A rate of $150 per night covers you and your dogs;

breakfast is not included, but you have your own kitchen to DIY. It's a straight shot down Hamby Road to the Big Sky Dog Park. It's bliss, is what it is. 63520 Cricketwood Rd.; 541/330-0747; www.cricketwood.com.

Entrada Lodge: You can feel your stress level decrease a notch or two as soon as you enter the warm, fuzzy lobby of this quiet lodge on the west side of town, mere steps away from the Cascade Lakes Scenic Byway and the Deschutes National Forest. Rates range $80–100. There's a short list of reasonable pet rules and a $10 pet charge. Continental breakfast is included. 19221 Century Dr.; 888/505-6343; www.entradalodge.com.

Hillside Inn: The Studio Suite is your sweet spot on the west side of town, a desirable, modern destination with a separate entrance and private patio. It's got the you-thought-of-everything factor, with kitchenette, Internet, Satellite TV, DVD, and hot tub for $170 a night, plus a $20 pet fee. It's a half mile from Drake Park, and closer still to great outdoor seating and eating. 1744 N.W. 12th St.; 541/389-9660; www.bendhillsideinn.com.

Riverhouse Resort: This extensive, popular hotel is always busy thanks to superior service and Danish-influenced rooms with sliding glass doors onto patios overlooking the Deschutes River. If you sign a simple pet policy, there is no charge for your pets. Rates range $100–135, higher for suites. 3075 N. Business Hwy. 97; 866/453-4480; www.riverhouse.com.

More Accommodations: Please look under *Chain Hotels* in the *Resources* section for additional places to stay in this area.

Sunriver

There are those who make an annual pilgrimage to the 3,300-acre resort town of Sunriver, due south of Bend, as a required homage to sun worship. What's there? Golf courses, tennis courts, 35 miles of paved bike paths, swimming pools, athletic clubs, stables, a marina, a nature center, and a shopping/dining village.

PARKS, BEACHES, AND RECREATION AREAS

🐾 Newberry National Volcanic Monument–Lava Cast Forest

🐾🐾 🐾 (See Central Oregon map on page 178)

It's not every day that you get to walk on a lava field, especially if you're not in Hawaii. A mile-long interpretive trail takes you through a forest where the trees are gone, but their impressions, molded in lava, remain. The trees acted as casts around which the molten lava surged when the Newberry Volcano erupted about 6,000 years ago. The path is paved, but the nine-mile road to the site is not. For the price of a bumpy ride on a washboard dirt road and a $5 parking fee, you're treated to one of the most unusual geological sites you're likely to see. The peaks of the Cascades accentuate the stark beauty, and in the spring, fiery Indian paintbrush and purple prairie lupine flowers contrast with the hardened black lava. Your dog will be too busy enjoying her leashed stroll to question the point of going to a treeless forest.

Travel south on U.S. Highway 97 and turn east on Forest Service Road 9720, directly across from the Sunriver exit. The trail is wheelchair accessible. Closed due to snow cover in winter. 541/593-2421.

PLACES TO STAY

Sunray Vacation Rentals: As the pet-friendliest agency in the Sunriver resort, Sunray believes you should be able to bring your loved ones with you for these rites of passage. There's a list of about 50 rentals that allow pets under "Pet Homes" on the left navigation bar. Find a handful that look good online, and then call and chat with a representative for availability and their recommendations. 56890 Venture Lane; 800/531-1130; www.sunrayinc.com.

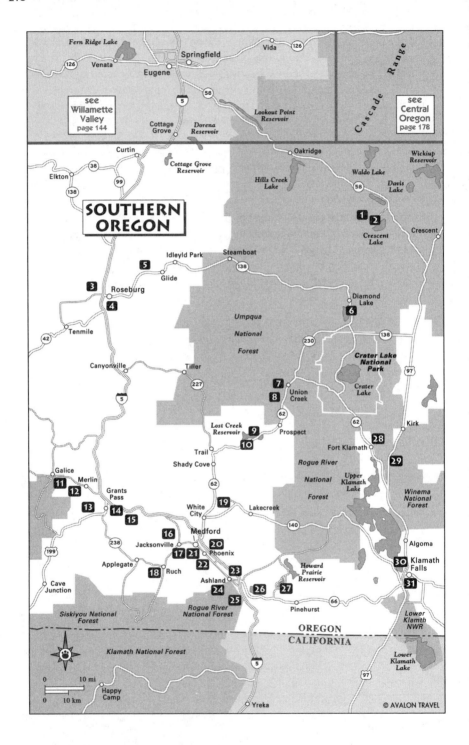

CHAPTER 7

Southern Oregon

The mighty Rogue and Umpqua Rivers, named for regional Native American tribes, are the source from which fun flows in Southern Oregon. The rivers begin high in the Cascade Mountains, winding and tumbling down to the ocean, providing hikes, campgrounds, and water sports of infinite variety along the way. Salmon, trout, and steelhead fishing and white-water rafting on the Rogue draw people from all over the world. Even so, except for a few hotspots, Southern Oregon is not as crowded as, say, the Oregon Coast. Rules are more relaxed, areas more open, and the lifestyle resonates in a lower key. While visitors crowd Crater Lake and the Oregon Caves National Monument—both places where dogs are *not* allowed—you can recreate unhampered in the backwoods.

The rivers connect to lakes, hundreds of them, and dozens of those have lake resorts. In addition to providing lodging or camping or both, they are complete destinations, offering boat and bicycle rentals, general stores, restaurants, and more places to picnic, play, and hike. The topography shifts from fertile valleys in the west to the Cascade Mountains as you head east. Be prepared with

PICK OF THE LITTER—SOUTHERN OREGON

BEST PARK
Whistler's Bend, Roseburg (page 216)

BEST DOG PARKS
Bear Creek Dog Park, Medford (page 228)
Ashland Boyd County Dog Park, Ashland (page 230)

BEST OFF-LEASH BEACHES
Crescent Lake Recreation Area, Crescent (page 214)

BEST TRAIL
Rogue Gorge Trail, Union Creek (page 219)

BEST EVENT
Puss 'n' Boots Costume Ball, Ashland (page 230)

BEST PLACES TO EAT
Blue Stone Bakery and Coffee Café, Grants Pass (page 224)
Allyson's Kitchen, Ashland (page 232)

BEST PLACES TO STAY
Sutherlin Inn, Roseburg (page 217)
Jacksonville Inn, Jacksonville (page 227)
Anne Hathaway's Garden Suites, Ashland (page 233)
CrystalWood Lodge, Fort Klamath and Crater Lake (page 235)

traction tires and/or snow chains for any elevation above 1,000 in the winter months, and ask for local road conditions before traveling.

NATIONAL FORESTS AND RECREATION AREAS

Rogue River–Siskiyou National Forests
🐾🐾🐾

The two million acres of the Siskiyou and the Rogue are managed together, and cover parts of Southern Oregon and Northern California. Biologists will tell you that it's the most floristically diverse forest in the nation and includes the carnivorous *Darlingtonia californica,* the fly-eating Cobra Lily. The "Recreation" section of the National Forest Website (www.fs.fed.us/r6/rougue-siskiyou) provides information on everything from guides and outfitters to detailed trail information. Or, stop into the Prospect Ranger Station (47201 Hwy. 62; 541/560-3400) and the Ashland Ranger Station (645 Washington St.; 541/552-2900).

Umpqua National Forest

The Umpqua covers almost a million acres on the western slope of the Cascade Mountains. This forest's most popular recreation opportunities are Diamond Lake, included in this chapter, and a 79-mile hiking and mountain-biking trail following the North Umpqua wild and scenic river. Playing with the interactive North Umpqua Trail Map online is almost as much fun as hiking the trail itself. The map is also available in print at the Roseburg Visitors Center and at the North Umpqua Ranger Station in the tiny town of Glide: 18782 N. Umpqua Highway; 541/496-3532; www.fs.fed.us/r6/umpqua.

Fremont-Winema National Forest

On the eastern slope of the Cascades, the 1.1 million acres of the Winema are wild and rugged, with fewer developed recreation opportunities. The two main trails, sections of the Pacific Crest Trail and the Mount McLoughlin Trail, are in Winema's wilderness. Mount McLoughlin isn't so much of a trail as it is a rock scramble guided by unreliable spray paint markers on loose boulders. You and your experienced trail dog really need to know what you are doing to wander in the Winema. The ranger station in Klamath Falls has more information: 1936 California Ave.; 541/883-6714; ww.fs.fed.us/r6/frewin.

Crescent

If dogs awarded sainthood to humans, Ronda Bishop would be on the short list. As the recreation program manager for the Crescent Ranger District of the

Deschutes National Forest, she has designated eight off-leash play areas around the beach at Crescent Lake.

Winter activities in the area include alpine and nordic skiing at the Willamette Pass Ski Area and miles of roads and trails for snowmobiling, snow shoeing, and skijoring. Crisp air and warm summer days are ideal for fishing, hiking, swimming, and taking to all those trails on a mountain bike.

PARKS, BEACHES, AND RECREATION AREAS

1 Crescent Lake Recreation Area

🐾🐾🐾🐾🐕 (See Southern Oregon map on page 210)

Do doubt about it, this is dogtopia. Cooper and Isis had to pinch each other to make sure they hadn't died and gone to doggy heaven. Crescent Lake is a 4,000-acre, crystal-clear, glacially fed water playground surrounded by silky sand beaches and mountain peaks that make you want to sing, "The hills are alive!" Keep your pets on leash when they are in the campgrounds and wear your mosquito dope in June and July. Day-use areas are open 6 A.M.–10 P.M. Crescent Ranger District: 541/433-3200.

Take the Crescent Cut-Off Road from the center of town in Crescent on U.S. Highway 97, turn right toward Oakridge on State Route 58, and go 3.5 miles to Road 60, to Crescent Lake Campgrounds-Resort-Marina. It's another 2.2 miles to the Y junction that is the start of all recreation around the lake. From Eugene, the lake is 70 miles southeast on State Route 58. The off-leash areas (OLAs) are:

North Simax: This is the only OLA on the south shore. There is paved parking, a latrine, picnic tables, and the most beautiful wide and long beach you can imagine with a gentle slope into the water. Go straight to the left when the road forks right to the campground.

Crescent Lake Campground: This area is only practical if you are staying in the campground. It is small and steep, to the right of the old boat launch. It's .3 mile to the right of the Y junction. There is a $5 parking fee at this area.

Day-Use Areas: There is limited dirt parking in two pullouts. If you're the first ones there, you'll probably get to keep the area to yourselves. No facilities. Go right at the Y intersection, 3.3 miles.

Tranquil Cove: The cove has picnic tables, garbage, gravel parking, a potty, and a designated swimming beach marked by posts driven into the ground. The OLAs are to the outsides of the pylons, left and right. Head right at the Y, four miles.

Tandy Bay: Walk a few yards through the woods at this bay to the beach, to a single picnic table with a phenomenal lake view and a peek at Diamond Peak behind you. The whole area is off leash. Right at the Y, 4.5 miles.

Spring Campground: This is the last access area off of the paved road. The OLA is to the right of the boat launch. In addition to a lovely crescent of beach, there are high grass fields for olfactory exploration. Right at the Y, 5.5 miles. There is a $5 parking fee at this area.

Contorta Point: The lake saves its best for last. This beach is an interesting mix of sand and crumbly volcanic pumice. Views of Diamond Peak take up the entire skyline. As of press time, there was no charge to stay at the undeveloped campground. Right at the Y,

7.5 miles, left at Cortorta Point turnoff, and 0.5 mile to the first campground road and OLA. The last two miles are on a dirt road.

🛂 Diamond Peaks Wilderness–Fawn Lake Trail

🐾🐾🐾 (See Southern Oregon map on page 210)

The official distance to Fawn Lake from the trailhead was three miles on the sign, but someone had crossed that out and written in four. It sure seems longer, perhaps because of the continuous elevation gain and hot, dusty trail. The higher you go, the better the views get, so the moderately steep trail isn't the only thing that will take your breath away. Signs will direct you if you want to branch off in the direction of Pretty Lake, Stag Lake, and Diamond Peak Lake for even more mileage and vistas. Water and some form of bug deterrent are essential traveling companions.

Park at the Crescent Lake Campground and watch for the busy road you must cross at the beginning of the hike. Parking is $5.

PLACES TO EAT

KJ's Café: Sure, dogs are allowed on the covered porch, where they can plead earnestly for a bite of your omelet, pancakes, burger, sandwich, or salad. KJ's also has a lengthy kids' menu, great chili, ice cream, and milk shakes. Milepost 69, Hwy. 58; 541/433-2005.

PLACES TO STAY

Crescent Lake Campground: Of the 44 tent/RV sites, #37 is the choicest spot, with direct access to the off-leash beach. Fees are $13 for premium lakefront sites and $11 for the rest, on a first-come, first-served basis. Follow the signs to the campground from Road 60. 541/433-3200.

Roseburg

Roseburg is the center point of The Land of Umpqua, a major river system that provides public parks, hiking trails, and campgrounds that are a source of dog delights in every form. The Roseburg visitors center (410 S.E. Spruce St.; 800/444-9584; www.visitroseburg.com) publishes a self-guided tour map that takes you in four directions, literally and figuratively—Historic South, Wine West, Cultural North, and Scenic East. Isis pointed her paw due east for the best outdoor adventures.

PARKS, BEACHES, AND RECREATION AREAS

🛃 Singleton Park

🐾🐾 (See Southern Oregon map on page 210)

The story goes that would-be farmer George Singleton had his eye on a plot of land owned by farmer Charles Curry. Charles finally relented and sold it to

George, when George did him a favor by fixing a cantankerous Curry farm tractor. Not a bad way to become landed gentry, especially of such a choice plot at the confluence of the North and South Umpqua rivers. This postage-stamp-sized park was the first land purchased by Douglas County in 1951. A jug of wine, a loaf of bread, and dog need be your only companions as you rest in the shade of the dark green leaves of the myrtlewood trees.

Part of the park's appeal is that it's out a ways, past vineyards, orchards, and farms. Take Garden Valley Parkway west, turn left on Curry Road and right on North Curry Road to the end.

🛑 Riverside Park

😛 (See Southern Oregon map on page 210)

When everyone is hot, sweaty, and tired from driving the super slab of I-5, you can all dog-pile out of the car onto the shady green lawns of this park in the backyard of the Roseburg visitors center. The grass slopes to the water, but your entrance is blocked by thick brush and trees, so you'll have to enjoy the river simply for its cooling breezes and refreshing sound. The gardens surrounding the park and center are full of rhododendron bushes, especially pretty in bloom in May.

From I-5, take Exit 124 onto State Route 138 and turn right on S.E. Oak Street, following the signs to the visitors center. Open dawn–dusk.

🛑 Whistler's Bend

😛😛😛😛 (See Southern Oregon map on page 210)

Like Cooper, your dog may gleefully and vocally greet the many sheep, wild deer, and turkeys you'll encounter on the rolling foothills surrounding this county park. The Wonder Wieners highly recommend this remote, beautiful spot along the North Umpqua River. The picnic area is on the north side of the bend, with front row seats on the wide, strong water. Watch the current carefully if you or your dog decide to take a dip. The swings and slides are shaded by myrtlewood and pine trees, which are also used as obstacles for a very challenging disc golf course. The only flush toilets are in the campground, around the bend on the south side, far enough away that you'll want to hop in the car to reach them.

The road to the park is 12 miles east of Roseburg on State Route 138. Follow the sign to turn on Whistler Park Road and travel patiently until it dead-ends into the park.

PLACES TO EAT

Anthony's Italian Café: Dine out or takeout, lunch and dinner at this pasta place feature at least 20 specialty dishes, plus pizzas, subs, soups, antipasto, and salads. Sip Chianti or bottled and tap beer with your meal on the large concrete patio. You won't regret accepting the challenge to save room for Mama Carole's cheesecake. 500 S.E. Cass Ave.; 541/229-2233.

Gay '90s Ice Cream and Deli: We don't know if the name of this café is referring to the 1890s or the 1990s. Your dog certainly won't care as long as you feed him bits of your sandwich and legendary Umpqua ice cream at one of three outdoor tables. 925 W. Harvard Ave.; 541/672-5679.

PLACES TO STAY

Big K Guest Ranch: City dogs looking for a taste of the country will find that this is as authentic as it gets, about an hour's drive northwest from Roseburg. The "driveway" winds along a dirt road for four miles through a 2,500 acre working ranch with 200 head of cattle, 400 ewes and lambs, and free-range turkeys. As you round the final bend, spread before you are a lodge and 20 cabins on a plateau among the hills overlooking the Umpqua River. The 10,000-square-foot lodge is grand in every way, with a dining hall, river rock fireplace, and a game room all flanked by stunning views through banks of massive windows. The wheelchair-accessible cabins are simple, with various bed arrangements. Plan to eat in the lodge, because there's nothing else for miles, and meals feature steak, salmon, quail, catfish, chicken, and homemade desserts. If your dogs are prone to wandering or chasing wildlife, you might want to keep them leashed, it's up to you. Rates range $325–340 per night, including meals. Hwy 138 W., Elkton; 800/390-2445; www.big-k.com.

Sutherlin Inn: Although it's 15 minutes north of Roseburg, we had to include this spotless motel, which offers the best quality for the price in this entire book, including Wi-Fi, cookies and bagels, cable TV, tubs, and a guest laundry, at rates starting at $40 (40 bucks!), plus a $10 pet fee. Rooms are spare and modern, and the beds are "chiropractor-approved." A lawn out back is handy for pit stops. 1400 Hospitality Pl., Sutherlin; 541/459-6800.

More Accommodations: Please look under *Chain Hotels* in the *Resources* section for additional places to stay in this area.

Diamond Lake

Diamond Lake has the most developed national forest facilities in Oregon. For more information before you go, call the visitors center at 541/793-3333.

PARKS, BEACHES, AND RECREATION AREAS

6 Umpqua National Forest–Diamond Lake

😹 😹 😹 (See Southern Oregon map on page 210)

The crystal waters of the lake sparkle at 5,182 feet, a mile above sea level. For sea dogs, there are boat rentals of all breeds—pedal boats, patio boats, dinghies with dinky motors, kayaks, canoes, and bumper boats. For landlubbers, an 11-mile paved, multi-use trail circles the entire lake. Humans can rent bicycles at the lake's resort to do the double-digit mileage. Resort management is low-key about allowing dogs off leash to run around the ball field and go swimming, but the trail passes through several government-managed campgrounds where you should leash up. Winter recreation includes innertubing, ice skating, and snowmobiling.

Diamond Lake is five miles north of Crater Lake on State Route 138.

PLACES TO STAY

Diamond Lake Resort: Dogs are welcome in both the durable cabins and rooms in the lodge for $5 each per night. Thick-furred animals will do fine in the cabins, heated only by woodstoves. Italian greyhounds and Chihuahuas might prefer the warmer lodge. The resort includes restaurants, a general store, and boat and bicycle rentals (snowmobile and Sno-Cat tours in winter). Motel rooms are $85–100, cabins are $150–190 for up to six people. 350 Resort Dr.; 800/733-7593; www.diamondlake.net.

Steamboat Inn: For a small dog, Isis has a fairly large vocabulary, yet even she ran out of adjectives to describe the beauty of this area along the North Umpqua River and this historic fly-fishing camp, revamped as an upscale haven for recreational activities near Crater and Diamond lakes. It's 38 miles east of Roseburg on Highway 138, and about 45 miles west of Diamond Lake. Pets are allowed in the glamorous Hideaway Cottages, 0.5 miles of solitude down the road from the main inn; and in the practical Camp Water Houses, leased from Oregon State Parks and the U.S. Forest Service. There are no pet fees or restrictions. Rates for two people are $210 a night. Dinners at the inn are legendary and cost $50–85 per person extra. Hiking and fishing excursions are often arranged for guests. 42705 N. Umpqua Hwy. 138, Steamboat; 800/840-8825 or 541/498-2230; www.thesteamboatinn.com.

Union Creek

Pick a trail, any trail, and you can't go wrong. All of them follow the splashy spectacle of the Rogue River and Union Creek, through rapids and waterfalls, lava tubes, beaver dams, and log jams. Some lead you to volcanic rock formations and pumice flats, or deep into canopies of Douglas fir. The trails can be accessed reliably June–October; during winter months, the region is a popular snowmobile and cross-country skiing playground. While hiking, you'll probably need to exercise restraint, otherwise known as a leash, to keep your dog out of the water. The adjectives used to describe the river—such as wild, raging, and swift—do not exaggerate, and no one wants to see their dog get swept away by strong currents.

PARKS, BEACHES, AND RECREATION AREAS

7 Natural Bridge Trail

🐾🐾🐾🐾 🐾 (See Southern Oregon map on page 210)

The Natural Bridge is a lava tube, carved through rock by the molten flow. The Rogue River now follows the same path, disappearing underground for several hundred yards before emerging in a roiling rage downstream. Viewpoints around the formation are accessible on a paved walkway. Near the viewpoint bridge is a trailhead that leads to a 3.5-mile trail following the Westside of the Upper Rogue River south to Woodruff picnic area. Much of the time you'll be treading on mossy lava rock, alternating between sheltering old-growth forest and open brush.

Travel nine miles north on State Route 62 from Prospect and look for signs to the Natural Bridge Viewpoint. If you crave more, continue south another 4.6 miles to the River Bridge campground, along a section known as the Takelma Gorge Trail.

8 Rogue Gorge Trail

🐾🐾🐾🐾 🐾 (See Southern Oregon map on page 210)

On a 0.25-mile paved loop, there are four scenic viewpoints that demonstrate the power of water over time to slice through solid rock. It is simply spectacular, even more so during spring runoff in June. A 3.5-mile trail starts at the southern end of the loop, traveling along the east side of the river down to the Natural Bridge area. The sometimes rocky, mostly level trail is easy, featuring rock formations called potholes, carved by churning river currents. Your dog will get a kick out of watching you drool for a change, your mouth agape, awed by the scenery.

Travel north on State Route 62 approximately 12 miles from Prospect to the parking lot. A latrine is the only amenity.

PLACES TO EAT

Beckie's Restaurant: Although they are tasty, no one would blame you if you skipped past the burgers, sandwiches, and chicken-fried steak and went straight to the homemade pies. Dogs feel no guilt when eating dessert first, nor for chowing down on steak and eggs for breakfast, and they've been doing it here for more than 80 years. Order to go and eat at the tables in front of the ice cream shop next door. 56484 Hwy. 62; 541/560-3563.

Prospect and Shady Cove

These tiny burgs are mere spots of community along the Rogue-Umpqua Scenic Byway (State Route 138), also known as the Highway of Waterfalls, leading to the wilderness, forests, and high mountain lakes of the Oregon Cascades. The area has drawn famous anglers, including Western novelist Zane Grey, to its fishing holes and nature trails. Pick up USFS maps for the hikes along the Rogue River at the Prospect ranger station (47201 Hwy. 62; 541/560-3400).

PARKS, BEACHES, AND RECREATION AREAS

🐾 Lost Lake Trail

🐾🐾🐾 (See Southern Oregon map on page 210)

The Dachsie Twins prefer skipping the crowds at Joseph Stewart State Park and traveling the far side of the lake on this trail instead. It's 2.4 miles from this trailhead to a viewpoint called The Grotto. Pick up a U.S. Army Corps of Engineers map of all the trails around Lost Creek Lake at the state park on your way. On the back of the map is a species list of hundreds of birds, mammals, flora, and fauna you may see. While you should leash your dog to keep her paws out of the poison ivy, there are places where she can slip into the water for a quick dip.

Start at the Lewis Road Trailhead, reached by traveling north of the state park on State Route 62, and turning left onto Lewis Road for a mile.

🔟 Joseph H. Stewart State Park

🐾🐾 (See Southern Oregon map on page 210)

This State Recreation Area is the place to go for family reunions and big gatherings. The whole place is like one big, happy family in the summer anyway, parked on wide, open plains aside Lost Creek Lake. It's a big park, mostly taken up by endless campsites. Dogs will undoubtedly prefer the separate day-use area, southwest of the campground, with room to roam along the lake, and a store, café, marina, and boat launch. There are 5.5 miles of trails in the park along the south shore, from the dam to the picnic area and up to the campground.

Take State Route 62 from Shady Cove northeast to Lost Creek Lake. Parking is $3. Open 6 A.M.–7 P.M.

PLACES TO EAT

Phil's Frosty: Bunches of umbrella-shaded picnic tables are outside the order window. Inside the hot pink shed is the standard fare you're supposed to eat on summer vacation. There are hot dogs, burgers, burritos, fries, and onion rings for the main course; doughnuts and hard and soft ice cream are for dessert. 22161 Hwy. 62, Shady Cove; 541/878-2509.

PLACES TO STAY

Edgewater Inn: The Rogue River runs right past your room at this spiffy motel, and your pooch can do the same at the dog run in the back. The rooms are fresh and simple with white pine furniture and Danish accents. Continental breakfast is included. Summer rates range from $115 for parking lot views up to $170 for a room with a king-size bed, spa, and patio on the river; winter rates are lower. The pet fee is $7. 7800 Rogue River Rd., Shady Cove; 541/878-3171; www.edgewaterinns.com.

Prospect Historical Hotel, Motel, and Dinnerhouse: Behind the original 1892 stagecoach inn is a simpler motel that is more suitable for families with dogs and children. Nice, clean canines (even gorillas, according to the policy) are allowed in the motel rooms at no charge. Dog treats are provided at check-in with a map of where to play and potty. There's a huge groomed field with a little creek to wade in. Rooms are $80–110, $10 pet fee per visit. 391 Mill Creek Dr., Prospect; 800/944-6490; www.prospecthotel.com.

Merlin and Galice

These two villages mark a section of the Rogue River that is most famous for rafting and salmon and steelhead fishing. Drive the historic Rogue River Loop, between Exits 61 and 71 off of I-5, to trace the struggles between early pioneers and native inhabitants during the Rogue Indian Wars of 1852–1856. The battles erupted largely due to the Oregon Donation Land Act, passed by congress to allow settlers to stake claims to Native American lands without consent or treaties. Today the river remains as turbulent as the area's history. Dozens of scenic pullouts line the waterfront, with fishing access near river riffles, which Isis learned is water lingo for miniature rapids. However, as a miniature dachshund, she does not feel it is appropriate to call her a *diffle*.

PARKS, BEACHES, AND RECREATION AREAS

🐾 Indian Mary Historic Reservation

🐾🐾🐾 (See Southern Oregon map on page 210)

What was once the smallest Native American reservation in the United States is now a 61-acre, well-kept county park. Indian Mary filed a homestead application in 1884 and was granted the land in honor of her father, known as

Umpqua Joe, who had warned settlers of a planned massacre, saving the lives of settlers and Native Rogues. The county purchased Mary's property from her descendants in 1958.

It is a showpiece park with lawns of golf-course-green perfection. Wet noses go into overdrive sniffing the many varieties of trees, including Japanese fern, maple, flowering cherry, Port Orford cedars, pines, fir, oak, walnut, and Pippin apple trees from an old orchard. Isis spent most of her time inspecting the tall grape arbor that divides the RV sites from the tent camping area. The park is on the banks of the Rogue River, with the picnic area closest to the water, and the campground loops above. The hosts who care for this park obviously take great pride in keeping it well maintained. Its level spaces are excellent for handicapped users. There are accessible camping plots and an ADA-rated fishing platform.

From I-5, take Exit 61 and follow Merlin-Galice Road five miles north of Galice. www.co.josephine.or.us (click "Parks" under "Departments").

🐾🐾 Griffin Park

🐾🐾 (See Southern Oregon map on page 210)

Despite the Swim at Your Own Risk signs, the river is long and calm beside this quiet, cozy park. And, leash laws aside, we saw dogs chasing Frisbees at their own risk, as well. Griffin pales in comparison to Indian Mary, but then again, it's not as crowded. Plastic climbing equipment and a wooden bridge over a tributary creek provide the kind of simple pleasures kids and dogs appreciate.

From U.S. Highway 199, go north on Riverbanks Road for six miles and turn right on Griffin Road.

PLACES TO EAT

Backroad Grill: The quality and variety of the gourmet food available at this restaurant "on the road to the Rogue" comes as a bit of a surprise is such a tiny, unassuming town. Even better yet, if you are staying at a place with an oven, many dishes are available in individually sized take-and-bake options. Try Chinese pork with peppers, pineapple, and water chestnuts; chicken Divan with Mornay sauce and Parmesan; or eggplant moussaka with feta, tomato, and béchamel sauce. After roughing it on the river, it doesn't get any better than this. Open 4–8 P.M. Wednesday–Sunday May–December 15. 330 Galice Rd.; 541/476-4019.

Galice Resort: Lunches are simple and filling at this roadside stop. Try a famous river burger, for example, the Widowmaker, with Swiss cheese and jalapeño peppers. The dinner menu adds great choices like vegetarian lasagna, breaded fantail shrimp, and homemade strawberry shortcake. In the summer, there's a big barbecue spread Friday and Saturday nights and a famous Sunday brunch buffet. Open seasonally, May–November. 11744 Galice Rd.; 541/476-3818; www.galice.com.

PLACES TO STAY

Indian Mary Campground: This county park has been named one of the 10 best camping spots in Oregon. There are 91 spaces, 35 of which are for tents on amazingly level, tidy plots. Tent sites are $13 in the off-season and $15 April–October. If you call ahead for reservations—and you'll need to in the summer—there is an additional $5 fee. 800/452-5687; www.reserveamerica.com.

Grants Pass

An 18-foot-tall caveman on the lawn of the visitors center (1995 N.W. Vine St.; 541/476-5510; www.visitgrantspass.org) welcomes you to this city, commemorating the oldest inhabitants of the area. Grants Pass brags about its ideal climate that gets warmer earlier than the rest of the valley but stays cooler as the summer heat beats down farther south. Parks in and around the city showcase the Rogue River, the whitewater rafting capital of Oregon. For a change of pace and more local color, travel the Rogue River Highway (State Route 99), which roughly parallels I-5 through the area.

PARKS, BEACHES, AND RECREATION AREAS

🔢 Schroeder Park

🐾🐾🐾 (See Southern Oregon map on page 210)

Schroeder County Park is a great destination that manages to give off a country vibe, even though it's within whistling distance of downtown. Separate areas of the park are neatly divided by rows of towering trees, hills, fences, and sculpted shrubs, adding to the secluded feel. The sports fields and playground are first, fenced off and with a separate parking lot. Next is the campground, a

🖉 DIVERSION

Ferron and Junior the mostly black Lab are co-owners of the only rafting guide service along the Rogue River that allows you to bring your dog along for the ride. **Ferron's Fun Trips** are aptly named, as long as your idea of fun includes getting wet. You can rent your own floating craft or take a tour guided by Junior and Ferron, which Cooper highly recommends. Ferron is a character who knows much about local wildlife, ecosystems, and history. Junior is an experienced guide dog who has been featured on an *Animal Planet* TV special. Take a fishing expedition for game fish, steelhead, and Chinook salmon or a mild Class 2 whitewater trip on the infamous Rogue. Guided raft trips are $50 per person for a half day, $80 for a full day, and include lunch. 541/474-2201; www.roguefuntrips.com.

loop with a large lawn in the center designed for croquet or badminton. Most dogs make a beeline for the picnic area, with about the dimensions of a football field, down the hill and alongside the river. There's a barrier-free fishing platform for anglers with special access needs.

From U.S. Highway 199 west of the city, turn right on Willow Lane for a mile to Schroeder Lane. 541/474-5285.

14 Riverside and Baker Parks

🐾🐾🐾 (See Southern Oregon map on page 210)

Several recreation areas along the Rogue River share the Riverside name, but this one is the coolest among them, especially for a picnic. The grass goes on for 26 acres, mature trees provide soothing shade, and the river burbles alongside.

The grounds include the Josephine County Peace Memorial, a rose garden, decent restroom facilities, and plenty of picnic shelters to go around. The big playground has a real tractor, scoop truck, and steamroller to climb on. Wheelchair-accessible pathways wind through the trees, and there are ample parking places. Across the parking lot, Baker Park adds a public boat ramp and more restrooms into the appealing mix.

From I-5, take Exit 58 to State Route 99, which becomes N.W. 6th Street through town. Cross the river and turn onto E. Park Street. Open 7 A.M.–10 P.M.

15 Tom R. and Watta B. Pearce Park

🐾🐾🐾 (See Southern Oregon map on page 210)

This 108-acre county park is elongated, providing multiple meadows, woods, fields, and trails along the Rogue River. There were dogs everywhere the day Coop 'n' Isis visited, including an agility course for corgis set up at the far end. The river access trail is short and sweet. You have to stay away from the little Wildlife Sanctuary, which leaves you about 107 other acres to enjoy. Caution: The river is faster and deeper than it looks. There's plenty to do without getting in the water.

Take Exit 55 from I-5. Turn left on Agness Avenue. At the stop sign, turn left on Foothill Boulevard. Take the right fork in the road onto Pearce Park Road when Foothill turns to go under the highway. It's an additional 1.1 miles to the park entrance. Open 8 A.M.–8 P.M. Parking is $2. 3700 Pearce Park Road.

PLACES TO EAT

Blue Stone Bakery and Coffee Café: The Blue Stone's menu is more extensive and healthier than a typical coffeehouse, with fabulous soups and choices like stuffed potatoes, chicken burritos, and the "Yougonnalikeit," a deluxe sandwich that approximates a Thanksgiving dinner between two slices of bread. Okay, so the pastries, cakes, and puddings aren't exactly healthy, but they are so fine! Outdoor seating and free wireless Internet are available. 412 N.W. 6th St.; 541/471-1922.

La Burritta: This restaurant serves large portions of all your Tex-Mex favorites, plus a wide selection of Mexican beers and margaritas, at your covered patio table. The management requests that you sit with your dog along the edge of the deck. The menu features an entire page of fajita and seafood specialties with plenty of zing. 941 S.E. 7th St.; 541/471-1444.

PLACES TO STAY

Redwood Motel: Three ground-floor rooms in the older section of this tidy motel are reserved for pets. Rooms are big, the TVs are huge, and the grass out back is wide and soft. Rates range $80–125 per night; the pet fee is $10, which buys a couple of biscuits at check-in. 815 N.E. 6th St.; 541/476-0878; www .redwoodmotel.com.

Riverside Inn: This resort is a grand affair, covering three city blocks. It's the only lodging on the river in town, and the five pet-friendly rooms have river views. Standard rates are $125–150, but there are often specials. The dog fee is $10. 971 S.E. 6th St.; 541/476-6873 or 800/334-4567; www.riverside-inn.com.

Schroeder County Park Campground: This is a serene and outdoorsy campground close to the city with 54 sites, 22 of them designated for tents in a separate loop. $15 for tents or $20 for hookup sites; 800/452-5687; www.reserveamerica.com.

More Accommodations: Please look under *Chain Hotels* in the *Resources* section for additional places to stay in this area.

Jacksonville

This well-preserved historic district was founded in 1852 by gold prospectors. When the railroad bypassed the town in the 1890s, so did commercial development, leaving the town captured in time. Citizens with excellent foresight began preserving and restoring this history in the 1960s, and now more than 100 of its buildings are listed on the National Historic Register. People have thoughtfully placed water bowls outside the homes and businesses everywhere to refresh your thirsty pup. You might want to avoid the town on Britt Music Festival Nights (www.brittfest.org), when throngs of concertgoers, without dogs in attendance, take up all the parking spots in town.

PARKS, BEACHES, AND RECREATION AREAS

16 Sarah Zigler Interpretive Trail

😸😸😸 (See Southern Oregon map on page 210)

This mile-long trail follows the Jackson Creek, where gold was first discovered in 1851. An excellent and extensive brochure and map is available. It's a good idea to follow the city's request to keep your dogs on leash, because poison oak grows heartily in the area (remember, "Leaves of three, let it be"). Coop saw lots of poop on the trail, so please do your part not to add to the problem.

From Oregon Street southbound into Jacksonville, turn right on C Street. The trail begins across the street from the visitors center parking lot, at the entrance to Britt Park.

🔢 Albert "Doc" Griffin Park
😊 (See Southern Oregon map on page 210)

Dogs don't mind tagging along on trips to this tidy and pretty park, designed mainly with kids in mind. Those kids will tell you that the "bestest" part of Doc's is the Spray Park, custom designed for water play on hot summer days. Dogs will have to settle for stray spray while sitting on the nearby lawn. There's also a big playground, a picnic pavilion, and clean restrooms.

Doc's is on Pine Street between 4th and 5th Streets.

🔢 Cantrall-Buckley
😊😊😊 (See Southern Oregon map on page 210)

Don't rely on first impressions to judge this county park in the country. The initial pull-out is an uninspiring dirt lot, with a single picnic table hidden in tall grass and a sandy riverbank down to a swimming hole. That's just a tease. Keep going, across a single-lane bridge, and you'll come to a campground on the left and an 88-acre picnic area on the right.

You'll want to go all the way down past the group picnic shelters to the south lawn on the banks of the Applegate River, where there's fun play equipment,

NATURE HIKES AND URBAN WALKS

When gold was discovered in Rich Gulch in 1851, the town of Jacksonville sprang up around the prospectors and the gold diggers hoping to profit from them. Development and modernization passed by when the railroads bypassed the town in favor of Medford, and the early character of Jacksonville remained largely unchanged as surrounding communities grew. In 1966, the charm of the city was permanently preserved when the entire town was designated as a National Historic Landmark.

Walk through the past on the **Jacksonville Historic Landmark Walking Tour,** with a brochure from the visitors center (N. Oregon and C Streets) or try a Jacksonville Woodlands Map ($2), listing 15 walking paths and woodland trails around the city, from 0.3 mile to one mile each. 541/899-8118; www.jacksonvilleoregon.org.

bathrooms and showers, a trail, and shade trees. It wouldn't be surprising to find a rope swing somewhere out over the 1.75 miles of river frontage. Take State Route 238 west from Jacksonville, turn left on Hamilton Road, for about a mile. Parking is $3. Open 10 A.M.–dusk. 541/899-7155.

PLACES TO EAT

Lutrell's Mustard Seed Café: A rose garden marks the entrance to Lutrell's outdoor patio. The food is named after family and friends; Pop's Covered and Smothered is hash browns and biscuits with sausage gravy, Renee has her own chicken burger, Joel's BLAT is a BLT with avocado, and Millie has a killer Philly. 130 N. 5th St.; 541/899-2977.

MacLevin's Whole Foods Deli, Bakery, and Ice Cream Parlor: This authentic Jewish deli is the place to nosh on pastrami, knishes, and potato latkes, oy vey! All-day breakfast and lunch are served at a couple of outdoor tables. Or, you could take your matzo ball soup, herring in sour cream, borscht, and lox to go. 150 W. California St.; 541/899-1251.

PLACES TO STAY

Jacksonville Inn: Cooper and Isis are on their very best behavior at this glamorous inn. It is rare that an establishment of this caliber accepts pets, and they'd like to keep it that way. Two guest rooms and one cottage combine tasteful Victorian opulence with modern conveniences in the heart of town. The owner requests that she be allowed to meet every dog, that they sleep in their own beds, not hers, and that they not be left alone in the room, which goes without saying. The inn has an elegant restaurant, casual bistro, and wine shop. Rooms are $160–200; decadent cottages are $270–465. You get what you pay for. 175 E. California St.; 541/899-1900; www.jacksonvilleinn.com.

Stage Lodge: Well-behaved pets are welcome at this "anti-motel" with real colonial furniture and designer bath fixtures. Rooms are all nonsmoking. Rates are $100–115; honeymoon suites with fireplaces and jetted tubs are $175. 830 N. 5th St.; 800/253-8254; www.stagelodge.com.

Cantrall-Buckley County Park Campground: It costs $10 to overnight at this quiet county campground, not including quarters for the coin-operated showers. The 42 first-come, first-served sites are well shaded, but too close together to be private. www.jacksoncountyparks.com.

Medford

The working-class cousin of Ashland, Medford is the largest and most commercial city in Southern Oregon. It is surrounded by a rich agricultural valley dominated by pear orchards and vineyards. Many of the region's delectable goodies can be found at famous **Harry and David** (1314 Center Dr.; www.harryanddavid.com). Medford is a good central location from which to explore the Applegate Valley, named for pioneers Jesse and Lindsay Applegate, trail-blazers of Southern Oregon in 1846. Not as quaint as Ashland or Jacksonville, Medford has its merits in less expensive lodging and nearby winery tours.

North of Medford in Eagle Point is the oldest and largest training facility for hearing-assistance dogs in the nation. Tours of **Dogs for the Deaf** are free, but you are welcome to make a donation to the privately funded facility. See how rescued pups are trained for a higher calling as service dogs for the deaf and hearing-impaired. There are areas where your pup can wait for you; visiting dogs would be too disruptive to those in training (10175 Wheeler Rd.; 541/826-9220; www.dogsforthedeaf.org).

PARKS, BEACHES, AND RECREATION AREAS

19 TouVelle State Park

😾 😾 😾 (See Southern Oregon map on page 210)

So much of this region calls for activity—trails to hike, mountains to climb, rivers to navigate—that it is refreshing to come across a park tailor-made for doing little other than lying in the shade of a tree alongside a quiet river. This State Recreation Site is one of the few places where the Rogue calms down, gliding past the foot of the Table Mountains. Large trees shade the rolling grassy slopes dotted with picnic tables. Even when busy, there's plenty of room for everybody. Relaxation runs rampant.

From State Route 62, turn west on Antelope Road and right on Table Rock Road. Parking is $3 per day.

20 Bear Creek Dog Park

😾 😾 😾 🐕 (See Southern Oregon map on page 210)

Bear Creek Park is a 100-acre expanse of rolling hills with a litany of fancy amenities, including a skate park, amphitheater, playground, tennis courts, barbecue areas, a BMX bicycle track, and restrooms. Best of all, it is the location of Medford's only off-leash area, a good-sized two acres, secured all around by a sturdy, tall fence with a double-entry gate. A blend of open field and tree-covered shade, bushes to sniff, and a dirt path around the perimeter suit every dog's needs. There's a garbage can, a picnic bench, and water to sip, but we didn't see a bag dispenser, so come prepared. We visited at the peak of the dry season, yet the grass was still lush, watered, and maintained.

The main parking lot is on Siskiyou Boulevard, but there's a back way to sneak in directly to the off-leash area. From I-5, take Exit 27 east onto Barnett Road. Turn left immediately on Alba Drive in front of the Dairy Queen and park at the Little League field. Follow the signs across a wooden footbridge to reach the dog park entrance. Hours are 6 A.M.–10:30 P.M. 541/774-2400; www.playmedford.com.

Alba Park

🐾🐾 (See Southern Oregon map on page 210)

It's easy to imagine this lovely little park as the social center of downtown Medford. Dedicated to the city by Charles and Callie Palm in 1934, it has the formal quadrangle design of that era, with a gazebo and a fountain in the center of diagonal sidewalks. Next to the fountain is a statue of a young man, surely it's Charles, kneeling to pet two Irish setters. The thick maple trees lining the square lawn must have been around since the beginning. As the historic heart of downtown Medford is rapidly being restored, Alba revels in its former glory. This rarified atmosphere is appropriate for a walk, but probably not for mutts who want to mess around.

Alba Park is at the corner of Holly and Main Streets.

22 Hawthorne Park

🐾🐾🐾 (See Southern Oregon map on page 210)

There's room to roam at Hawthorne, enough for Friends of the Animal Shelter to hold a benefit parade annually on the expansive lawn. Picnic tables are smartly placed under the few shade trees. Isis adores the elaborate rose garden, where No Pruning signs admonish humans tempted to take flowers home. Dogs, that means no digging, either.

The park is across the street from Medford Center Mall, which has a Cold Stone Creamery ice cream shop. At the corner of Jackson and Hawthorne Streets. Open 6 A.M.–10:30 P.M.

PLACES TO EAT

Corks Wine Bar and Bottle Shoppe: Drink outdoors and enjoy antipasti, cheese and fruit plates, hummus and crackers, and chocolate truffles with your dog at a patio table or even up on the roof deck, near the restored Craterian Ginger Rogers Theatre. Corks carries only the best Washington and Oregon wines, of which there are many to please your palate. 235 Theater Alley; 541/245-1616; www.corks-wineshoppe.com.

PLACES TO STAY

In this area, chain hotels listed in the *Resources* section offer the best choices for dogs and their owners.

Ashland

This cultured, artistic town is world famous thanks to a guy named Bill who wrote great plays. Founded in 1935, the Oregon Shakespeare Festival has grown and evolved to present music, dance, and theater far beyond the Bard. The Plaza, a triangle in the center of town, is the hotspot for theater, shopping, and an entire row of restaurants with "creekside dining," a block-long outdoor patio. It's public space, where dogs can join you while you dine.

It's a shame that dogs are not allowed in Ashland city parks, excluded even from famous Lithia Park. However, the dirt roads and trails in the mountains above the town are fair game, and you'll meet many canine locals up in them thar hills. Gardening is a high art in evidence everywhere, especially at the many lovely B&Bs.

PARKS, BEACHES, AND RECREATION AREAS

23 Ashland Boyd County Dog Park
🐾🐾🐾🐾 🦮 (See Southern Oregon map on page 210)

The ABCD park, for short, is completely fenced, grassy, and graced by shade trees and scattered bushes. There's a covered shed (with a couch inside) for waiting out the rain, and a plastic swimming pool and water fountains for both species. A dozen or so lawn chairs are scattered around for impromptu seating in addition to a couple of picnic tables. Smack dab in the middle is a built-in trash bin with a bunch of garden shovels leaning against it. Why bother with bags or mitts when you can simply shovel the you-know-what?

The OLA is two parks in one: a two-acre, sloping lawn for the big boys, and a separately fenced, little spot with its own entrance for small or timid dogs. Cooper figures that now is as good a time as any to reveal his darkest secret: He is afraid of dog parks. Gasp! How can it be? For starters, practically everybody is bigger than he is and, sadly, his scars bear witness to prior dog attacks before he was rescued. What a treat to have his own space, complete with a miniature copse of trees for him to anoint.

From the center of town, turn east onto Oak Street for about a mile, turn left on Nevada, and right onto Helman, which looks like a driveway, past the

🐾 DOG-EAR YOUR CALENDAR

Every year in late October, the Friends of the Animal Shelter (FOTAS) in Ashland host an annual **Puss 'n' Boots Costume Ball** and silent auction to benefit the Jackson County Animal Shelter in nearby Phoenix, Oregon. The cost is a worthwhile $35 per person, with all funds raised going to pay the salary of a full-time coordinator who wrangles more than 100 volunteers to keep the shelter running smoothly.

In nearby Jacksonville, the annual **Mutt Strut** parade is held in May, sponsored by the Jacksonville Animal Hospital, with all funds raised also going to FOTAS. 541/774-6646; www.fotas.org.

Ashland Greenhouses. You can also connect to the Bear Creek Greenway Trail from this location. Open dawn–dusk. 541/488-5340; www.abcdogpark.com.

🐾 Ashland Watershed Area

🐾🐾🐾 (See Southern Oregon map on page 210)

It took some digging in the dirt, but Cooper and Isis finally got the local sheriff to spill the beans on the best kept secret in these parts. We're not sure what to call these wooded areas above town, but eat your heart out long-distance dogs, there's probably 20 miles of dirt roads and trails up here, free for all. Sheriff said to be aware of the homeless people that sometimes camp up here, and you're even more likely to encounter and be bothered by prolific poison oak, so stay on the dirt pack.

Don't mind the green gate, past it is an old rock quarry you can roam around; don't mind the yellow gate, past it are old police training grounds you can use as an impromptu agility course. Another trail, just before both gates, leads beside, over, under and in Asford Creek.

From State Route 99 southbound into town, as soon as it becomes E. Main Street turn right on Granite Street, one street north of the plaza. Drive out Granite about 1.5 miles or until you can't go any farther, past the water tank, past where the pavement ends, and just to the right at the intersection with Glenview Drive. There are several head-in parking areas. Even if you don't make it to the trails, the Ashland Creek Loop dirt road above town provides a bird-dog's-eye view of the city, frequented by local joggers and their sidekicks.

🐾 Siskiyou Mountain Park and Todd Oredson Woods

🐾🐾🐾 (See Southern Oregon map on page 210)

If you enjoy the nightlife, shopping, and culture of staying in Ashland *and* you want to do some more serious trekking, you're in luck. Above the city on the west side are 270 acres of single-track trails connecting the Pacific Crest Trail and the Creek to Crest Byway (no animals on the byway, by the way). You can't really tell where the "woods" leave off and the "park" starts; it's all one big, happy, hiking ground. Just stay on the trail and off private property when signs request, and you're good to go. You might want to leave a trail of breadcrumbs to eat on your way back, as most of this area is unmarked.

South of town, Highway 99 becomes Siskiyou Boulevard. Take the right fork in the road to stay on Siskiyou when you pass the turnoff for State Route 66 to stay. Park on Park Street before Dragonfly Lane, being careful to curb your wheels on this very steep hill. Tamarack Place is another parking possibility; be courteous of the residents and their driveways and mailboxes. Walk uphill on the left fork of the gravel trail, then on the left fork of the dirt trail, to access the woods.

26 Emigrant Lake

🐾🐾🐾 🦴 (See Southern Oregon map on page 210)

Word on the street is that Emigrant Lake is packed with local dogs on weekends. The catch is that they're not allowed in the County Recreation Area, a.k.a. the RV park. Go past the park entry and you'll see at least a half dozen dirt roads with Day Use Area signs. The roads are rough, you're lucky if there's a latrine, and parking is in a dirt patch. Yet, persevere! Rediscover what it means to bound around. Indulge your dock-dog fantasies. There are no leash restrictions; there *are* meadows filled with wildflowers and lots of comfortable entry points along the lake for dog paddling; and you don't have to pay the $3 that dogless people are paying to park in the RV park. Songer Wayside has the best parking.

From I-5, take Exit 14 west on State Route 66 about six miles to the lake. Park closes at sunset.

27 Hyatt Lake

🐾🐾🐾🐾 (See Southern Oregon map on page 210)

The Hyatt Lake Recreation Complex is located a dizzying mile above sea level, so unless you're from Colorado, don't be alarmed if you're a little out of breath. Here's another tip: The higher you go in altitude, the less alcohol it takes to get buzzed. The lake is crystal clear, remote, and surrounded by wilderness and snow-capped peaks. The playground and picnic areas are rudimentary except for a large fire ring, ideal for a bonfire and weenie roast. Cooper suggests you spend time hiking the section of the Pacific Crest Trail that parallels the west side of the lake, accessible from behind the park office. It's especially awe inspiring to play in the winter snow up here in this rarefied air.

From Ashland, take State Route 66 east for 17 miles, past the top of Green Springs Pass. Turn onto Hyatt-Prairie Road and follow the signs. Parking is $3.

PLACES TO EAT

Allyson's Kitchen: It's predictable in this town for things to be named after Shakespearean characters, and Allyson has followed suit in dubbing her sandwiches MacBeth, Shylock, King Lear, etc. Clichéd names aside, they are otherwise exciting and really good. Daily specials are even better, such as chicken and pumpkin tortellini. Order downstairs and they'll bring your food to your sidewalk table. 115 E. Main St.; 541/482-2884.

Greenleaf Restaurant: Of all the restaurants on the plaza, Isis favors this one. The menu is five pages long, with something for even the pickiest palates. Food dishes lean toward the healthy side, and it's all fresh and delicious. 49 N. Main St.; 541/482-2808.

Pangea Grills and Wraps: Meals wrapped in tortillas make for handy, on-the-go lunches and dinners. Get your taste buds tingling with Greek and Mediterranean flavors, then cool down with a mango or peach smoothie.

Order at the counter and relax at a sidewalk table. Your food is brought to you, along with a water dish and some dog biscuits for your dining companion. 272 E. Main St.; 541/552-1630.

Water Street Café: It's a great concept, well suited to a resort town: open-air dining with healthy food ordered from an outdoor bar. Salads, wraps, smoothies, and espresso soothe the savage stomach. Open April–November. Downtown at the corner of Water and Main Streets; 541/482-0206.

PLACES TO STAY

Anne Hathaway's Garden Suites: Guests with pets who opt for the Garden Suites across the street from the main house will find spacious rooms, private entrances, decks overlooking an English garden, kitchenettes, whirlpool tubs, and continental breakfast in a clubhouse. We like Viola, with an enclosed sun porch, and Calla, with its front porch. Everyone will experience the unforgettable, warm hospitality of the innkeepers, which extends to the pets in the form of treats, pick-up bags, and a welcome letter from resident chocolate Lab Cappy. All this brilliance comes at amazing rates as low as $115 in the off-season to $160 in the summer, plus a $10 nightly pet fee. No pets on the antique beds or furniture please. 586 E. Main St.; 800/643-4434 or 541/488-1050, www.ashlandbandb.com.

Ashland Creek: Isis feels she is expensive, but worth it; thus, she finds the Taos Suite ($200/$250/$325 depending on season) at this top-of-the-line establishment to be in suitably good taste. A cool Mexican tile floor graces all 1,200 square feet of the California-king bedroom, two full baths, kitchen, and living and dining rooms. The deck overhangs the creek where the waterwheel used to enter the old mill. Pets may be welcome in other suites on a case-by-case basis, but never on the furniture or beds. The pet fee is $10. 70 Water Street; 541/482-3315; www.ashlandcreekinn.com.

Green Springs Inn: The road to get here, about 17 miles east of Ashland, is worth the price alone. State Route 66 inspires adjectives such as precipitous and convoluted as it winds through deep forests above green valleys to arrive at the top of Green Springs Mountain. Two lodge rooms, #2 downstairs with an outdoor jetted tub and #5 upstairs with an indoor one, are icing on the cake. The rooms are recovering from neglect under new owners in 2008, but they are fine for people who don't want to rough it for recreation at Hyatt Lake. Dogs enjoy almost infinite walking opportunities. Rooms are $120, and there's no pooch tariff. Steaks at the inn's restaurant and summer bonfires add to the enjoyment. 11470 Hwy. 66; 541/482-0614; www.greenspringsinn.net.

Lithia Springs Resort and Gardens: About five minutes north of town, the Lithia Springs' unique garden setting with a backdrop of forested hills is an ideal location for pets who need room to stretch their legs. The owner began allowing dogs in 2008, choosing Irish Suite #4 and ADA-accessible English Cottage #12 for them. Both are roomy and have easy access to the backyard for birding, hiking, and general lolling about. Rates range $140–250; $20 one-time pet fee. 2165 W. Jackson Rd.; 800/482-7128; www.ashlandinn.com.

Plaza Inn and Suites: The Plaza is a sophisticated, modern choice in downtown. Dogs under 60 pounds are allowed in a second building, smaller but equally fancy. Cascade Rooms rates range $90–220 and include a European breakfast. The pet fee is $25. 98 Central Ave.; 541/488-8900; www.plaza innashland.com.

Hyatt Lake Campground: Tent sites are on an opposite shore from the RV sites, with walk-in or drive-in availability. Sites are deeply wooded and widely spaced apart for privacy. Most have views; #T15 is the best. Available June–October. Fees are $12 Monday–Thursday and $15 Friday–Sunday. Hyatt–Howard Prairie Rd. off Hwy. 66; 541/482-2031; www.blm.gov/or (see "Outdoor Recreation" under "Visit Us" on left navigation bar).

More Accommodations: Please look under *Chain Hotels* in the *Resources* section for additional places to stay in this area.

Fort Klamath and Crater Lake

Crater Lake is Oregon's only national park, and as such, your dog is not allowed on trails or in buildings. She can still experience the best part of this natural wonder with you, a 33-mile Rim Road drive encircling the 4,000-foot-deep basin, the remnants of the Mount Mazama volcano that erupted an estimated 7,700 years ago. You have to travel the route slowly as the curves hug the mountains and the water, leaving lots of time for her to hang her head out the window and take in the territory. The full drive is open only during the warmest summer months; the southern entrance and a short drive up to a lake viewpoint and historic lodge are open year-round. The entrance fee is $10 per vehicle (www.nps.gov/crla).

PARKS, BEACHES, AND RECREATION AREAS

28 Jackson F. Kimball

🐾🐾 (See Southern Oregon map on page 210)

Locals will tell you that the best time to visit this State Recreation Site is in September, after the first hard frost kills off the mosquitoes that will drink you dry during spring and summer. A 50-foot path leads to the Wood River Head-waters; on one side is a creek not much wider than a road, and on the other is a panorama of snow-capped mountains and towering pines that our host at CrystalWood Lodge said was "straight out of a John Wayne Western." Despite including a river and a marsh, it is called a dry camp, because none of the water is drinkable. Bring some with you on this short, sweet stop.

From State Route 62, north of Fort Klamath, turn west on Dixon Road and left at the T intersection onto Sun Mountain Road.

29 Collier Memorial

🐾🐾🐾 (See Southern Oregon map on page 210)

The main attraction at Collier is the logging museum, with the largest collection of equipment in the country on 147 acres of state park land. The museum is outdoors, allowing your dogs to enjoy it with you. Self-guided tour brochures are available. The rusting hulks of machinery are left in situ, rain or shine, although it doesn't rain much in this high, dry country. Across the highway, the poor trees in the campground look thirsty and scrawny. The picnic area is greener, with watered lawns leading to the banks of the Williamson River and Spring Creek. Cooper was driven to an ecstatic frenzy by the excess of chipmunks and tiny prairie dogs in the park. If he hadn't been on leash, Isis doubts she would have ever seen him again.

Collier is 30 miles north of Klamath Falls on U.S. Highway 97. Open dawn–dusk. 541/783-2471.

PLACES TO STAY

CrystalWood Lodge: Every detail of this B&B is designed to welcome dogs. After all, owners Liz and Peggy have 21 dogs of their own. You are welcome to meet the troops, 14 of whom who finished the 2008 Iditarod dogsled races in 14 hours. Copies of *Fido Friendly* and *Bark* magazine are in every room, as are kennels, lint/hair remover brushes, and designer doggie-bag holders. You are not required to use the kennels. Extra sheets are provided if your dogs sleep in bed with you. The property encompasses 130 acres, with five miles of trails your hosts have cleared and access to the 10-mile Klamath Lake Canoe Trail. The lodge, an original homestead, is also a phenomenal place for bird-watchers, anglers, and hunters. It's easy to reach, yet secluded between the Winema National Forest and the Upper Klamath National Wildlife Refuge.

You won't mind being sent to the doghouse here, full of games for kids and a self-service dog-wash station. The room rates, ranging $85–215, include unparalleled hospitality and breakfast. In short, Coop 'n' Isis think it's one of the best place for dogs to stay in the region. 38625 Westside Road; 866/381-2322; www.crystalwoodlodge.com.

Klamath Falls

In the Oregon High Country, the only way you and your dog will get cabin fever is by staying in too many of them. Between the Rogue Valley and Klamath Falls are the Cascade Mountains, famous for more than 100 alpine lakes, at least a dozen of which have cabin resorts on their shores.

Klamath County is a high-desert region. You'll leave behind the dreary, drippy Pacific Northwest to an average of 300 days of sunshine yearly. The heat rises up through the ground as well, as most of the city is warmed by underground geothermal energy, a pleasant reminder of an explosive volcanic legacy. In winter, when it's not sunny, it's snowing. Keep traction tires or chains on hand.

PARKS, BEACHES, AND RECREATION AREAS

❸⓪ Link River Nature Trail

🐾 🐾 🐾 (See Southern Oregon map on page 210)

In the summer, a morning stroll along this 1.7-mile gravel trail is best, before it gets too hot to enjoy the meandering river and the many birds. For longer walks, the Link Trail connects to the Lake Ewauna Wingwatchers Nature Trail for another mile. You might see blue herons, white pelicans, mallards, and red-winged blackbirds.

To reach the trailhead parking lot, turn west on Nevada Avenue from U.S. Highway 97. The small, gravel parking area is on the left, shortly after the road becomes Lakeshore Drive and before you round the bend and cross the bridge. Dog walking has recently been allowed in Moore Park as well, further down the same road.

❸❶ Veterans Memorial Park

🐾 🐾 (See Southern Oregon map on page 210)

In this hot, dry town near the California border, this city park may be the only place where you can picnic in the shade of large trees. The football-field-sized lawn also has steps for sitting in the sun, restrooms, and big steam engine trains on display.

It's on the south end of downtown at the bottom of Main Street, which has a couple of great places to grab a picnic lunch before heading to the park.

PLACES TO EAT

Café Paradise: Mexican food and American fare sit side-by-side on the extensive menu, and it's all good. Cooper is biased toward the Mexican side of the border, with to-drool-for quesadillas and deep-fried ice cream. There's easy ordering through a to-go window. 1401 Esplanade; 541/850-2225.

The Daily Bagel: The custom bagel sandwiches, named after big-city U.S. newspapers, are so fat they're almost impossible to fit your mouth around. You're highly likely to drop sandwich filling from your sidewalk table, and nothing would please your pooch more. This news-worthy stop also offers daily soups and Ben and Jerry's ice cream bars. 636 Main St.; 541/850-1809.

PLACES TO STAY

Maverick Motel: This downtown establishment prefers to accept dogs for a couple of days only, not weeks or months. Each pet is $6 per stay, and rates

DIVERSION

You don't have to roam the wilds of Alaska to experience the thrill of dogsled racing. At **Briar's Patch Sled Dogs,** veteran musher Liz Parrish and her team of long-distance racing dogs will take you on an extreme sport wilderness trip, where you'll get to enjoy all of the excitement without doing any of the work.

You won't forget the thrills, from the tension-building moment the dogs are harnessed, bootied, and put into position to the bedlam that erupts as the command is given to "GO!" After whooshing through the forest, you'll return with rosy cheeks and a serious case of perma-grin without the perma-frost. Even in the summer, these eager working dogs are happy to pull you in a rugged, all-terrain cart.

One-hour rides ($60 adult/$35 child) include warm refreshments; half-day ($170 adult/$80 child) and all-day ($300 adult/$145 child) excursions also include lunch. Talk to Liz about dog-sitting for your pups while you're out. 38625 Westside Rd. (based at CrystalWood Lodge); 541/892-3639; www.briarspatchsleddogs.com.

---

range $60–100. Rooms are crisp and clean, with a full list of amenities including continental breakfast and afternoon cookies and milk. Afternoon naps are also encouraged. 1220 Main St.; 541/882-6688 or 800/404-6690; www.maverickmotel.com.

Running Y Ranch Resort Lodge: If you enjoy running with a high-brow crowd, as Isis certainly does, you'll love this upscale Western ranch on the grounds of Oregon's only Arnold Palmer–designed golf course. Everything is as nice as you'd expect, from the leather furniture, timbered ceilings,

and flagstone floors to the views of the greens and surrounding mountains. Rates are $180–210 per night, plus a $25 pet fee. Pet-friendly vacation rental homes are also available. 5500 Running Y Rd.; 541/850-5500 or 888/850-0275; www.runningy.com.

More Accommodations: Please look under *Chain Hotels* in the *Resources* section for additional places to stay in this area.

RESOURCES

Emergency Veterinary Clinics

For better geographic coverage, this list includes clinics that have an emergency veterinarian on call in addition to 24-hour animal clinics.

NORTH COAST

Cloverdale Veterinary Clinic: Doctor on call. 34610 Hwy. 101, Cloverdale; 503/392-3322.

Emergency After-Hours Hotline: Shared answering and referral service for Cloverdale/Tillamook area. 888/437-5278.

Pioneer Veterinary Hospital: Doctor on call. 801 Main Ave., Tillamook; 503/842-8411.

The Tillamook Veterinary Hospital: Doctor on call. 1095 N. Main St., Tillamook; 503/842-7552.

CENTRAL COAST

Animal Medical Care of Newport: Doctor on call. 162 N.E. 10th, Newport; 541/265-6671.

Oceanlake Veterinary Clinic: Doctor on call. 3545 N.W. Hwy. 101; Lincoln City; 541/994-2929.

Osburn Veterinary Clinic: Doctor on call. 130 E. Railroad Ave., Reedsport; 541/271-5824.

Osburn Veterinary Clinic: Doctor on call. 1730 Kingwood, Florence; 541/902-2013.

Emergency Veterinary Hospital: These coastal communities also refer people to the 24-hour clinic in Eugene-Springfield. 103 W. Q St., Springfield; 541/746-0112.

SOUTH COAST

Gold Beach Veterinary Clinic: Doctor on call. 94211 3rd St., Gold Beach; 541/247-2513.

Hanson and Meekins Animal Hospital: Walk-in only, no appointments. Doctor on call after hours. 45 E Lockhart Ave., Coos Bay; 541/269-2415.

Morgan Veterinary Clinic: Doctor on call. 230 Market Ave., Coos Bay; 541/269-5846.

Ocean Boulevard Veterinary Hospital: Doctor on call. 1710 Ocean Blvd. N.W., Coos Bay; 541/888-6713.

Town and Country Animal Clinic: Doctor on call. 15740 Hwy. 101 S., Brookings; 541/469-4661.

GREATER PORTLAND

Dove Lewis Emergency Animal Hospital: 24-hour clinic. 1945 N.W. Pettygrove, Portland; 503/228-7281. Southeast location: after hours 6 P.M.–8 A.M., Mon.–Fri. and weekends. 10564 S.E. Washington St. in Plaza 205; 503/262-7194; www.dovelewis.org.

Southeast Portland Animal Hospital (VCA): 24-hour clinic. 13830 S.E. Stark, Portland; 503/255-8139.

WILLAMETTE VALLEY

Dallas Animal Clinic: Doctor on call. 135 Fir Villa Rd., Dallas; 503/623-3943.

Emergency Veterinary Hospital: 24-hour clinic. 103 W. Q St., Springfield; 541/746-0112.

Newberg Veterinary Hospital: Open seven days a week, plus doctor on call after hours. 3716 Hwy. 99W. Newberg; 503/538-8303.

River's Edge Pet Medical Center: 24-hour animal emergency service. 202 N.W. Hickory St., North Albany; 541/924-1700.

Salem Veterinary Emergency Clinic: After hours 5 P.M.–8 A.M. and weekends only. 3215 Market St. N.E., Salem; 503/588-8082.

Willamette Veterinary Clinic/Animal Emergency and Critical Care Center: 24-hour clinic. 1562 S.W. 3rd St., Corvallis; daytime: 541/753-2223; after-hours emergency: 541/753-5750.

CENTRAL OREGON

Animal Emergency Center of Central Oregon: After hours 5 P.M.–8 A.M. and weekends only. 1245 S. Hwy. 97, Suite C3, Bend; 541/385-9110.

Sisters Veterinary Clinic: Doctor on call. 371 E. Cascade Ave., Sisters; 541/549-6961.

SOUTHERN OREGON

Animal Emergency Service: Doctor on call. 2726 S. 6th St., Klamath Falls; 541/882-9005.

Basin Animal Clinic: Doctor on call. 1776 Washburn Way, Klamath Falls; 541/884-4558.

Southern Oregon Veterinary Specialty Center: 24-hour clinic. 3265 Biddle Rd., Medford; 541/282-7711; www.sovsc.com.

Chain Hotels

The following chains are generally pet friendly; but not every location of every chain allows dogs. If a specific location is listed below, you can expect a warm welcome for your weimaraner; for any unlisted location, call ahead and check with management before arriving with your dog in tow. The listings are organized as follows: restrictions on size, number, or location of pets; pet fees (pet fee is per pet per night unless stated otherwise); and nightly room rates.

BEST WESTERN

The largest hotel chain in the world has a good track record of accepting pets, but not all Best Westerns take pets, and their fees and regulations vary. 800/528-1234; www.bestwestern.com.

Albany–Albany Inn: No restrictions; $10 pet fee; $60–130; 315 Airport Rd.; 541/928-6322.

Ashland–Bard's Inn: Two dogs; $15 pet fee; $90–225; 132 N. Main St.; 541/482-0049.

Ashland–Windsor Inn: No restrictions; $15 pet fee; $80–180; 2520 Ashland St.; 541/488-2330.

Astoria–Lincoln Inn: Three dogs, at managers discretion for size and temperament; $10 pet fee; $80–325; 555 Hamburg Ave.; 503/325-2205.

Bandon–Inn at Face Rock: Dog rooms do not have ocean view, but the beach is dog friendly. No restrictions; $15 for the first dog, $5 each additional dog, per stay; $110–300; 3225 Beach Loop Rd.; 541/347-9441; www.innatfacerock.com.

Bend: No restrictions; pet fee $10, $50 if not declared; $80–150; 721 N.E. 3rd St.; 541/382-1515.

Brookings–Beachfront Inn: No restrictions; $5 pet fee; $120–295; 16008 Boat Basin Rd.; 541/469-7779.

Cascade Locks–Columbia River Inn: No restrictions; $10 pet fee; $80–150; 735 Wanapa St.; 541/374-8777.

Coos Bay–Holiday Motel: Two dogs under 35 pounds; $10 pet fee; $95–180; 411 N. Bayshore Dr.; 541/269-5111.

Corvallis–Grand Manor Inn: Dog-specific rooms, closer to side rooms; $10 pet fee; $85–225; 925 N.W. Garfield; 541/758-8571.

Eugene–Greentree Inn: Two dogs, small pets only, special treat bag given at check-in; $30 deposit per dog, refundable depending on room condition; $90–105; 1759 Franklin Blvd.; 541/485-2727.

Eugene–New Oregon Motel: Two dogs, do not leave dog unattended, special treat bag given at check-in; refundable $30 deposit per dog, depending on room condition; $90–105; 1655 Franklin Blvd.; 541/683-3669.

Eugene South–Creswell Inn: No restrictions; small off-leash area on property; $10 flat fee for all dogs; $75–130; 345 E. Oregon Ave.; 541/895-3341.

Eugene (Springfield)–Grand Manor Inn: No restrictions, do not leave pets unattended; $10 pet fee; $95–175; 971 Kruse Way; 541/726-4769.

Florence–Pier Point Inn: Two dogs; $10 pet fee; $90–400; 85625 Hwy 101 S.; 541/997-7191; www.bestwestern.com/pierpointinn.

Grants Pass–Grants Pass Inn: Content, well-behaved dogs may be left unattended for short periods, such as dinner. Biscuits given at check-in. No restrictions; $10 flat fee per stay; $80–140; 111 N.E. Agness Ave.; 541/476-1117.

Grants Pass–Inn at the Rogue: Grassy hill for on-leash walks; no restrictions; under 20 pounds is $10 per dog per night and $30 refundable deposit; over 20 pounds is $20 per dog per night, and $50 refundable deposit; $65–100; 8959 Rogue River Hwy.; 541/582-2200.

Gresham–Pony Soldier Motor Inn: Small and medium dogs only; no pet fee; $80–130; 1060 N.E. Cleveland Ave.; 503/665-1591.

Hillsboro (Forest Grove)–University Inn and Suites: No restrictions; $10 pet fee; $90–200; 3933 Pacific Ave.; 503/992-8888.

Hood River–Hood River Inn: Treats given at check-in; no restrictions; $12 pet fee; $80–180; 1108 E. Marina Way; 541/386-2200.

Klamath Falls–Klamath Inn: No restrictions; no pet fee; $80–120; 4061 S. 6th St.; 541/882-1200.

Madras–Rama Inn: Treat bag given at check-in. Pets under 30 pounds, four dogs, no pit bulls; $20 per dog per stay; $70–100; 12 S.W. 4th St.; 541/475-6141.

McMinnville–The Vineyard Inn Motel: Limited pet rooms, must call ahead; $10 pet fee; $99–141; 2035 S. Hwy 99W; 503/472-4900.

Medford–Horizon Inn: Across the street from Medford's off-leash dog park; $20 pet fee; $85–130; 1154 Barnett Rd.; 541/779-5085.

Newport–Agate Beach Inn: Treats, dog sheets/bedding given at check-in; two dogs; $15 per dog per stay; $100–225; 3019 N. Coast Hwy.; 541/265-9411.

Portland–Inn at the Meadows: Biscuits available at front desk. Two dogs, 50 pounds or less; $25 flat fee per stay; $70–160; 1215 N. Hayden Meadows; 503/286-9600.

Roseburg–Garden Villa: Bags are available at the front desk and there is a walking trail behind hotel; $15 per dog per stay, plus credit card or $125 cash refundable deposit; $75–120; 760 N.W. Garden Valley Blvd.; 541/672-1601.

Roseburg–Rice Hill: Two pets maximum; $10 pet fee; $70–95; 621 John Long Rd.; 541/849-3335.

Salem–Black Bear Inn: No restrictions; $12 pet fee; $70–110; 1600 Motor Ct. N.E.; 503/581-1559.

Salem–Pacific Highway Inn: Two dogs; $20 pet fee up to $40 maximum per stay; $90–95; 4646 Portland Rd. N.E.; 503/390-3200.

Sandy–Sandy Inn: Two dogs; $10 pet fee; $85–125; 37465 Hwy. 26; 503/668-7100.

Seaside–Oceanview Resort: Treat bags given at check-in. Dogs not permitted in whirlpool suites; $20 pet fee; $90–300; 414 N. Prom; 503/738-3334; www.oceanviewresort.com.

Sisters–Ponderosa Lodge: Very pet-friendly. Doggie basket given at check-in with sheets, towels, bags, and treats. Lodge is near Deschutes National Forest and has walking trails next to pet wing. Two dogs; $15 per dog per visit; $90–240; 500 Hwy. 20 W.; 541/549-1234.

St. Helens–Oak Meadows Inn: Four dogs depending on size; $10 per dog per visit; $75–145; 585 S. Columbia River Hwy.; 503/397-3000.

The Dalles–River City Inn: Small dogs only, two dogs; $10 pet fee; $65–110; 112 W. 2nd St.; 541/296-9107.

Tigard–Northwind Inn and Suites: Four dogs, each less than 30 pounds, at discretion of front desk staff; $10 pet fee; $80–170; 16105 S.W. Pacific Hwy.; 503/431-2100.

Tillamook: Ground-floor rooms only, two per room; $10 pet fee; $90–170; 1722 N. Makinster Rd.; 503/842-7599.

Wilsonville–Willamette Inn: Two dogs under 25 pounds; no pet fee; $90–100; 30800 S.W. Parkway Ave.; 503/682-2288.

Woodburn: One dog per person; $10 pet fee; $70–130; 2887 Newberg Hwy.; 503/982-6515.

COMFORT INN AND SUITES

Not all Comfort Inns allow pets, and each location's rules and fees vary. The fees assume payment with credit cards in case of damages. Cash transactions may require additional refundable deposits. 800/228-5150; comfortinn.com or petfriendlyhotels.choicehotels.com.

Albany–Suites: No restrictions; $15 pet fee, or $30 per stay; $65–160; 100 Opal Ct. N.E.; 541/928-2053.

Coos Bay: Two dogs under 25 pounds; $15 per night; $70–170; 1503 Virginia Ave.; 541/756-3191.

Cottage Grove: No restrictions; $10 pet fee; $65–120; 845 Gateway Blvd.; 541/942-9747.

Eugene/Springfield: No restrictions; $25 pet fee; $100–160; 3550 Gateway St.; 541/746-5359.

Garibaldi: Under 50 pounds, maximum two pets; $20 pet fee; $60–160; 502 Garibaldi Ave.; 503/322-3338.

Grants Pass: No restrictions; $10 pet fee and $100 refundable deposit; $60–130; 1889 N.E. 6th St.; 541/479-8301.

Gresham: No restrictions; $15 pet fee; $75–100; 2323 N.E. 181st Ave; 503/492-4000.

Klamath Falls: No restrictions; $10 pet fee; $60–150; 100 Main St.; 541/882-4666.

Lincoln City: Pets under 20 pounds; $20 pet fee; $80–350; 136 N.E. Hwy. 101; 541/994-8155.

McMinnville: Three dogs under 50 pounds; $10 pet fee; $100–160; 2520 S.E. Stratus Ave.; 503/472-1700.

Seaside: Under 50 pounds; $25 per stay; $80–350; 545 Broadway; 503/738-3011.

The Dalles: Two dogs under 20 pounds; $10 pet fee; $65–145; 351 Lone Pine Dr.; 541/298-2800.

Wilsonville: Three dogs; $15 pet fee; $80–140; 8855 S.W. Citizen Dr.; 503/682-9000.

DAYS INN

Rules and regulations vary. 800/DAYS INN (800/329-7466); www.daysinn.com.

Bend: Two small to medium pets only; $6 pet fee; $70–100;
849 N.E. Third St.; 541/383-3776.

Corvallis: First floor only; $5 pet fee; $60–82; 1113 N.W. 9th St.; 541/754-7474.

Eugene: No restrictions; $10 pet fee; $55–113; 1859 Franklin Blvd.;
541/342-6383.

Gresham–Days Inn and Suites: Limit four dogs, $10 pet fee; $60–75;
24134 Stark St.; 503/465-1515.

Portland–North: Limit three dogs; $15 flat fee per stay; $65–85;
9930 N. Whitaker Rd.; 503/289-1800.

ECONO LODGE AND RODEWAY INN

Rules and regulations vary. 800/55 ECONO (800/553-2666);
www.econolodge.com or www.petfriendlyhotels.choicehotels.com.

Albany: Two dogs; $10 pet fee; $55–90; 1212 S.E. Price Rd.; 541/926-0170.

Bend–Roadway Inn: No restrictions; $10 pet fee; $60–100;
437 N.E. 3rd St.; 541/382-7711.

Corvallis: Quantity allowed depends on size, call ahead; $5 pet fee;
$45–50; 345 N.W. 2nd St.; 541/752-9601.

Klamath Falls: No restrictions; no pet fees, but deposit required if paying
with cash; $35–110; 75 Main St.; 541/884-7735.

Lincoln City: Dogs under 25 pounds, but no rottweilers, Doberman
pinschers, or pit bulls; $15 pet fee low season, $25 pet fee high season;
$40–150; 1713 N.W. 21st St.; 541/994-5281.

Medford/Ashland: Two under 20 pounds; $10 pet fee; $55–90;
50 Lowe Rd.; 541/482-4700.

Newport: No restrictions, don't leave unattended; no pet fee; $39–99;
606 S.W. Coast Hwy.; 541/265-7723.

Portland/Hillsboro: One dog under 50 pounds; $10 pet fee; $50–70;
622 S.E. 10th Ave.; 503/640-4791.

Salem–Rodeway Inn: Three dogs; $5 pet fee; $45–100;
3340 Astoria Way N.E.; 503/393-6000.

HOLIDAY INN, HOLIDAY INN EXPRESS

Pet room availability and rates may vary for special occasions. 800/HOLIDAY (800/465-4329); www.holiday-inn.com or www.ichotelsgroup.com.

Albany–Express: Three dogs; $15 pet fee per night, or $30 per visit for longer stays; $85–160; 105 Opal Ct.; 541/928-8820.

Astoria: Two dogs; $15 pet fee; $80–180; 204 W. Marine Dr.; 503/325-6222.

Bend: No restrictions; $10 pet fee; $85–130; 20615 Grandview Dr.; 541/317-8500.

Corvallis: First-floor rooms only; $25 pet fee; $90–110; 781 N.W. 2nd St; 541/752-0800.

Cottage Grove: No restrictions; $15 pet fee; $75–95; 1601 Gateway Blvd.; 541/942-1000.

Eugene/Springfield–Express: Designated rooms only; $10 pet fee; $80–120; 3480 Hutton St.; 541/746-8471.

Grants Pass: No restrictions; $10 pet fee; $80–130; 105 N.E. Agness Ave.; 541/471-6144.

Portland–Airport (I-205): Two dogs, lower floors only; $25 non-refundable deposit per stay; $105–275; 8439 N.E. Columbia Blvd.; 503/256-5000.

Roseburg: First-floor rooms; $10 pet fee; $70–95; 375 W. Harvard Ave.; 541/673-7517.

Troutdale: Quality Excellence Award Winner; pets up to 50 pounds; $10 first night, $15 additional nights; $90–110; 1000 N.W. Graham Rd.; 503/492-2900.

Wilsonville: No restrictions; $15 pet fee; $80–125; 25425 S.W. 95th Ave.; 503/682-2211.

KOA CAMPGROUNDS

Aggressive dogs of any breed are not welcome at any KOA. If your dog shows behavior that is protective and unfriendly to strangers, please leave it at home. If you bring your dog and it exhibits this type of behavior, the owner or management of the KOA will ask you to find other camping accommodations. KOA Kampgrounds have policies against accepting breeds that have been identified by its insurance provider as having a history of unfriendly and aggressive behavior to other dogs and humans, specifically pit bulls and pit bull mixes, rottweilers, and Doberman pinschers.

KOA does not charge pet fees. Dogs are not allowed in Kamping Kottages or Kabins. 406/248-7444; www.koa.com.

Albany/Corvallis: Very dog-friendly. Tents $25–35; 33775 Oakville Rd. South; 541/967-8521.

Astoria/Seaside: Tents $25–55; 1100 N.W. Ridge Rd.; 503/861-2606.

Bandon/Port Orford: Tents $25–30; 46612 Hwy. 101; 541/348-2358.

Bend/Sisters: Tents $30–45; 67667 Hwy. 20 W.; 541/549-3021.

Cascade Locks/Portland East: Tents $25–30; 841 N.W. Forest Ln.; 541/374-8668.

Klamath Falls: Tents $25–30; 3435 Shasta Way; 541/884-4644.

Lincoln City: Tents $25–35; 5298 N.E. Park Ln.; 541/994-2961.

Madras/Culver: Tents $20–30; 2435 S.W. Jericho Ln.; 541/546-3046.

Medford/Gold Hill: Tents $25–30; 12297 Blackwell Rd. (Gold Hill Exit 40); 541/855-7710.

Oregon Dunes: Tents $20–35; 68632 Hwy. 101; 541/756-4851.

Salem: Tents $25–30; 8372 Enchanted Way; 503/363-7616.

Waldport/Newport: Tents $20–35; Alsea Bay Bridge, Waldport; 541/563-2250.

LA QUINTA

There are no restrictions or pet fees at the following locations, unless otherwise noted. 800/NU ROOMS (800/687-6667); www.laquinta.com or www.lq.com.

Albany: Limit four dogs; no pet fee; $70–140; 251 Airport Rd. S.E.; 541/928-0921.

Ashland: No restrictions; no pet fee; $70–140; 434 S. Valley View Rd.; 541/482-6932.

Bend: Four beings per room (pets and people); no pet fee; $60–150; 61200 S. Hwy. 97; 541/388-2227.

Eugene: No restrictions; no pet fee; $80–135; 155 Day Island Rd.; 541/344-8335.

Grants Pass: Two dogs per person; no pet fee; $60–130; 243 N.E. Morgan Ln.; 541/472-1808.

Newport: Two dogs; no pet fee; $65–150; 45 S.E. 32nd St.; 541/867-7727.

Portland–Lloyd Center: Two dogs; no pet fee; pets may be left unattended if crated; $75–130; 431 N.E. Multnomah St.; 503/233-7933.

Portland–Northwest: No restrictions; no pet fee; $70–130; 4319 N.W. Yeon Ave.; 503/497-9044.

Wilsonville: No restrictions; no pet fee; $80–90; 8815 S.W. Sun Pl.; 503/682-3184.

Woodburn: Two dogs; no pet fee; $65–85; 120 N. Arney Rd.; 503/982-1727.

MARRIOTT

Rules and regulations vary. The Marriott chain includes Courtyard by Marriott, Residence Inns, SpringHill Suites, and TownePlace Suites. 800/228-9290; www.marriott.com.

Eugene-Springfield–Residence Inn: No restrictions; $75 nonrefundable fee; $150–180; 25 Club Rd.; 541/342-7171.

Hillsboro–Residence Inn: No restrictions; $10 pet fee; $180–200; 18855 N.W. Tanasbourne Dr.; 503/531-3200.

Hillsboro–TownePlace Suites: Two dogs; $10 pet fee (changes for longer stays); $90–160; 6550 N.E. Brighton St.; 503/268-6000.

Lake Oswego–Residence Inn: No restrictions; $80–160; $75 nonrefundable pet fee; 15200 S.W. Bangy Rd.; 503/684-2603.

Portland–Downtown RiverPlace Residence Inn: Two dogs; $10 pet fee; $150–220; 2115 S.W. River Pkwy.; 503/552-9500.

Portland–Lloyd Center: No restrictions; $75 per stay; $105–175; 1710 N.E. Multnomah St.; 503/288-1400.

MOTEL 6

Official policy for Motel 6 is that all properties accept one pet per room, exceptions are noted below. There are no pet fees, unless listed otherwise below. There is a 10 percent discount for booking online. 800/4MOTEL6 (800/466-8356); www.motel6.com.

Albany: $45–70; 2735 Pacific Blvd. S.E.; 541/926-4233.

Bend: Two dogs; $45–80; 201 N.E. 3rd St.; 541/382-8282.

Coos Bay: No restrictions; $45–85; 1445 Bayshore Dr.; 541/267-7171.

Corvallis: $45–65; 935 N.W. Garfield Ave.; 541/758-9125.

Eugene–South: No restrictions; $45–70; 3690 Glenwood Dr.; 541/687-2395.

Gold Beach: Really nice, looks like a lodge. No restrictions; $50–75; 94433 Jerry's Flat Rd.; 541/247-4533.

Grants Pass: Two dogs; $40–65; 1800 N.E. 7th St.; 541/474-1331.

Klamath Falls: Two dogs; $40–65; 5136 S. 6th St.; 541/884-2110.

Lincoln City: $45–85; 3517 N.W. Hwy. 101; 541/996-9900.

Medford–North: Two small dogs; $50–75; 2400 Biddle Rd.; 541/779-0550.

Medford–South: $40–70; 950 Alba Dr.; 541/773-4290.

Portland–Airport: One dog free, second dog $10 per night; $45–65; 9225 S.E. Stark St.; 503/255-0808.

Portland–Central: Two small dogs; $45–70; 3104 S.E. Powell Blvd.; 503/238-0600.

Portland–North: One under 30 pounds, extra dogs $10 each; $45–65; 1125 N. Schmeer Rd.; 503/247-3700.

Redmond: Two small dogs; $60–85; 2247 S. Hwy. 97; 541/923-2100.

Roseburg: Pets and Wi-Fi are free. National award winner. $45–70; 3100 N.W. Aviation Dr.; 541/464-8000.

Salem: Three dogs; $40–60; 1401 Hawthorne Ave. N.E.; 503/371-8024.

Seaside: $45–90; 2369 S. Roosevelt Dr. (Hwy 101); 503/738-6269.

Springfield: Two small; $45–70; 3752 International Ct.; 541/741-1105.

The Dalles: One dog free, second dog is $10 per night; $40–80; 2500 W. 6th St.; 541/296-1191.

Tigard: One dog free, second dog is $10 per night; $45–60; 17950 S.W. McEwan Ave.; 503/620-2066.

Troutdale: $40–60; 1610 N.W. Frontage Rd.; 503/665-2254.

QUALITY INN

Rules and regulations vary. 800/228-5151; www.qualityinn.com.

Albany: Dogs up to 14-inch shoulder height (that's what they said); $10 pet fee; $80–105; 1100 Price Rd. S.E.; 541/928-5050.

Bend: No restrictions; $10 pet fee; $110–140; 20600 Grandview Dr.; 541/318-0848.

Eugene/Springfield: Three dogs; $5 pet fee; $80–180; 3550 Gateway St.; 541/726-9266.

Klamath Falls: No restrictions; $10 pet fee; $85–135; 100 Main St.; 541/882-4666.

Roseburg: Three dogs; $10 pet fee, plus a $50 refundable deposit; $70–100; 427 N.W. Garden Valley Blvd.; 541/673-5561.

RAMADA INN

Rules and regulations vary. 800/2RAMADA (800/272-6232); www.ramada.com.
Medford: No restrictions; $20 pet fee per stay; $75–95; 2250 Biddle Rd.; 541/779-3141.

RED LION

There are no restrictions or fees for pets at these locations, unless stated otherwise below. Booking online guarantees the lowest available rates. 800/RED LION (800/733-5466); www.redlion.com.

Astoria: Limited to two small dogs or one medium to large dog; $20 total per night; $99–179; 400 Industry St.; 503/325-7373.

Bend: No restrictions; $10 per night; $85–125; 1415 N.E. 3rd St.; 541/382-7011.

Coos Bay: Under a 100 pounds, max two; $10 per night; $135–190; 1313 N. Bayshore Dr.; 541/267-4141.

Eugene: Under 30 pounds; $20 per night; $90–250; 205 Coburg Rd.; 541/342-5201.

Hillsboro: "No elephants or snakes"; $20 per night; $90–170; 3500 N.E. Cornell Rd.; 503/648-3500.

Klamath Falls: No restrictions; no pet fee; $60–90; 3612 S. 6th St.; 541/882-8864.

McMinnville: Five pet-friendly rooms; $10 pet fee; $100–135; 2535 N.E. Cumulus Ave.; 503/472-1500.

Medford: No restrictions; $10 pet fee; $110–130; 200 N. Riverside Ave.; 541/779-5811.

Portland–Airport: $15 per dog per stay; $100–130; 5019 N.E. 102nd Ave.; 503/252-6397.

Portland–Jantzen Beach: $35 one-time flat fee; $110–130; 909 N. Hayden Island Dr.; 503/283-4466.

Salem: Maximum two pets, under 30 pounds each; $20 total per visit; $80–135; 3301 Market St. N.E.; 503/370-7888.

SHILO INNS

There is a standard limit of two pets per room at these locations, unless stated otherwise below. Shilo's standard pet fee is $25 total per stay. All Shilo Inns have 3- by 4-foot dog beds available; just ask at the front desk. 800/222-2244; www.shiloinn.com.

Astoria-Warrenton: $100–260; 1609 E. Harbor; 503/861-2181.

Beaverton: $100–155; 9900 S.W. Canyon Rd.; 503/297-2551.

Bend: $100–240; 3105 O.B. Riley Rd.; 541/389-9600.

Eugene/Springfield: $80–150; 3350 Gateway; 541/747-0332.

Grants Pass: $70–120; 1880 N.W. 6th St.; 541/479-8391.

Klamath Falls: $110–200; 2500 Almond St.; 541/885-7980.

Medford: $90–115; 2111 Biddle Rd.; 541/770-5151.

Newberg: $90–125; 501 Sitka Ave.; 503/537-0303.

Newport: $115–200; 536 S.W. Elizabeth; 541/265-7701.

Portland–Rose Garden: Three dogs; $90–180; 1506 N.E. 2nd Ave.; 503/736-6300.

Salem: $115–130; 3304 Market St. N.E.; 503/581-4001.

Seaside: Under 50 pounds; $90–190; 900 S. Holladay Dr.; 503/738-0549.

The Dalles: $130–170; 3223 Bret Clodfelter Way; 541/298-5502.

Tigard: $100–1365; Washington Square, 10830 S.W. Greenburg Rd.; 503/620-4320.

Tillamook: $115–150; 2515 N. Main St.; 503/842-7971.

STARWOOD HOTELS

In 2003, all Starwood Properties, including Sheraton, Westin, and W Hotels, made it corporate policy to accept and pamper pets after an independent study proved how loyal pet owners are to accommodations that accept their four-legged loved ones. There are no fees and no restrictions unless stated otherwise below. www.starwoodhotels.com.

Portland–Sheraton Airport: $25 nonrefundable pet fee; $120–180; 8235 N.E. Airport Way; 503/281-2500.

Portland–Sheraton Four Points Waterfront: Two dogs under 60 pounds; $50 fee per stay; $150–210; 50 S.W. Morrison St.; 503/221-0711; www.fourpointsportland.com.

Portland–Westin: Two dogs; $160–240; 750 S.W. Alder St.; 503/294-9000.

SUPER 8

Rules and regulations vary. 800/800-8000; www.super8.com.

Bend: Two dogs; $10 per pet per stay; $75–85; 1275 S. Hwy 97; 541/388-6888.

Corvallis: Three dogs; $10 pet fee; $70–90; 407 N.W. 2nd St.; 541/758-8088.

Grants Pass: No restrictions; $25 refundable deposit; $50–75; 1949 N.E. 7th St.; 541/474-0888.

Gresham: Two dogs; $10 dog fee; $60–80; 121 N.E. 181St Ave.; 503/661-5100.

Klamath Falls: No restrictions; $25 refundable deposit; $60–75; 3805 Hwy. 97 N.; 541/884-8880.

Portland–Airport: No restrictions; $10 pet fee; $65–90; 11011 N.E. Holman St.; 503/257-8988.

Redmond: No restrictions; $5 flat fee; $65–80; 3629 S.W. 21st Pl.; 541/548-8881.

Roseburg: Pride of Super 8 award; no restrictions; $10 pet fee; $55–70; 3200 N.W. Aviation Dr.; 541/672-8880.

Salem: No restrictions; $10 pet fee; $60–80; 1288 Hawthorne Ave. N.E.; 503/370-8888.

The Dalles: Three dogs; $10 pet fee; $60–85; 609 Cherry Heights Rd.; 541/296-6888.

Wilsonville: Limit four, 30 pounds or less; $10 pet fee; $65–75; 25438 S.W. Parkway Ave.; 503/682-2088.

Woodburn: No restrictions; $10 pet fee; $60–70; 821 Evergreen Rd.; 503/981-8881.

TRAVELODGE

Rules and regulations vary. 800/578-7878; www.travelodge.com.

Grants Pass: One dog under 35 pounds; $5 pet fee; $75–130; 1950 N.W. Vine St.; 541/479-6611.

Newberg: Allowed in specific rooms only; $7 pet fee; $65–90; 2816 Portland Rd. (99W); 503/537-5000.

Portland–Airport: One dog; $10 pet fee; $65–100; 3828 N.E. 82nd Ave.; 503/256-2550.

Roseburg: Two dogs under 30 pounds; $10 pet fee; $75–90; 315 W. Harvard Ave.; 541/672-4836.

Salem: Two dogs, in selected rooms only; $65–80; $10 pet fee; 1555 State St.; 503/581-2466.

Transportation

Broadway Cab: This taxi company in Portland will allow dogs if you call and let the driver know in advance. 503/227-1234.

Extended Trails

Pacific Crest Trail: Crisscrossing California, Oregon, and Washington on its way from Mexico to Canada, this American National Scenic Trail extends 2,650 miles. It transverses six ecozones, from high desert to old growth and arctic alpine. The Oregon section is typically wooded, generally the shortest and easiest terrain of the trail. Through the North Cascades, the Washington section boasts dramatic mountainous scenery and notoriously fickle weather patterns. The Pacific Crest Trail Association is in California: 5325 Elkhorn Blvd., 5325 Elkhorn Blvd.; PMB #256, Sacramento, CA 95842-2526; 916/349-2109; www.pcta.org.

Willamette Valley Scenic Bikeway: The entire route is 130 miles, separated into five sections on the website. It runs generally north–south, from Champoeg State Park near Newburg to Armitage County Park, just above Eugene. It largely highlights the agricultural history of the lush valley, passing vineyards, hazelnut orchards, fruit orchards one after another. Any segment can be walked on leash with dogs. Call the Oregon DOT Bike and Pedestrian program at 503/986-3555 or go to www.oregon.gov/oprd/parks/bike.

Oregon Coast Trail: This is a 360-mile route from the tip of the state at the mouth of the Columbia River to the bottom at the California border. The majority of the trail is on the beach, sometimes so close you need a tide table to cross headlands when the tide is out. Some of it wanders inland through state forests and parks, and in between, landowners along the coast have generously provided easements and permits through property to make connections. Some of it is dirt and gravel, some paved, and some so narrow through brush you need a scent hound to pick up the trail. If you want to take on the whole thing, or major portions of it, buy a detailed point-to-point guide available at bookstores and magazine outlets. Select the "Maps and Publications" link on the Oregon State Parks and Recreation website at www.oregonstateparks.org and look for the 2005 Coast Trail Brochure.

OC&E Woods Line State Trail: At 100 miles long, this state trail is Oregon's longest linear park, stretching from Klamath Falls east to Bly and north to Sycan Marsh. The wide, level path is built on the rail bed of the Oregon, California, and Eastern Railroad (hence the OC&E). It's open to all nonmotorized travelers, so be prepared to yield right-of-way to horses and bicyclists, inline skaters, and joggers. The farther you go, the more you'll run into the farm and ranch lands of the Klamath Basin, with great views of Mount Shasta to the south. The first 15 miles of the trail are paved, but softer paws will prefer the wood-chip trail that parallels the asphalt. 800/551-6949; www.oregon stateparks.org.

National and State Parks

Recreation.gov: The feds have established a new, easy-to-remember website to consolidate information and reservations for public lands such as National Parks and National Forests. Find a recreation spot on a massive, interactive map, get wilderness permits, and make campground reservations at the National Recreation Reservation Service (NRRS). www.recreation.gov.

Department of Fish and Wildlife: Contact this organization for angling, shellfish gathering, and hunting licenses. Print an application online and fax to 503/947-6117. Main phone: 503/947-6000 or 800/720-6339; Licensing: 503/947-6100; www.dfw.state.or.us.

Oregon State Parks: Oregon calls its state parks by many names, and only a few charge a $3 daily parking fee. Camping fees vary by location. Dogs are required to be on a six-foot or shorter leash. Reservations are made by calling 800/452-5687 or through www.reserveamerica.com.

Internet Resources

North Coast
Bow Wow Dog News: This free newspaper is distributed in Oregon Coast and Southwest Washington beach locations. Also available online at www.bowwowdognews.com.

Greater Portland
PDX DOG: For pets and their peeps, www.pdxdog.com is a social networking site for dog lovers who want to share—photos, tales, tips, hints—you name it. PDX is the airport designation for Portland, used locally as a nickname for the city. You can find local dog businesses that advertise on the site.

Portland Pooch: This online guide to the Portland dog scene has great information and the best descriptions and directions to all of the area's dog parks. www.portlandpooch.com.

Southern Oregon
FOTAS: Friends of the Animal Shelter holds benefits and dog events in and around Ashland, Medford, and Jacksonville to raise funds for the county animal shelter. www.fotas.org.

INDEX

www.moon.com

DESTINATIONS | ACTIVITIES | BLOGS | MAPS | BOOKS

MOON.COM is ready to help plan your next trip! Filled with fresh trip ideas and strategies, author interviews, informative travel blogs, a detailed map library, and descriptions of all the Moon guidebooks, Moon.com is all you need to get out and explore the world—or even places in your own backyard. While at Moon.com, sign up for our monthly e-newsletter for updates on new releases, travel tips, and expert advice from our on-the-go Moon authors. As always, when you travel with Moon, expect an experience that is uncommon and truly unique.

MOON IS ON FACEBOOK—BECOME A FAN!
JOIN THE MOON PHOTO GROUP ON FLICKR

Acknowledgments

First and foremost, I want to express my abiding love and gratitude to Dread Pirate Steve for saying "As you wish" to every demand made of him.

I'd like to extend thanks to my PCC Natural Markets peeps Mike, Jill, and Nancy for tolerating my bizarre and constant schedule requests. Apologies go to all my family and friends, who regularly watch me disappear into the wilds of Oregon, and into the depths of my home office, never knowing when I might emerge from either.

To Pam, Tana, Loni, Robin, Christine, and anyone else whose name I've lost in computer email crashes, thank you for housing, feeding, and touring our traveling dog and pony show.

Kudos to everyone, everywhere, who works or volunteers in animal rescue, spay and neuter education, and land conservation. Finally, this book would be greatly diminished if it weren't for the efforts of every dog advocate who campaigns for, creates, and cleans up off-leash areas.

Keeping Current

Note to All Dog Lovers:
While our information is as current as possible, changes to fees, regulations, parks, roads, and trails sometimes are made after we go to press. Businesses can close, change their ownership, or change their rules. Earthquakes, fires, rainstorms, and other natural phenomena can radically change the condition of parks, hiking trails, and wilderness areas. Before you and your dog begin your travels, please be certain to call the phone numbers for each listing for updated information.

Attention Dogs of Oregon:
Our readers mean everything to us. We explore Oregon so that you and your people can spend true quality time together. Your input to this book is very important. In the last few years, we've heard from many wonderful dogs and their humans about new dog-friendly places, or old dog-friendly places we didn't know about. If we've missed your favorite park, beach, outdoor restaurant, hotel, or dog-friendly activity, please let us know. We'll check out the tip and if it turns out to be a good one, include it in the next edition, giving a thank-you to the dog and/or person who sent in the suggestion. Please write us—we always welcome comments and suggestions.

The Dog Lover's Companion to Oregon
Avalon Travel
1700 Fourth Street
Berkeley, CA 94710
www.dogloverscompanion.com